Memory and Re-Creation
in Troubadour
Lyric

Memory and Re-Creation in Troubadour Lyric

AMELIA E. VAN VLECK

University of California Press

BERKELEY LOS ANGELES OXFORD

University of California Press
Berkeley and Los Angeles, California

University of California Press, Ltd.
Oxford, England

© 1991 by
The Regents of the University of California

Library of Congress Cataloging-in-Publication Data

Van Vleck, Amelia Eileen.
    Memory and re-creation in troubadour lyric / Amelia E. Van Vleck.
        p.   cm.
    Includes bibliographical references.
    ISBN 0-520-06521-2 (alk. paper)
        1. Provençal poetry—History and criticism.   2. Songs, Provençal—
    History and criticism.   3. Provençal language—Versification.
    4. Oral tradition—France—Provence.   5. Troubadours.   I. Title.
    PC3304.V36   1991
    849'.1209—dc20   90-31357
                                                                           CIP

Printed in the United States of America

9 8 7 6 5 4 3 2 1

The paper used in this publication meets the minimum requirements of American
National Standard for Information Sciences—Permanence of Paper
for Printed Library Materials, ANSI Z39.48-1984. ∞

CONTENTS

ACKNOWLEDGMENTS

This book began in 1979, the year of the Los Angeles MAP conference on the troubadours. Joseph J. Duggan introduced me to the current discussion of troubadour *chansonniers* and their multiple versions, and to the work of Rupert Pickens, William D. Paden, Jr., and Hendrik van der Werf; he set up a puzzle that seemed likely, if solved somehow, to make a good thesis. The ideal dissertation director, he offered unsolved questions, challenges rather than answers, encouragement, and caution at wise intervals. To say that he has been supportive from first to last, even through the long process of revision, would be the barest understatement. I cannot thank him enough.

Suzanne Fleischman worked closely with me on the first versions, catching small and large mistakes both in my Old Provençal and in my English. She and Joe Duggan together convinced me that philology would make my book sound without necessarily making it stuffy.

I am indebted to members of the faculty in Comparative Literature, French, and Classics at Berkeley, both for the climate of ideas they created and for specific suggestions regarding my work. R. Howard Bloch's suggestions for revision helped guide the transformation from Ph.D. thesis to book. Hans Ulrich Gumbrecht, Michael Nagler, and Florence Verducci read the 1982 manuscript with care and offered fresh viewpoints for the revision.

The statistical analysis owes a great deal to Shirley Wodtke and Edgar M. Van Vleck, who helped me with the technical aspects of both the original survey and the expanded version. My father, not just a scientist but a singer and the first Manrico in *Il trovatore* I ever heard, constantly proves that when performers forget, they invent: the song must go on.

My thanks to Bill Paden for reading the 1982 version and uncovering the most serious chinks in its armor. I haven't patched them all, but I appreciate the strengthening influence of a sincere and serious challenge.

Rupert Pickens and Sylvia Huot, who gave detailed critiques of the whole manuscript, helped enormously in the revision. I would also like to thank my colleagues at Syracuse University for their insights and encouragement in this revision, especially Paul Archambault, who clarified what needed rewriting and what didn't. Equally kind and skillful people helped me bring an end to *mouvance:* Russ C. Smith finalized the graphs; Mark N. Taylor initialized the index and shared its tedium. Doris Kretschmer, Rose Vekony, and Anne Geissman Canright of the University of California Press kept my text moving toward fixity.

To Mrs. Winifred Seely Myers Love of Syracuse, I am most grateful for the time and the security that her endowed Faculty Fellowship has given me. She had the generous idea to give a scholar a good start: a rare and precious gift in hard times for academe.

Finally, thanks to the many friends whose conversation, comments, and support have improved the quality of this book.

ABBREVIATIONS

Troubadour poetry is quoted from the following editions, except where otherwise indicated. Numbers after abbreviated names refer to poem number and line number as printed in the cited edition. Poems not in these editions are referred to by the number assigned them in Pillet and Carstens's *Bibliographie der Troubadours*. For example, "P.-C. 262,4" refers to Jaufre Rudel's "Pro ai del chant enseignadors": Jaufre is poet number 262, and "Pro ai . . ." song number 4, in the *Bibliographie*.

Aim Bel	Aimeric de Belenoi: Dumitrescu 1935
Arn D	Arnaut Daniel: Toja 1960
Arn Mar	Arnaut de Mareuil: Johnston 1935
B Pal	Berenger de Palazol: Newcombe 1971
B Vent	Bernart de Ventadorn: Appel 1915
B Mar	Bernart Marti: Hoepffner 1929
B Born	Bertran de Born: Paden, Sankovitch, and Stäblein 1986
D Prad	Daude de Pradas: Schutz [1933] 1971
F Mars	Folquet de Marselha: Stronski [1910] 1968
Gm Berg	Guilhem de Berguedà: Riquer 1971
Gm Mont	Guilhem de Montanhagol: Ricketts 1964
Gm St-D	Guilhem de St-Didier: Sakari 1956
Gm IX	Guilhem IX: Pasero 1973
Gr Bor	Giraut de Bornelh: Kolsen 1910
J Rud	Jaufre Rudel: Pickens 1978
Js Pcb	Jausbert de Puycibot: Shepard 1924
Mcb	Marcabru: Dejeanne 1909. See also Roncaglia 1951a, 1951b, 1957; and Ricketts 1968
P d'Alv	Peire d'Alvernhe: Del Monte 1955
P Rog	Peire Rogier: Nicholson 1976
P Vid	Peire Vidal: Avalle 1960

Pons G	Pons de la Guardia: Frank 1949
R d'Aur	Raimbaut d'Aurenga: Pattison 1952
Rm Mir	Raimon de Miraval: Topsfield 1971
R Berb	Rigaut de Berbezilh: Várvaro 1960

Craft, Sentiment, and Mechanism in the Medieval Lyric

The troubadours of medieval southern France still have an audience: not just of scholars, but also of poets, musicians, and others pursuing an interest in poetry or music. Until recently, an unduly large proportion of our attention to the troubadours (as well as to their northern French counterparts, the trouvères) has been directed at the amatory theories they elaborated.[1] Even to scholars, their love terminology seemed systematic, and its apparent precision seemed to afford glimpses into a spiritual knowledge beyond our own. As a result, their poetry was overrun by a scholarly quest for the meaning of love, their usual "theme." Still, love per se remained unelucidated by these inquiries, and post-Romantic scholars blamed the poets' insincerity for the mere words, to them a disappointing shadow, they found at the center of troubadour and trouvère lyric, where the object of the quest—*amors*—should have been finally snared.

With the announcement in 1949 that "the theme is but a pretext" for the interplay of conventions and forms in Old French love lyric (Guiette [1949] 1960, 15), medievalists began to learn new and productive ways of reading trouvère poetry. In turn, this formal approach developed by Guiette, Dragonetti, and Zumthor has inspired better readings of Old Provençal lyric. We can now admire songs that nineteenth- and early-twentieth-century critics found repellent, for example, the songs of Raimbaut d'Aurenga, whom Alfred Jeanroy called "the first of our funambulist poets" and blamed for offering "a foretaste of the nerve-wracking sestina" (1934, 43). The modern reader sees artistic strategy where Jeanroy saw impropriety—where formal argumentation, elaborate sound patterns, and conscious weaving of the familiar with the original draw attention to the poem itself. For Jeanroy, whatever cast doubt on the sincerity of the poet's amorous homage also rendered suspect its delicacy and good taste and, thus, even its literary value. Today, beauty need not equal biographical truth, and we accept poetry made more of words than of emotion.

One of the major contributions of this formal approach is to expose and discourage anachronism: the superimposition of favorite biases, filters through which even the best-trained eyes often view the lyrics of the troubadours. Chief among the older biases is a view of poetry derived from romanticism: poetry is private, personal, and autobiographical. That this view has been sustained by the *vidas* and *razos* (the fictional "lives of the poets" and the "stories" "explaining" their work) probably reflects the outlook of their thirteenth-century biographers rather than of the twelfth-century troubadours (see Poe 1984). With the aid of the formal approach, which takes medieval lyric composition as a professional game of words, not as the embodiment of personal passions, we can outgrow the unacknowledged fancy that the troubadour Jaufre Rudel's "faraway love" was modeled after Dante's Beatrice; we can realize that troubadour poetry (unlike "all good poetry," according to William Wordsworth) was not "the spontaneous overflow of powerful feelings"—at least, not if we tentatively accept the poet whose "love is a pretext" and compare him to the poets whom Wordsworth most detested: "Poets, who think that they are conferring honour upon themselves and their art, in proportion as they separate themselves from the sympathies of men, and indulge in arbitrary and capricious habits of expression, in order to furnish food for fickle tastes, and fickle appetites, of their own creation" (Knight 1896, 49).

Wordsworth's accusation hits an unexpected mark with the poetry of "programmatic accumulation of motifs"—motifs that are themselves mere "forms of content" attached to "forms of expression." The poet does not sing, but "actualizes":

> A given song of the troubadour Peire Vidal is entirely composed, as if in a game, of a programmatic accumulation of motifs which the poet must expound. The probability of the motifs, then, depends less upon their choice than upon their mode of realization. Several among them are nothing more

than forms of content, to each of which are attached several forms of expression, with greater or lesser chances of actualization.

(Zumthor 1972, 230)

The discovery of a "network of lexical fields" in the Northern *grand chant courtois* has, in a sense, restored trouvère song to intelligibility for our late-twentieth-century minds. Zumthor's implied analogy with electronic circuitry familiarizes poetry based on permutation and combination, on the endless recurrence of standard courtly motifs "which activate one another," just as constant use familiarizes the heartless machinery we depend on. Probability and randomness make themselves at home in the literary critical terminology applied to medieval poetry. The mechanistic view of literature is, in fact, becoming one of our own computer-age reading biases for literature, as much as the emotional view dominated nineteenth- and early-twentieth-century criticism. This is not necessarily a disaster, as long as we do not begin to suppose that word frequency, actualization, or probability were matters of concern to medieval poets.

As if in reaction to this mechanistic view, we are now seeing a timely emphasis on the voice as the "body" of poetry (Zumthor 1982, 1987; Ong 1982). The voice, as the nearest thing to our sense of touch, is much more "physical" than the visual representations of words; in this sense, poetry created for oral performance stands in something of a "physical" (more than intellectual) relationship with its audiences. It is also active, in the sense that through speech—and even more through song—one body physically acts on another; the "performative" aspect of troubadour lyric thus takes on new significance.

It is tempting to map the successful formal approach to trouvère lyric directly onto the quite different terrain of troubadour poetry. And yet, though it may prove genuinely valid, we can impose a poetics of the northern *chanson* on the southern *canso* only after testing its appropriateness. Not merely a difference in language separates the troubadours and the trouvères, but a difference in the cultural climate for both poetics and politics. The social position of women, for instance, differed greatly in that women in the south could legally own land. "Langue d'oc" expresses a poetic tradition other, and slightly older, than the derived traditions of "langue d'oïl." When Zumthor argues for a high degree of correspondence in the vocabulary of the two languages ("one could easily establish a lexicon of these equivalencies"; 1972, 191), he encourages the reader to generalize a theory intended to describe the songs of the trou-

vères. Yet few would maintain that a description of the Old French conventional love lyric can be generalized to Occitan lyric before 1150–
1170.[2] The period of "duality of form and, especially, of content" (1972,
190), which Zumthor bypasses, actually offers a variety that is not necessarily dual. The "programmatic" stage has not yet been reached, and
troubadour poets debate vigorously and ingeniously over the merits of
potential "programs."

To include Occitan poetry in the *poésie formelle* described by Guiette,
Dragonetti, and Zumthor, we would have to ignore a fundamental difference between the troubadours and the trouvères: originality and individuality were of prime importance to the troubadours, whereas the
trouvères strove primarily to refine convention. The works of Marcabru,
Peire d'Alvernhe, Giraut de Bornelh, Raimbaut d'Aurenga, and Arnaut
Daniel scarcely resemble the poetry of the trouvères: "Major poets did
not only *not* seek to conform to tradition, but attempted to shape a developing literature to their own individual concepts of eloquence" (Paterson
1975, 6). As we shall see, these poets whom Paterson singles out for their
individuality are important figures in a movement favoring authorial
originality and the conservation of "the legitimate versions" of their
songs. Still, even troubadours who open their works to adaptation and
re-creation emphatically contradict the conception of the vanishing author, whose voice "is stifled in a composite, neuter, oblique text, destructive of personal identities," and whose stylistic signatures are swept away,
along with his name, in the wave of medieval anonymity: "The author
has disappeared: there remains the subject of the enunciation, a speaking
insistence integrated in the text and inseparable from its functioning:
'that' speaks" (Zumthor 1972, 69).

We need only recall Peire d'Alvernhe's "Cantarai d'aquestz trobadors"
to realize how far from this *je impersonnel* were the troubadours of Peire
d'Alvernhe's generation, thus confirming Paterson's view:

> Cantarai d'aquestz trobadors
> que canton de maintas colors
> e·l peier cuida dir mout gen;
> mas a cantar lor er aillors
> q'entrametre·n vei cen pastors
> c'us non sap qe·s mont'o·s dissen.
>
> D'aisso mer mal Peire Rotgiers,
> per qe n'er encolpatz primiers,

car chanta d'amor a presen;
e valgra li mais us sautiers
en la glieis'o us candeliers
tener ab un gran candel'arden.
(P d'Alv 12, 1–12)[3]

I will sing about these troubadours, who sing in many "colors," and even the worst of them thinks he recites very nicely;
but they will have to sing elsewhere, for meanwhile I see a hundred shepherds such that not one of them knows whether he is
going up or down.

Thus Peire Rogier is unfortunate, because he will be the
first accused, since he sings about love in public; and he would
be better off with a psalter in church, or holding a candlestick
with a large burning candle.

This joke about Peire Rogier's originality, the insinuation that he should
resort to singing from a psalter instead of composing his own songs, can
be funny only if originality was the norm. At the same time, as a bit of
literary criticism, the stanza acknowledges a difference in intention between persona and poet, both of them caricatured: the image of Peire
Rogier as a choirboy "holding a large burning candle" suggests a contrast
between the apparent innocence of Peire's lyrics and their implicit sexual
content, intimidated but no less "ardent" in sacred territory—granted
that sometimes a candle is just a candle. Peire d'Alvernhe creates just such
a distinctive portrait for each poet; some of these vignettes are known to
be based on lines from their subjects' songs, and the caricatures mock the
way each represents himself to his audiences.[4]

"Individual concepts of eloquence," defended by poets "que canton de
maintas colors," were expressed partly through personalities; the special
trademark of each poet's "performing self" is more than a mark of genre
specialization. It is the stamp of authorship, more or less firmly imprinted
on every troubadour poem. When transmitters did not know who composed a poem, they would usually attribute it to someone: out of 2,542
troubadour songs only about 250 come down to us as "anonymous"; we
know the names of some 460 troubadours (Pillet and Carstens 1933).

One peculiarity of medieval poetry that might be presumed to depend
completely on authorial self-effacement and anonymity—the "essential
mobility of the medieval text"—is if anything more pronounced in troubadour poetry than in other medieval lyric traditions. Zumthor's general

description of medieval manuscripts applies in every detail, and in the extreme, to the songs of the troubadours:

> Variants in the flower of the text: words, isolated turns of phrase, variants bearing on more considerable fragments, added, omitted, modified, substituted for others; alteration or displacement of parts, variants in the number and sequence of elements. (1972, 71)

For a body of poetry so preoccupied with individual style, how can this general trend in medieval literature hold true? How can it happen that "the notion of textual authenticity seems to have been unknown" (Zumthor 1972, 71)? Yet Zumthor's concept of *mouvance*, of the changeable medieval text or, as he puts it, "the text creating itself" (p. 73), becomes more and more relevant to troubadour poetry the more we learn about its transmission. The question then becomes, how did these adamantly individualistic poets reconcile themselves to the fact (if they knew it) that their songs would weather and change and be restored, like barn murals, perhaps within their own lifetimes?

The "openness" of texts governed throughout their transmission by *mouvance*, as opposed to the "closure" of texts resisting its tyranny, is one of the central distinctions addressed here. "Open texts" are relatively unfamiliar to twentieth-century readers, whose assumptions were shaped mainly by print media rather than by oral or electronic modes of "publication." Yet it will become apparent that the "open text" was a norm against which certain troubadours—rather unsuccessfully—rebelled. It was also a norm that many troubadours embraced and fostered.

This book concerns itself with the style of troubadour poetry as it might have been influenced by available modes of transmission. An attentive reader soon realizes that transmission preoccupies the troubadours: even when the phrase "to send a messenger" is absent, the closing lines (*tornada*, equivalent to the French *envoi*) "send" the song to one or several specific persons or places, or to a general audience. Conscious as they were of their songs' destinations, the poets anticipated their songs' destinies as well. The idea that some troubadours might have tried to interfere with *mouvance*—to stop the "moving text"—suggests intriguing possibilities: for example, I will show that *trobar clus* (closed poetry) was a style associated with the effort to control the quality of circulation and thus (with only moderate success and intermittent application) to allow poets to compose fixed texts. By contrast, some poets evidently welcomed *mouvance*. Jaufre Rudel seems to invite revision by future singers (Pickens 1977). This finding, when we pursue its implications through a large body of evidence, leads to the important discovery that Jaufre was not alone among his contemporaries and successors in adopting this attitude, so alien to the modern view of poetry. As we shall see, many other poets offer the same invitation and encourage, or at least facilitate, the recasting in performance of their poetry.

If the unity and the permanence of perfection associated with fixed poetry were not valued by the troubadours, then we must ask what the troubadours did value as essential to their lyric composition. To answer these questions, I examine several sources of knowledge about the circulation of troubadour song.

The transmitters reveal their methods in at least two ways. The compilers who made the anthologies, as well as the theoreticians who from the thirteenth century gave expert advice to young poets, occasionally offer straightforward comments on their experience in learning, composing, or collecting songs. Other transmitters—anonymous performers, scribes, and compilers—have left us only indirect evidence: traces of their work surviving in manuscript variants. I survey the more direct evidence in Part One, "Making and Sending: A View from Within the Literary Texts."

Circumstantial evidence is investigated in Part Two, "The View from Without: Performance and Poetics Reflected in the *Chansonniers*," where, through a statistical analysis of the works of twenty-three troubadours, I trace some important causes of stanzaic transposition, the feature of troubadour *mouvance* that most seriously disarms literary interpretation. Part Two looks at the transmission of troubadour lyric from the outside, from the perspective of our time as we attempt to recapture the medieval text. It begins to sort out what can be deduced from the number and formal properties of extant copies. Here the "chirographic folk," as Ong (1982) would call them, record the creations of a performing art and appropriate it to the newly ascendent culture of the book. Discrepancies among the recorded versions of the same "poem" illuminate its life as performance as well as the circumstances of its encryption in script.

Chapter 4, "*Mouvance* in the Manuscripts," discusses the results of a statistical survey aimed at correlating such features as manuscript survival, rhyme complexity, and stanza length with the mutability of a given poet's work. The combination of evidence from transmitters and evidence from poetry is enlightening, once we can assume an early transmission that was largely oral. When transmission shows that a particular rhyme scheme was "easy to learn," then the poet can display willingness to accommodate the transmitters either by mentioning that his song is *leu ad aprendre* (which may be a true statement or an ironical one) or by using the "easy" schema without comment. Chapter 5, "Rhyme and *Razo:* Case Studies," evaluates the stabilizing effects of certain rhyme schemes, using both statistics and detailed analysis of exemplary songs whose manuscript transmission shows how these schemata fared in practice. In some cases these songs tell us explicitly what kind of "stability" the poet hoped to give his song. The recasting of songs was so predominant a feature of transmission that it was accepted even by those who could conceive of the idea of a closed text.

More valuable than the testimony of the transmitters is that of the poets themselves. Part Three, "Poetics and the Medium," explores the vocabulary of metaphors and images with which the poets allude to *mouvance* and textual integrity, to the "closed" and "open" text, to the genesis of a song's perfection or of its flaws. In seeking the poet's "intention" as to the way a song would circulate, the modern reader can never be sure that a given text represents the "authentic," original song in the poet's "own words."[5] Yet that text can at least offer the stylistic statement of someone who represents himself (or herself) as the author, who dons the persona of the original poet. At worst, it is the statement of a transmitter active at a time when the song was still a "living thing."

Troubadour songs tell us, subtly or overtly, what the poets expected from their transmitters; I focus on those statements of style that display the poets' awareness of their mode of transmission and their efforts to adjust to it or rebel against it. Instructions, criticisms, and praises for their transmitters: these constitute the poets' most direct "testimony" and thus provide key evidence for Part One. The poets also answer the question of who the primary transmitters were, allowing us to assess the role assigned by poets to professional and nonprofessional singers. Taking into account the rhetorical setting for such statements of style, one can still find there the reflection of actual performance practice.

Part Three returns to literary questions. Here I apply what has been learned about transmission to reexamine twelfth-century controversies about poetics. If we can now share some of the poets' assumptions about transmission, we can also read more clearly their references to it. I address in this way not only the set of literary terms surrounding *trobar clus* and *trobar natural* with their concurrent issues of "closure" and "legiti-

macy" or "authenticity," but also an array of images that stand metaphorically for notions of textual integrity and mutability.

The book culture that arose in the mid-thirteenth century and had by
the fourteenth transformed the idea of the "text" from a verbally woven
thing to a visually fixed object comprised part, but not all, of the transmitting cultures responsible for the texts that survive in manuscripts today. This new book culture began to produce the *chansonniers* about a
century after the poets in my study composed their lyrics. Thus, many of
the conclusions drawn here will not apply to later poets, from 1250 onward, who lived to see their works anthologized and for some of whom
the songlike quality of poetry became perhaps rather a topos than a reality. It is likely that a performing tradition carried on twelfth-century troubadours' songs long after their deaths, independent of manuscript makers
who captured on parchment the versions that they "gathered from the
air" from time to time in the period when manuscripts were being made.
The present study thus applies primarily to poets of the twelfth century
and to the transmitters who succeeded them.

The study of the visual aspect of songbooks as books and as artifacts
offers us new perspectives on the reception of troubadour lyric among literate clerics who made the parchment anthologies (see Huot 1987). The
copyists' conception of what a lyric is does not necessarily conform in
every detail to the poets' conception or to the audiences' conception. But
to the extent that we can learn how a given anthologist understood his
task, we discover a link in the chain of transmission and its influence over
the form in which he passed down troubadour songs.

To discover how troubadour style might have been shaped by the
poets' expectations about jongleurs, audiences, and the system of circulation, one needs to examine an abundance of poets' comments on style
and transmission. For this reason I concentrate on a period in the development of this poetry when self-conscious artifice prevailed, when the
poets participated in frequent exchange of literary ideas, when they liked
to explain their poetics to audiences capable of appreciating such information. The generation of 1170 is ideal for this purpose. Like *trobadors*
before and after them, they send poems to one another for approval, they
deliver harangues in person, they engage in contests, they exchange *ten-
zones,* and they borrow stanzaic patterns from friends in hopes of out-
doing them. Their "individuality" is abetted rather than isolated by the
awareness of active competition and controversy: the starling returns

with a reply rather than flying off "lonely as a cloud" into the private outlands of independence. Undeniably by 1170, many troubadours did "cultivate a traditional poetry of form"; however, they prized freshly made forms instead of moving toward a small canon of fixed forms. At this time, poets became especially liberal with allusions to their own art: its techniques, its purposes, its hazards. Their individuality springs from their participation in a literary community, with each of their *maintas colors* contributing to the spectrum.

I have chosen some of the poets essential to this inquiry from among those Peire d'Alvernhe teases in his satire of their "many colors." Between June and September 1170, according to Walter T. Pattison's hypothesis (1933), there converged at or near Puivert (Aude) Eleanor II's wedding party, a large group of noblemen, and a following of troubadours:[6]

> Lo vers fo faitz als enflabotz
> a Puoich-vert, tot iogan rizen.
> (P d'Alv 12, 85–86)

The poem was made for the stuff-bellies[7] at Green Peak, all in fun and laughter.

The poem lets us glimpse a bright literary constellation as it once actually convened. It is the sense of literary comradeship reflected in Peire's satire, as well as his assurance that all will join in criticizing and appreciating the unique style and character of each singer, that leads me to begin with this group of poets.

Of the twelve *trobadors* mentioned aside from Peire d'Alvernhe himself, only four names are recognizably those of famous poets. I have already drawn attention to Peire's "inculpation" of Peire Rogier. This poet has been dated to the third quarter of the twelfth century, partly because he spoke as an "experienced senior" to Raimbaut d'Aurenga (born ca. 1144) as early as 1167.[8] He may have been the eldest at the gathering and thus earned first place (and an ironic portrait as an innocent choirboy); however, the descriptions in "Cantarai d'aqestz trobadors" provide no real evidence for a poet's age.

Everything about the passage introducing us to Giraut de Bornelh suggests age: he is described as "a dry wine-skin in the sun" and compared to "an old woman carrying a bucket" looking sadly into a mirror. Yet Giraut, "master of the troubadours," outlived all the other known poets in the group: his documented activity spans nearly forty years (fl. 1162–1199). With these dates, he could have been one of the younger poets gathered in 1170. It is well known that for the troubadours, *jovens* (youth) was a frame of mind rather than a time of life; Peire d'Alvernhe's comments on Giraut, then, tell us more about Giraut's style than about his seniority at the gathering.

The high esteem in which Bernart de Ventadorn was held by his contemporaries can perhaps be gauged by the diminution he undergoes in Peire's satire. "A handsbreadth shorter than Bornelh," Bernart is described not as an adult but as the child of his mother and father. The "ardor" of Bernart's love songs is implicitly ascribed to the heat of his mother's baking-oven. Again, his "youth" is figurative: Bernart's activity as a poet is documented between 1147 and 1170, the gathering at Puivert being his last recorded appearance. Bernart is without doubt the most famous troubadour today, so much so that an inordinately large proportion of discussion of "the troubadours" in general is based on the favorite two or three of his poems.

Of Raimbaut d'Aurenga, Count of Orange and the ninth poet in Peire's gallery, much more is known because of the importance of his family, whose financial doings—testaments, property transfers, oaths of allegiance, receipts of rent—are comparatively well documented.[9] Peire accuses Raimbaut of overvaluing the *pipautz* ("derelict" singers) who come to him for charity. It is true that Raimbaut entertained at his castle Courthézon at least two other troubadours—Peire Rogier and Giraut de Bornelh. But we must not suppose him a wealthy patron; he spent most of his life in debt and died at an early age (about twenty-nine) in 1173, probably from the epidemic of influenza in that year. The jongleur with the beautiful voice, Levet, was present at the signing of his testament. So was another young poet—and his presence at Raimbaut's deathbed has escaped the notice of both troubadours' editors—whose imaginative invention owed much to Raimbaut, both in his versification and in his comic style. That poet was Guilhem de St-Didier, who deserves much more attention than he gets from modern scholars.[10]

Finally, Peire d'Alvernhe describes himself; there are two versions, and in neither of them does Peire spare himself the satirical treatment he has applied to the others. His voice is so bad, he says, that he sings "like a frog in a well." Alternatively, he sings "both above and below." Either way, hardly anyone can understand his words:

Peire d'Alvernge a tal votz
que chanta con granoill' en potz,
e lauza·s mout a tota gen;

> pero maistres es de totz,
> ab c'un pauc esclarzis sos motz,
> c'a penas nuils hom los enten.
>
> (P d'Alv 12, 79–84)[11]

Peire d'Alvernhe has such a voice that he sings like a frog in a
well, and he praises himself much before all kinds of people;
but he is the master of all, if only he would clarify his words a
little, for scarcely anyone understands them.

Peire's documented literary career stretches from 1149 to 1170; like Bernart de Ventadorn, he makes his last recorded appearance in this literary "gallery."

Bernart Marti, whose poetry much resembles that of the influential older poet Marcabru (fl. 1130–1149), perhaps attended the Puivert gathering under the name Bernatz de Saissac (Roncaglia 1969a). His dispute with Peire d'Alvernhe over the practicality of "whole poetry" (*vers entiers*) is only one of many signs that he participated in working out the literary issues confronting the poets of 1170. In Peire's self-description, he is still defending himself against Bernart's accusation of wrongly claiming *de totz maistria* (mastery of all); even now Peire affirms that he is *maistres de totz,* although others (especially Bernart Marti) have misunderstood his words of self-praise—he should have "clarified his words a little." These stylistic controversies, and others like them, are discussed in Chapters 6, "Nature Enclosed" (on *trobar clus, trobar natural,* and related problems), and 7, "The Metaphorical Vocabulary of *Mouvance* and Textual Integrity".

I also include in my study several near-contemporaries of the poets in Peire's gallery, especially those who either contributed to the stylistic debates of circa 1170 or profited from them, whether by providing models for innovation or by borrowing and refining the techniques of others. The most important of these contemporaries are Rigaut de Berbezilh (fl. 1141–1160),[12] Guilhem de St-Didier (fl. 1165–1195), and two Catalan poets, Pons de la Guardia (fl. 1154–d. 1188) and Guilhem de Berguedà (fl. 1138–1192).

Two figures have been included not because of contemporaneity with the poets of 1170 but because of the methods of their modern editors: Jaufre Rudel (fl. 1125–1148) and Peire Vidal (fl. 1183–1204). Both Rupert T. Pickens and d'Arco Silvio Avalle address questions of transmission, textual instability, and writing; the two editors' opposing hypotheses about the poets' efforts to "preserve their songs" reflect a division far more important for the issues dealt with here than the chronological gap between the two poets. While Jaufre Rudel's editor suspects that the poet invited revision of his poems, Peire Vidal's editor claims that the poet compiled his own book to fix his texts for posterity. The two styles of editing depend on two opposite ways of understanding "the lyric text," the mode of transmission, and the importance of authenticity. It will make a great difference for the editing of Provençal song whether other poets, by their own account and their transmitters', tend to resemble Jaufre Rudel as Pickens sees him or Peire Vidal as Avalle sees him.

Finally, no investigation of troubadour poetics can be complete without Arnaut Daniel (fl. 1180–1195). A case can be made for his association with the poets of circa 1170, especially with Raimbaut d'Aurenga, but even without such "literary contacts" he would be useful for this study.[13] He perfects many of the techniques proposed and debated in 1170, and he enjoys describing the goals and processes of composition.

My statistical survey includes twenty-three poets, from Guilhem IX, the first troubadour, to performers of the mid-thirteenth century. After that time there is a historical burgeoning of the influence of literacy and the book culture on poetry, even poetry that relied on conventions developed by the troubadours. My thesis, that the twelfth-century troubadours were ambivalent toward the concept of the fixed text and tried alternately to promote it and to undo it, no longer applies when later poets take reading as the model of reception and writing as the model of composition.

PART ONE

Making and Sending

A VIEW FROM WITHIN THE

LITERARY TEXTS

———

ONE

Amar/Trobar

THE VOCABULARY OF LOVE AND
POETICS

A prerequisite to gathering and interpreting stylistic statements is the ability to recognize such statements when they appear. Having absorbed both the formal approach to trouvère and troubadour lyric and recent historical studies, scholars no longer assume that every troubadour worshiped a high-ranking lady who so stirred his emotions that they "overflowed" into verse. A few have begun to suspect that the Provençal poets' "lexicon of love" is in large part a lexicon of poetry—that the verbs *amar* and *trobar* are almost interchangeable. One of the best formulations of this hypothesis is by Edward I. Condren: "Because of what seems to have been a tacit understanding that the troubadour's love was almost always fictional, and because of the explicit belief that love was always the source of poetic power, it does not seem impossible that the word love and the entire vocabulary used to talk about it came to signify for some the creation of poetry" (1972, 191).

The circumspection of Condren's statement appears to have come from a wish to make only such claims as could be strongly substantiated in a brief article, not from lack of conviction. In fact, this view of love and poetry is ubiquitous in troubadour lyric; Condren finds it in songs by Bernart de Ventadorn, Jaufre Rudel, Peire Vidal, Gui d'Ussel, Guilhem de Montagnagol, and, most unmistakably, Raimbaut d'Aurenga. Condren clearly shows how at least one element of the troubadour's expression of love for "the implied lady"—his "desire" (*talan*)—can function within the lexical field of *trobar*: it is the poet's intention, his will to compose, his "desire" to make the best possible song.

Paul Zumthor's quantitative analysis of the usage of the pair "to love/ to sing" (*aimer/chanter*) in a hundred trouvère songs identifies four ways in which these terms were used interchangeably by the northern French poets. Zumthor is much less reserved than Condren about his conclusion: "However one envisions this situation, it seems to me obvious that the connotative (if not the denotative) clusters represented by 'to sing' on the one hand, and 'to love' on the other, comprise a vast zone of intersection. I would scarcely hesitate to press the metaphor further and to announce bluntly that 'to love' 1 (referring to the subject of the song) is included in 'to sing'" (1971, 135). Zumthor cautiously includes the Occitan poet Bernart de Ventadorn, "whose songs more than the others' furnished the trouvères with the procedures of their art," among the poets conscious of "the circularity of the song," where "the poem is a mirror of the self . . . a mirror which is his eyes [i.e., the singer's eyes], which are Love, which is the Song" (p. 139).

One might object that the troubadours are exempt from Zumthor's conclusions because his concept of the "circular song" depends on the "impersonal I" of the trouvères: only when the "I" and the "you" of the poem recede can "it," the song, become its own self-fulfilling motivation. For the troubadours of around 1170, a highly individualized "I" dominates the song, and it is only the lady who vanishes. This objection can be met in at least two ways. First, "I sing" and "I love" can be equivalent or intersecting activities without weakening the identity of the speaker; on the contrary, the absence of an identified love object intensifies the song's reference to the performing self, and to what it performs. Second, the "individualism" of the troubadours serves their art: these poets have crafted for themselves stage personalities perhaps based on, but probably not identical with, their private characters (Sutherland 1965; Stevens 1978).

Although the intersection of *amar* and *cantar* cannot, without a great deal more and better evidence, settle the historical question of the origins of troubadour lyric,[1] I am convinced that it can assist us in reading troubadour lyric. It can, for example, explain "the split role of the persona"—as lover and as singer—of the most famous (and most apparently sincere in his *fin'amors*) of all the troubadours: Bernart de Ventadorn. In an analysis emphasizing the distinctness of the two roles rather than claiming identity for them, Mariann S. Regan (1974) arrives at surprising results: singer and lover receive unequal emphasis, because time and again in Bernart's songs the dissatisfactions of the unfulfilled lover are transcended and diminished by the artistic fulfillment of the singer.

For the most part, then, the argument that the vocabulary of *amor* intersects that of *trobar* has been restricted to the words *amar/trobar/chantar* themselves and their derivatives. Those who have carried the argument beyond this restriction have limited their claims to a single word (for example, as Condren explains *talan*, "desire" = "intention"), to a single poet's work, or to a single poem.[2]

Nevertheless, the vocabulary of *fin'amors* (pure love) has been thoroughly studied and categorized, both in specialized articles and in comprehensive studies. In a review of such a work, Jean-Charles Payen (1978, of Cropp 1975) complains that "the ideological dimension" is lost when the poets' words are defined solely with reference to the experience of the lover and not of the whole man in his social and historical setting. The entire courtly vocabulary should be reinterpreted, Payen argues, with sensitivity to a broader range of connotation. I would add to this, since "the lover" is essentially a fictitious persona in this poetry, and since "the whole man" is not represented in the spectacle of the *canso,* that the "ideological dimension" through which the courtly vocabulary most needs reinterpretation is the artistic ideology of the *cantador/trobador* (singer/poet).

Before presenting details of this dual vocabulary, where words of love function to describe poetic activity, let me stress that in the chapters to follow I use this mode of interpretation sparingly and with caution. Just as one cannot assume that a poet is always singing about a lady, one cannot assume that he is always singing about his art. My overall purpose has not been to write the dictionary of poetic terms, but to discover how the medium of transmission—no less than the individual creators—made choices of style, form, and flexibility in troubadour song. It is helpful to be able to recognize the subtle affirmations of stylistic preference, and not only the explicit ones. To this end, I will briefly sketch some of the ways in which the troubadours use this ambivalent vocabulary to weave together their two dominant subjects.

We have already seen the most important field of terms that take both *amor* and *trobar* as their object: the poet's will, his motivation to attain his object.[3] These terms have in the past been construed as always marking the influence of a lady. They are all words for intention. The most important of these are *voler, talan, dezir* (will, wish, desire), as well as *cor* and *coratge* (heart); the category includes words that indicate the attitude of volition, such as *ardir* (burn), *s'eslaissar* (rush [to]), and *s'esforsar* (force oneself [to]). Raimbaut d'Aurenga combines the poet's "desire" and the activity that fulfills it in one word: *rima* ("I burn" or "I rhyme").[4] *Joy* is already well recognized as the creative impulse of poetry; few scholars still translate it *jouissance*.

The mental labor that precedes *trobar* is expressed by a group of words that have usually been taken as signs of the lover's pain, distress, and preoccupation with the lady.[5] To the courtly definitions of these words one should add an artistic connotation, since the poet "meditates" on both love and song. *Pessar* and *cossir* (think, worry) direct themselves toward "creating the song" as often as toward "loving a lady." The selection of words and rhymes is governed by *chausimen* (discernment), the ability to *triar son melhs*. The first, *chausimen*, is easily confused with *jauzimen* (enjoyment);[6] this word and *triar* (separate, discern) have both been read as referring exclusively to the selection of lovers or moral codes rather than of rhymes. *Albir* refers to a more decisive stage of thought (cf. *mos albirs*, "in my judgment"). A poet rapt in "thinking up" his song is "thoughtful": *pensius, cossiros,* or *cabals*.[7]

Poetic control is generally expressed as a bond tied by *Amors*, by an unspecified feminine agent, or by the poet. Such verbs as *lassar* and *liar* (tie, bind), *tener en fre* (keep in rein), *metre cadena* (enchain), and *serrar* (constrain) take as their object sometimes *motz* or *vers* (word, poem) and sometimes the speaker, *me, mos cors* (my heart/body) or his *volers* (will, desire). *Esmerar* (to purify) is something the poet does either to his song or to himself; the same is true of *melhurar* (to improve). The song can also take the reflexive form of these verbs and "purify itself" or "improve itself." Both the poet and his poem "grow" (*cresc*). Loss of poetic control, which the poet usually denies, participates in the same vocabulary as does discourtesy toward ladies: *faillir/faillensa* (fail, failure), *franher/frachura* (break, fracture), *desmezura* (breach of good measure). The usage of such terms suggests that at times the poet becomes identified with his poem: *mos cors s'esmera* (my heart/body purifies itself) makes very little sense if we imagine the poet taking a bath; he is purifying "himself," which is his "performing self," and thus his "performance":

> Per que·us deu ben esser plus car
> mas mos cors ves vos s'esmera
> si que res no·i pot camjar.
>
> (R d'Aur, 26, 49–51)

> Therefore I should be more dear to you, since my being [*cor*] refines itself toward you in such a way that nothing can be changed in it.

The claim "nothing can be changed in it" is strongly associated with claims for the stability of the song. Thus, the poet's identification with his song can alert us to subtle declarations about his choice of style and his hopes for its success.

The poet's enemies—and he spends much of his time defaming them—are those who "speak ill," the *lausengiers*. Marcabru has also called them *trobador bergau*, "hornet troubadours." They are rivals, bent on destroying or stealing the poet's reputation, love, and songs. They do not "speak ill" merely by gossiping, but by singing badly: they twist one's words. Much like the comic figure of the blundering jongleur, and often indistinguishable from him as an *avol chantador* (bad singer), the *lausengier* makes songs *pejurar* (get worse), and instead of singing he shouts (*cridar*), twitters (*braire*), or bleats (*bramar*). His evil speech (*mal dich*) brings *dan, mal trach,* and *trebalh*—damage, abuse, and trouble. Some words for gossip serve also as words for publication: *mazan* (the noise of rumor) can mean applause; *ressos* (echo) can mean good fame or ill; *espandre* (spread) can refer to the circulation of a rumor or of a song.

The virtues making up the troubadours' "implied lady" are attributes of songs:

> Ai, bon'amors encobida,
> cors be faihz, delgatz e plas
> frescha chara colorida
> cui Deus formet ab sas mas!
> (B Vent 30, 50–53)

> Ah, desired good love, body well made, delicate, and smooth, fresh, colorful face, that God shaped with his hands!

If there is a lady here, she is an aspect of *Amors* (Love), as is the song; she has not quite materialized. *Bon'amors* conjures up a body and a face, both praised with the same words that poets use to boast about their songs: the body is "well made, delicate, and smooth" like a good melody, and the face is "fresh" and has "color," like a rhetorical trope. The greatest distinction between this being and a song is that she is God's handiwork, rather than Bernart de Ventadorn's. Yet since for us she exists only as this description, even she is Bernart's construct. Like the *canso* (love song), the implied lady is frequently described as *doussa, clara, franca,* and *gaia*—sweet, clear, free, and gay. It does not matter who she is, as long as she, like a song, is "refined and purified":

> S'ieu lieys pert per son folhatge
> ieu n'ay autra espiada
> fina, esmerada e pura.
>
> (Mcb 28, 31–33)

> If I lose her through her folly, I have glimpsed another one—
> refined, purified, and spotless.

She is *coind'e avinen, plazen, rizen* (appealing and comely, pleasant, and laughing). So are many songs. If her love seems too steadfast ever to change, the speaker calls it *veraia, certa,* and *segura*—true, sure, and secure. So he may call his most stable songs. If she is "difficult," he complains that her behavior toward him is *fer, greu,* and *escur*—hard, difficult, and dark, like obscure poetry. He will not associate with a woman he considers *vilana* (lowly), or with *obra vilana* (lowly work).

Benefits conferred by the "implied lady" are implicitly verbal or musical as well as erotic. She "accords" favors or "accords with the speaker"—*acort* and *acordar* refer to "setting words to music." The *benenansa* and *melhurament* she offers "advance" the singer or "improve" the song. *Solatz, plazer,* and *gaug*—company, pleasure, and amusement—are to some extent conversational favors, bestowed in words. The speaker petitions for *merce,* the reward or prize for a good poem in the form of applause and money, of approving speech, or of a kiss.[8] The addressee may "reward" the poet in other ways: by "understanding" him (*entendre*), by "retaining" him (*retener*), or by "understanding" and "retaining" the song, memorizing it (*aprendre*), and "knowing" its contents (*saber*).[9]

Once having tried this approach, the reader will develop a sense of whether these meanings are applicable in a given context. I offer the method of "translation" from *amor* to *trobar* as a useful tool, capable of bringing out one of the "ideological dimensions" of troubadour language: the dimension of the poet's artistic intent. The troubadours are extremely self-conscious, and they are conscious of at least two and perhaps three "selves," for they portray the lover, the poet, and the song with which he identifies himself and which is the means of conveying all three portrayals. Their audience, moreover, was quite sophisticated by

1170. *Entendadors* were *amateurs* who "understood" this art not only through practice in careful listening but in many cases through practice in singing and composing songs too. They were interested in the techniques of expression as much as in the thing expressed.

Reading what may appear to be a declaration about love as a declaration about the love *song* calls for a kind of interpretation with which the troubadours are quite familiar. Their idea of the poem as *drogoman* or *messatge*—as "translator" or "messenger," as diplomatic envoy—shows their awareness that the poem allows them to move between two worlds, giving form and sense to the shapeless "sighs and tears" of inarticulate emotion:

> Ma chansos er drogomanz
> lai on eu non aus anar
> ni ab dretz oillz regardar,
> tan sui conques e aclus.
> (R Berb 2, 45−48)

> My song will be an interpreter, there where I dare not go nor dare look with direct gaze because I am so vanquished and downcast.

The idea of "the song as go-between" proposes a solution to the difficult double task of rendering the lover's "spontaneous emotion" believably in the highly artificial medium of rhymed verse with responding strophes. The song arbitrates between language and eros, imparting some of each of the other. Through its language, especially through the language of double reference, the poem can work out a treaty, act as diplomat, between separate "registers" of language; as ambassador, fluent in the idioms of both sender and receiver, it can "translate" from one code to another, addressing a feudal petition as an amorous one, interpreting the senses for the mind, making the language of poetic technique intelligible to "native speakers" of the language of social intrigue. The "game for one player" (whose object is artistic perfection) and the "game for two players" (whose object is fulfillment in love) share in language that applies to the larger "work" of the community—religion, economics, politics, as well as humbler activities like building and baking.

Bernart Marti does not despair over the incongruity of his two masks or over the need to end the lover's soliloquy with a request for praise of the poet's skill. He sees himself as a kind of civil servant, a political arbiter. The verb *entrebescar,* among other meanings, denotes the patterned intertwining of sound and sense. Bernart makes of it, and of *Amors,* a sort of whimsical proper name; he describes his own diplomacy as a poet who sings both of love and of poetry:

> N'Eblon man ves Margarida
> lo vers per un mesatgier,
> qu'en lui es amor jauzida
> de don'e de cavalier.
> Et ieu soi sai ajustaire
> de dos amicx d'un vejaire,
> n'Aimes e·n L'Estrebesquiu.
>
> N'Aimes e·n L'Estrebeschaire
> son dui amic d'un vejaire
> . . . ab l'entrebeschiu.
>   (B Mar 7, 57–66) [10]

To Sir Ebles near Margarida I send the verse by way of a messenger, for through it love is enjoyed between ladies and knights. And, here, I am the adjustment officer between two friends of one mind, Sir Love and Sir Intertwine.

Sir Love and Sir Intertwine are two friends of one mind . . . with intertwining.

For Bernart, as for many other troubadours, love is a matter of language. Except for the most intimate moments, it consists entirely of speeches, pleas, promises, agreements, avowals—in short, of words. Bernart does not confine this observation to the sublimated spiritual love that one often hears ascribed to the troubadours, those pleas and flatteries from afar. Even the kiss, the "reward" (*merces*) of the petition for love, is for him a "linguistic act":

> C'aisi vauc entrebescant
> los motz e·l so afinant:
> lengu'entrebescada
> es en la baisada.
>   (B Mar 4, 60–64)

Thus I intertwine the words and the music, refining [completing] them: tongue [language] intertwined is in the kiss.

Bernart suggests that a good song provides its own "prize" for the *cantador,* if the *amador*'s prize is a lady's kiss. The "intertwining tongue" boasts simultaneously of the lover's success and of the poet's craft. Bernart shows us the one moment when lovers, after so much talking, are "tongue-tied."

Ultimately, eros is subsumed into language, and not the other way around. This book concentrates, therefore, on what the poets tell us about their words rather than about their loves. What was "the lyric" to them? What were its ideals, its limitations? The first step in understanding their conception of poetry is to understand their medium.

TWO

Writing and Memory in the Creation and Transmission of Troubadour Poetry

No other body of poetry confronts its editors with so overgrown a wilderness of autonomous versions, nearly every surviving copy a unique variation, as does troubadour song. Some variants ornament the poem, others whitewash it; some betray a slip of the pen or of the eye, others record the ear's perception of two radically different meanings in approximately the same sound;[1] still others, in a manner not explicable as the mechanical error or "vandalism" of scribes and compilers, evince a thorough recasting of the work. For example, a total of thirty-two distinct versions, distributed among six surviving songs of Jaufre Rudel, are now available in an edition of Jaufre's work by Rupert Pickens (1978). Readers accustomed to the monomorphic poem (either an editor's "best" choice or a composite) might hope that Jaufre's works were anomalous in their mobility. But it is not so: a study of 518 troubadour poems found "that nearly 40% of these songs show permutation in stanza order" (Paden 1979, 3). The percentage is much higher if we consider other kinds of variation: abridgments, alternative *tornadas*, and "fractured" stanzas.[2] Further, the variability in form and content of each poem in the Jaufre canon, if it developed in transmission and not through authorial redaction alone, implies a set of distinctly unmodern assumptions that pervaded the entire transmitting culture from a very early stage through a very late one.

The notion of *mouvance*, of "the text in process of creating itself," is borne out by the *chansonniers'* testimony to extensive change in most troubadour lyric. By comparison with Jaufre Rudel's, many of Bernart de Ventadorn's songs appear to be even more "fluid" because many more copies have survived. To take an extreme case, his "Non es meravelha s'eu chan / Melhs de nulh autre chantador" ("It is no wonder if I sing better than any other singer") comes down in nineteen manuscripts (excluding stray *coblas*), and Carl Appel had to choose for his edition among eleven different arrangements of strophes (1915, 187). The thought that its self-congratulatory incipit made it a favorite among *chantadors,* who tailored it to suit themselves, is hard to resist. For the literary text, no less than for the musical notation, we must imagine either that the compilers of the *chansonniers* innovated drastically as often as they transcribed mechanically,[3] or that most of these variations already figured in the "texts" before extant compilations were written.

The customary anonymity of medieval poets might be held responsible for textual instability in other medieval literary traditions. Since the songs of the troubadours purport not to be anonymous works, the question of the authenticity of many disparate versions must draw the serious reader, as well as the editor, into a study of the process of transmission itself. D'Arco Silvio Avalle faced this problem in his edition of Peire Vidal's poems (1960) and arrived at a system of authentication based on comparing the *chansonniers'* selections and orderings of Peire's poems. Deducing an autograph collection—that is, an anthology written by the poet himself, the "libro del Vidal" of Avalle's introduction—the Italian scholar believed he could rate the extant manuscripts according to their stemmatic relationship to it. Pickens set out to follow this example in his edition of Jaufre Rudel, "by rigorous application of Lachmannian principles":

> It soon became apparent, however, that not only can "authentic" texts not be discovered, much less "established" with a sufficient degree of certainty, but that, given the condition of the manuscripts and the esthetic principles involving textual integrity affirmed by Jaufre himself as well as by his transmitters, the question of "authenticity," insofar as the meaning of the texts was concerned, was largely irrelevant. (Pickens 1978, 40)

What I intend to explore in this discussion of the transmission of troubadour poetry is the degree to which other poets and their transmitters shared the "esthetic principles involving textual integrity" that Pickens observes in the songs of Jaufre Rudel. There are two separate questions here: first, whether the troubadours did invite their transmitters to revise their poems; and second, whether the transmitters were inclined to do so even without an invitation.

A great deal depends on the breadth or narrowness of the "gap between creation and transmission" [4]—that is, the degree to which, or the way in which, poets and transmitters agreed or were at variance on the subject of textual integrity. If the mutability of poems from one *chansonnier* to another reflected no more than one of the worst manuscript traditions in literary history, all because its scribes were so singularly and reliably erratic, then we would find no continuous lineage of "principles involving textual integrity." Rather, we would have to assume that the "chirographic folk" (Ong 1982) had disregarded the original poets' aesthetic principles in favor of their own and had allowed their pens to slip with extreme indulgence when it came to troubadour poetry.

One may overestimate the gap between creation and transmission, whether a gap of chronology or of mentality, if one forgets that a poem composed in 1150 must have been "transmitted" in one way or another before it was anthologized in 1254. True, many elements the poets valued in their songs had worn thin by the time the anthologies were written. The blank staves in the manuscripts where music should have been noted in; the bookish tracts from the period of compilation recommending a poetics so far removed from that of the classical troubadours that it used their works as a source of exemplary "vices"; the utter incomprehension of the late scribe of MS Q who filled all the blanks between *cansos* with fragments of miscollated *tensos*—all these instances point to more than the ordinary hazards of medieval dissemination. [5]

Yet the inconsistency of extant written sources reflects health rather than sickness, insofar as it reflects an ongoing practice of singing troubadour lyric. Ong (1982, 81) points out the "startling paradox" that associates writing with death: writing destroys memory, and the letter kills. If there was a continuous performing tradition, perpetuating an aesthetic upheld by the troubadours themselves, then the diversity of current versions as manifested in writing, beginning around 1250, does not record the decadence of a dying art but the energy of a very lively one:

> There is no reason to suppose that a nearly equal amount of diversity was not current before 1250. . . . Manifestations of texts are like bubbles accidentally rising to the surface which do little to evidence the currents and crosscurrents below. Thus, one cannot reasonably assume that a text by an author active around 1150 which is manifested in 1250 is any more "authentic" than one written down in 1350. Everything depends upon the

quality of the traditions from which samples were selected by anthologizers. (Pickens 1978, 20–21)

"Authentication" may in some cases be available only in the poet's implicit consciousness and approval of the song's tendency to be essentially re-created in each act of its transmission.

Fortunately, the poets express themselves abundantly on the subject of the diffusion of their works: they speak of their intention to *send* their songs just as frequently as they announce the plan to *compose* a song. The place of honor given the topic of transmission within the poetry itself spotlights the very medium of the lyric as essential to its purpose and to the communication it contains. The *exordium* and the *envoi* often locate the addressee and the means of the song's conveyance inside the poem rather than outside it, just as the speaker himself is inside the song. Eloquence is the fabric of *fin'amors* (as well as of *castimen* in the *sirventes*); in the medium of the poem, *dichs e fachs* (words and deeds) unite, for the speech itself is a deed in the negotiation it depicts. To "send the message" is to complete the song, entrusting it to the audience where it will do its persuasive work, give aesthetic pleasure, and live on. The fact of sending, then, has a legitimate place in the matter of the song: it is as well established a motif as praise of the lady and condemnation of those who speak falsely.

Medieval Editors: Jaufre de Foixa, Bernart Amoros, and Bernard de Clairvaux

Medieval compilers and theorists, when they expressed their principles of textual permanence, more than once cited the poets as the "wise men" whose example they have tried to follow. Jaufre de Foixa, in his *Regles de trobar,* appeals to authority (in this case, one who abdicates his authority) for a precedent to his own willingness to be corrected:

> E si alcuna causa de repreniment hi ha ques eu non entenda, a mi platz fort que la puesquen esmenar segons rayso; car N'Aymerich de Peguilha m'o ensenya en una sua canço dient en axi:
>
>> Si eu en soy desmentitz
>> C'aysso no sia veritatz
>> No n'er om per mi blasmatz
>> Si per ver m'o contreditz;

Ans vey sos sabers plus grans
Si·m pot venser d'ayso segons rayso
Qu'eu non say ges tot lo sen Salamo.

(Marshall 1972, 56)

And if there is any unintentional cause for reproach here, I would be very pleased if they could emend it according to reason, for Aimeric de Peguilhan teaches me this [attitude] in one of his songs, speaking thus: "If I am deceived in this, so that this be not the truth, then no man shall be criticized by me [on my account] if for the sake of truth he contradicts me;

rather, I recognize his knowledge as greater if he can win out over me with reason, for I by no means know all the wisdom of Solomon."

Only someone who "knows the truth" better than Aimeric, then, would venture to correct any false statements in his work; Aimeric authorizes such corrections, implying that criticism itself demonstrates superior knowledge. Jaufre de Foixa extends this principle, a matter of truth, to "any cause for reproach" that might require "emendation" in his treatise. He invites his readers to change his text if they find errors in it (again, the ability to criticize proves wisdom); more interesting, he believes that the troubadour Aimeric extended the same invitation. The special privilege of the highly qualified reader here reaches its peak: permission to rewrite the book.

In similar fashion, the medieval compiler Bernart Amoros cites one of the poets, *uns savis* (a wise man), to confirm his idea that only the best qualified, those most nearly approaching the wisdom of Solomon, should undertake to emend a text: when the *emendador* "does not have understanding," then even the finest work is likely to be spoiled (see text below, points 7 and 8). In a sense, Bernart Amoros and Jaufre de Foixa share a tolerant view of intelligent, informed "improvements" to the text: Jaufre welcomes emendation "segons rayso" (according to reason), and Bernart allows it, implicitly, wherever an "emender" has "ben aüt l'entendimen" (truly grasped the intended meaning). Each admits that his own version is not always letter-perfect.

In the light of current thinking about *mouvance* and transmission, Bernart Amoros's "curieuse note" takes on a significance hardly suspected since its publication by Ernest Stengel (1898, 350).[6] Bernart's preface to a collection of troubadour songs survives in the paper manuscript *a*. As a first-person account of how a medieval compiler of troubadour poetry might operate, describing the choices open to him and the principles he followed, the passage from beginning to end offers rare and valuable information about medieval editing—an art that otherwise, in the *chansonnier* tradition, kept silent about itself and in its very anonymity disavowed its creativity as well as its conservatism, concealing its efforts behind fair copy under authors' names. Matfre Ermengaud—if (as Gustav Gröber believed) he did prepare *chansonnier* C for copying—prefaced it with no such frank statement of method.[7] Because of the premises he takes for granted, as well as the ideas he presents as his own personal insight, Bernart Amoros's foreword is reproduced here in full.[8]

Eu Bernartz Amoros clergues scriptors d'aquest libre si fui d'Alvergna don son estat maint bon trobador, e fui d'una villa que a nom Saint Flor de Planeza. E sui usatz luenc temps per Proenza per las encontradas on son mout de bonz trobadors, et ai vistas et auzidas maintas bonas chanzos. (2) Et ai apres tant en l'art de trobar q'eu sai cognoisser e devezir en rimas et en vulgar et en lati, per cas e per verbe, lo dreig trobar del fals. Per qu'eu dic qe en bona fe eu ai escrig en aqest libre drechamen lo miels q'ieu ai saubut e pogut. (3) E si ai mout emendat d'aquo q'ieu trobei en l'issemple, don eu o tiejn e bon e dreig, segon lo dreig lengatge. (4) Per q'ieu prec chascun que non s'entrameton de emendar e granren que si ben i trobes cors de penna en alcuna letra. (5) Chascuns homs, si truep pauc ne saubes, [no] pogra leumen aver drecha l'entencion. Et autre(s) fail non cuig qe i sia bonamen. (6) Que granz faillirs es d'ome que si fai emendador sitot ades non a l'entencion. (7) Qe maintas vetz, per frachura d'entendimen, venon afollat maint bon mot obrat primamen e d'avinen razo. (8) Si com dis uns savis:

> Blasmat venon per frachura
> D'entendimen obra pura
> Maintas vetz de razon prima
> Per maintz fols que-s tenon lima.

(9) Mas ieu m'en sui ben gardatz. Que maint luec son qu'eu non ai ben aüt l'entendimen, per q'ieu non ai ren volgut mudar, per paor q'ieu non peiures l'obra. Que truep volgra esser prims e sutils hom qi o pogues tot entendre, specialmen de las chanzos d'En Giraut de Borneill lo maestre.[9]

I, Bernart Amoros, cleric, writer of this book, came from Auvergne, from which many good troubadours have come; and I was from a town that has the name Saint Flor de Planeza. And I have spent a long time [traveling] through Provence and through regions where there are many good troubadours, and I have seen and heard many good songs. (2) And I have learned so much in the art of poetic composition that I can recognize and distinguish, in rhymes both in the vernacular and in Latin, by case and by verb, the right *trobar* from the false. Therefore I say that in good faith I have written this book, correctly, to the best of my knowledge and ability. (3) And I have emended much of what I found in the exemplar, which I consider both good and proper to do, according to correct language. (4) Therefore I beg every man not to undertake to emend a great deal unless you truly find a slip of the pen in some letter. (5) Every man, if he knows too little, will not easily be able to get the intended meaning right. And I do not think that another man's error should properly be there. (6) For it is a great failing in a man who makes himself an emender unless he first has the intended meaning. (7) For many times, through a flaw in understanding, many good verses of the first workmanship and elegant reasoning have come to a bad end. (8) As a wise man says: "Through flaws in understanding of the first *razo,* pure works often come to be blamed, on account of many fools with erasers in their hands." But I took good care not to do this. For there are many passages where I did not really grasp the intention, and for this reason I did not wish to change anything, for fear that I might make the work worse. For a man will have to be extremely superior and subtle in order to understand everything, especially the songs of Giraut de Bornelh, the master.

In describing his background and travels, Bernart Amoros is not indulging in mere vanity: he is giving his credentials. By using the *vida* form for his autobiographical introduction, he presents himself as the peer of the troubadours, like them an initiate in the art of lyric composition. He counts on his reader's believing that the proximity of his birthplace to the origin of so many good troubadours, as well as his extensive travels in Provence and Auvergne, enhances his qualifications to distinguish "lo dreig trobar del fals." Certainly *trobar* was still a living art at the time of Bernart's visits, since it is clear from the passage that Bernart was not limited to traveling from library to library examining manuscripts: not only did he *see* many songs; he *heard* them also. He implies that the troubadours' native lands were a particularly abundant and reliable source of their songs; we may infer that each region not only preserved copies of its natives' works (the songs Bernart "saw") but also maintained them in a performing tradition (the songs he "heard").

When Bernart says that he has "learned so much in the art of composition" that he can *devezir* (make decisions) both "en vulgar e en lati" (in the vernacular and in Latin), he does not necessarily mean only that he has become a good critic, an informed member of poetry's audience. He may also mean that he can versify. Five Latin hexameters bearing his name survive, at the end of a collection of Latin proverbs; they demonstrate that his enthusiasm extends to his having learned to create original lines in the style of what he edited:

> Anno milleno ter centum ter quoque deno
> Adjuncto terno complevit tempore verno
> Dictus Amorosus Bernardus, in his studiosus,
> Librum presentem, proverbia mille tenentem,
> Milleque quingentos versus hic ordine junctos.[10]

> In the year one thousand three hundred and thirty and three added, in the springtime, the man called Bernart Amoros, a devoted student of these matters, completed the present book containing a thousand proverbs, and a thousand five hundred lines of verse here adjoined in order.

Bernart knew his contemporaries—both copyists and compilers—better than we know them today, and if he thought it necessary to make a special plea for careful, responsible copying, we can be sure that he expected *emendadors* by the dozen. He himself was one, and in good conscience. He begs that others correct *only* "slips of the pen," implying that writers of the day were in the habit of correcting more serious errors, perhaps even the kinds of errors (*vicis*) for which the grammarians constantly reproach the *anciens trobadors*. What saves Bernart Amoros, at least in his own eyes, is that he made his emendations "in good faith," following both "correct language" and "the intended meaning." In his view, one *must* resort to mechanical transcription when one has not understood the passage. He admits that this has been his practice "especially with the songs of Sir Giraut de Bornelh the master." But how does Bernart proceed when he does understand the passage before him and finds it "flawed"? He emends "much." And it requires all the powers of this learned man, who has taken pains not only to learn the grammar but also to listen to as many songs as possible in their native lands, and who can write original verse if necessary, to make these emendations "rightly, to the best of my knowledge and ability."[11]

Sylvia Huot, who has recently commented on Bernart Amoros's preface, argues that this late-thirteenth-century text reflects an attitude that "can exist only within the framework of a written literary tradition; it is foreign to the semi-improvisational oral tradition." The case for this conclusion is well-stated in Huot's book: "For Bernart, vernacular and Latin poetry alike exist as a written tradition, governed by strict rules of poetic and grammatical form. His concern with textual emendations further reflects a consciousness of the poem as having a fixed form, composed by a gifted individual; the task of the copyist is to restore and preserve the work of the masters" (1987, 333). Yet Bernart's concern is not so much with preserving the literal utterances of the gifted individual (and Giraut de Bornelh is the only poet Bernart mentions as particularly deserving of non-emendation) but with preserving the "rightness" of the poem. As for the claim that Bernart's attitude belongs exclusively to a written tradition, we should not discount Bernart's "seeing and hearing" of many songs. It may be that in his "fieldwork" he conceived of himself as seeking the "right" version of any given song, assuming that the "right" version would of course coincide with the "authentic" or "authorial" version. Nonetheless, Bernart obviously was exposed to the "semi-improvisational oral tradition" and was keenly aware of the existence of variant versions.

It is unlikely that Bernart Amoros's plea for literal copying by the tasteless scribes of posterity reflects a sudden, late upsurge in zealous emendation. Even in the twelfth century we find much concern about the reproduction of musical texts. Bernard de Clairvaux addresses the preface of his treatise on song (*De cantu*) both to future copyists and to future singers: "omnibus transcripturis hoc Antiphonarium, sive cantaturis in illo" (to all those who will transcribe this Antiphonary, or who will sing in it). St. Bernard apparently detects *mouvance* in the traditional antiphonary of the Cistercians and wishes to correct this situation, finding it unseemly for *laudes Deo*. Observing that the songs have long been entrusted to those who sang them,

> Cantum quem Cisterciensis Ordinis ecclesiae cantare consueverant, licet gravis et multiplex absurditas, diu tamen canentium commendavit auctoritas
>
> The song which the assemblies of the Cistercian order are accustomed to sing—though granted it is a serious and manifold absurdity—has nevertheless for a long time been entrusted by authority to those singing it,

he urges that some regularity be adopted in singing by monks who, in all other respects, follow the Rule:

> Dignum siquidem est, ut qui tenent Regulae veritatem, praetermissis aliorum dispensationibus, habeant etiam rectam canendi scientiam, repudiatis eorum licentiis, qui similitudinem magis, quam naturam in cantibus attendentes, cohaerentia disjungunt, et conjungunt opposita; sicque omnia confundentes, cantum prout libet, non prout licet, incipiunt et terminant, deponunt et elevant, componunt et ordinant. Unde nemo miretur aut indignetur, si cantum aliter quam huc usque audierit, in plerisque mutatum invenerit. (Migne 1844–1902, vol. 182, cols. 1121ff.)

> If in fact it is proper that those who uphold the truth of the Rule, ignoring the directions of others, yet still have true knowledge of how to sing, refusing the liberties taken by those men, who, paying more attention to similitude than to nature in songs, disjoin coherences and conjoin opposites; and thus, confounding everything, as they will and not as they should, they begin and end the song, lower and raise it, put it together and put it in order. Thus, no one is astonished or indignant if he hears a song different from the way it was in the past, and finds changes in several places.

St. Bernard is speaking both of the melodies and of the words to these church songs; he finds an "excusatio facilis" (easy excuse) for "mutatio litterae" (change in the letter) in the fact that most of the repeated phrases in the antiphonary are nowhere to be found in the Scriptures. His desire to establish a fixed text for nonscriptural material, and the weight of the opposition to fixity in song that his preface is designed to overcome, show how deeply ingrained must have been the distinction between divinely inspired texts (to be reproduced *prout licet*) and mere human, transitory utterances (to be reproduced *prout libet*). Yet Bernard de Clairvaux seeks to give his own edition of the antiphonary some of the lustre and integrity of a sacred text. Like Bernart Amoros, the saint explains that he has made many necessary changes and now desires that no one after him undertake the same charge.

Raimon Vidal, in the *Razos de trobar,* observes that troubadour poetry has captured the imagination, and the memory, of the listening public. Audiences are not mere audiences—they participate. *Everyone* from the highest walk of life to the lowest has taken a daily interest in poetry, both composing and singing it:

Totas genz cristianas, iusieuas et sarazinas, emperador, princeps, rei, duc, conte, vesconte, contor, valvasor, clergue, borgues, vilans, paucs e granz, meton totz iorns lor entendiment en trobar et en chantar, o q'en volon trobar o q'en volon entendre o q'en volon dire o q'en volon auzir; qe greu seres en loc negun tan privat ni tan sol, pos gens i a paucas o moutas, qe ades non auias cantar un o autre o tot ensems, qe neis li pastor de la montagna lo maior sollatz qe ill aiant an de chantar. Et tuit li mal e·l ben del mont son mes en remembransa per trobadors. Et ia non trobares mot [ben] ni mal dig, po[s] trobaires l'a mes en rima, qe tot iorns [non sia] en remembranza, qar trobars et chantars son movemenz de totas galliardias.

(cited in Poe 1984, 69)

All people—Christians, Jews, and Saracens, emperors, princes, kings, dukes, counts, viscounts, *contors,* vavasseurs, clerics, bourgeois, peasants, small and great, every day apply their attention to poetry and song, either that they want to compose it or they want to understand it or they want to recite it or they want to listen to it; so that you could hardly find yourself in any place so private or so isolated, be there few or many people, that you would not hear singing one person or another or all of them at once, for even the shepherds of the mountains, the greatest amusement that they have is to sing. And all the goods and evils of the world have been placed in remembrance by the troubadours. And never will you find anything, well or badly said, once a troubadour has set it to rhyme, which will not forever be in memory, for poetic composition and singing are movements of all gladness.

But few of these amateurs know how to compose *properly* ("la drecha maniera de trobar"), so Raimon must take it upon himself to set them straight. As for his own book, Raimon is equally conservative and monumentalist: "Per qu'ieu vos dig qe en neguna ren, pos basta ni ben ista, no·n deu om ren ostar ni mais metre" (Therefore I tell you that in no detail, since it suffices and is good as it stands, should a man take anything out or put in anything more). Let the public wreak havoc on troubadour poetry, but let it leave untouched the manual for undoing that havoc! Raimon Vidal's *Razos* have been dated by Jeanroy at ca. 1200—half a century before the writing of the earliest extant troubadour songbook. We may notice that in Raimon's list of all the things people want to do to poetry—hear it, understand it, compose it, recite it—we do not see the words *read* and *write*. The song was a matter for *remembranza*—memory.

If troubadour poetry was "a dying art" after 1254 in its native land, surely it continued to be a living art in its adoptive *patriae*—in Italy, Catalonia, northern France—in the regions, that is, where most of the early *chansonniers* were compiled. Ferrari de Ferrara, Bernart Amoros, and Miquel de la Tor were all, to some extent, practicing poets as well as makers of books. Ferrari de Ferrara

> fo giullar et intendez meill detrobar proensal che negus om che fos mai en lombardia e meill entendet la lenga proensal e sap molt be letras e scriuet meil ch'om del mond e feis de molt bos libres e de beil. . . . Mas non fes mais .II. cancos e una retruensa mais seruentes e coblas fes el asai de las meillor del mon e fe un estrat de tutas las cancos des bos trobador del mon.
>
> (Teulié and Rossi 1901–1902, 13:60–61)

was a jongleur and understood better how to compose poetry in Provençal than any man who was still living in Lombardy, and he better understood the Provençal language and knew letters very well and wrote better than any man in the world and made some very good and beautiful books. . . . But he only composed two love songs and one *retruensa,* but he composed plenty of sirventes and *coblas,* some of the best in the world, and he made a selection of all the love songs of the good troubadours of the world.

The sixteenth-century scholar Giovanni Barbieri, according to his book on the origins of rhymed poetry, had the same text, with a few additions, on page 5 of his *libro slegato* (Barbieri 1790, 84). In the biography of Peire Cardenal (d. ca. 1272), Miquel de la Tor solemnly certifies that he personally wrote the sirventes of Peire following the vida, that he was in Nîmes when he wrote it, and (as if he knew Peire) that the poet was more than a hundred years old when he died. Beyond that, the only trace of Miquel's work is preserved in Barbieri's testimony, and that only in a book published more than two hundred years after Barbieri wrote it.[12] Barbieri quotes poetry from a book he calls the "Libro di Michele" and cites the following statements from it (Italian phrases are Barbieri's):

> Maistre Miquel de la Tor de Clarmon del Vernhesi escrius aquest libre estant en Monpeslier &c.
>
> E ne scrisse ancora delle sue in soggetto del suo amore, di cui dice in una Canzone:
>
> > En Narbone era plantatz
> > L'albre quem fara murir,

Et en Monpeslier es cazatz
En molt bon luec se nes mentir.
(Barbieri 1790, 120–121)

"Master Miquel de la Tor, from Clermont in Alvernhe, wrote this book
while he was in Montpellier etc." And he wrote more of his own [poetry]
on the subject of his own love, of which he says in a canso: "In Narbonne
was planted the tree which will make me die, and in Montpellier it [the
tree] fell, in many a good place and that's no lie."

Like Bernart Amoros, these men in their biographies evince the conviction that to compile and copy troubadour lyric poetry one should be
able to compose it. Ferrari de Ferrara tried his hand at various genres but
specialized in the sirventes (political satire)—yet his compilation is one of
cansos. Miquel de la Tor, scholar though he was, adopts the ethos and
idiom of the poet/lover ("que·m fara murir") with his boast that his song
(the "tree," the body of knowledge he has mastered in Montpellier) has
been well distributed ("es cazatz en molt bon luec"). Poets and compilers,
these men's expertise in troubadour poetry came not only from reading
but also from performing and listening to others perform.

For these reasons we must now challenge the accepted theory (of
Gröber, Avalle, and Marshall) that all the poetry anthologized in the
chansonniers descends exclusively from authorized *Liederblätter* (song
sheets) distributed, multiplied, and modified only through repeated copying *from copies*.[13] There is no proof that twelfth-century jongleurs habitually referred to written copies as they sang their renditions; indeed, there
is evidence that many of these performers were illiterate (Paden 1979,
4–5; Paden 1984, 97–98). It is also, as Hendrik van der Werf points out,
very likely that some copies were taken down from performances rather
than from written texts. The act of transcription itself, given medieval
methods of reading, may have tended to reenact performance. Van der
Werf, in his study of variants in musical notation, observes that

there was no one prescribed way of performing a certain chanson, nor was
there the uniformity in musical notation that we know now. Furthermore,
we may conclude that the scribes did not copy at sight symbol for symbol.
Instead, the differences between certain manuscripts suggest that a scribe
may have sung to himself a section from the draft in front of him—not
necessarily the melody of exactly one entire line—and then copied from
memory what he had heard rather than what he had seen. Consequently he

put himself in the position of a performer notating his own performance.

(1972, 30)[14]

Bernart Amoros implies strongly that the correctness of the text he writes owes as much to the fact that he has "seen and heard" many songs as to "so qu'ieu trobei en l'issemple" (that which I found in the exemplar). Might not a copyist, familiar with a song *as song* more than as tuneless poetry, also sing the words to himself as he wrote, copying what he sang rather than what he saw? Might not he sing, moreover, what he had heard in preference to what he had read? The adaptability of spelling to conform to the scribe's own pronunciation of the language would surely not detract from this point of view: one might cite, for example, the "nonidentical twin" manuscripts G and Q in their presentation of the poems of Rigaut de Berbezilh: the six songs are given in exactly the same order, with a line-for-line correspondence that suggests a case where both copies were made from the same original, yet there is almost no letter-for-letter correspondence in their spelling (Bertoni 1912, 187–196; Bertoni 1905, 85–90).

Our modern literalism, influenced by the printing press, conceives of the "faithful copy" in quite a different sense from Bernart Amoros's transcription "en bona fe" (in good faith). It is true that "matters of editorial technique" need to come more to the attention of readers of troubadour poetry; it is also true that "at least in certain kinds of lyric poetry, the exact letter of the text matters a very great deal indeed" (Marshall 1975, 11). But do those "certain kinds of lyric poetry" to which Marshall refers properly include all troubadour songs, early and late, whether they forbid the jongleur to *camjar lo ver* or request that he improve it? This exactitude, this reverence for the "well-wrought Urn," for these "letters" and "texts," certainly is essential to our modern conception of lyric poetry. Nonetheless, we now have reason to doubt that the troubadours defined "lyric poetry" exactly as twentieth-century poets do. Marshall believes that written composition and purely written transmission allow us to reconstruct an authentic original text; underlying this belief are the assumption that such a text once existed and the hope that, like modern poets, the troubadours strove to perfect one original version and then, through written circulation, to claim it as inviolable literary property:

> in so far as we can reconstruct the textual history of individual poets or songs, that history seems to be one of written texts, without interference (or with no demonstrable interference) from memorial transmission. So far

as we can now ascertain, written copies were in circulation virtually from the moment of composition and formed ultimately the basis for the manuscript collections which have come down to us. (Marshall 1975, 14)

Since, as a matter of fact, "demonstrable interference from memorial transmission" is evident not only in the quality of variants in the *chansonniers* but also in the testimony of the troubadours themselves, we should reexamine this reconstructed "textual history . . . of written texts." A crucial question in evaluating the poets' own ideas of a "faithful copy" is the extent to which their own use of writing, and of other methods of promoting literalism and fixing their words, made the exact letter of the text matter to them. As we shall see, the twelfth-century poets know about writing but show little sign of using it either to compose or to fix their texts. They occasionally use "fixative" rhyme schemes, but only 10 to 20 percent of the time. They frequently speak to the addressee as to a future reciter of the song, and they occasionally ask for the kind of emendation "in good faith" that will, if necessary, "improve" their lyrics.

Images of the Writing Poet

Evidence that the troubadours used writing as an aid in composing, recording, and transmitting their songs often poses interpretive problems, for it is far rarer than the evidence for memorizing "carriers." There remains the possibility that even the more formally complex poems could have been composed in the author's head and then noted down afterward. This may be difficult for us to accept, in an era when the lyric is considered a form that aspires to perfection "to the letter." Ezra Pound, a modern poet who knew the labors of composition in exacting forms of rhymed and metered verse, could not imagine Bertran de Born other than as a writing poet. He suggests that when fact runs out we "try fiction," and envisions Bertran scribbling at a table on strips of parchment, swearing as he revises, "testing his list of rhymes," scratching and erasing quarrelsome words. Pound's vision comes complete with green eyes and a "red straggling beard." [15]

Ezra Pound's image of composition is borne out by some allusions in the works of the troubadours and undercut by others. Much of Gröber's (1877) evidence for the use of *Liederblätter* (individual song sheets) during composition comes from the time of Giraut Riquer, when written transmission had begun seriously to monumentalize in the permanent anthologies. The conclusion that pen and paper necessarily made it easier to "test one's list of rhymes" may owe its credibility to what "seems" true to the modern vision (which lacks some of the medieval acuity in audition) of lyric poetry. Pound's description of Bertran is a self-portrait, and the green eyes and red beard are not the only features borrowed from the modern poet to fill in what we do not know about the medieval one.[16] As Gröber puts it, it *seems* inconceivable that paper and pen would not have "helped" in so complex an art: "The poetry and composition of the troubadours in no way seems to have been so easy that parchment and pen would not have provided a welcome aid to the fixing of their thoughts" (1877, 338).

Miniatures in the *chansonniers* often depict the Occitan poets writing, most often on a long scroll. The artist's conception does not distinguish between the poet composing verse on paper and the poet making a record of what he has composed. Sylvia Huot observes that in the trouvère MSS O, M, P, and W, "the scroll is an iconographic motif suggesting song as such—the lyric text, destined ultimately for oral performance. . . . The scroll as a visual image carried connotations of orality from its use as the medieval equivalent of the 'voice balloon': a figure held an unfurled scroll bearing the words that he or she was meant to be saying." The trouvère MS A, by contrast, depicts books (Huot 1987, 78–79). She also finds, in trouvère manuscripts, that "in every image of 'song making,' the song is represented by a scroll." While in one manuscript the scroll is inscribed with the opening line of the song being illustrated, in two others the figures holding the scrolls are not looking at them, and in two cases the scrolls are rolled up (p. 78). The manuscripts in Huot's study date from the end of the thirteenth century and later. Although these pictures of the scroll-using poet could have been influenced by the assumptions of the growing book culture for which they were painted, it is true that, executed so soon after the flourishing of the classical troubadour tradition, and many of them decades before its last revival, they may spring from factual knowledge of the poets' usage.[17]

The image of the writing troubadour is also validated by several allusions in the works of the poets. Jaufre Rudel's famous lines remain ambiguous:

> Senes breu de pargamina
> Tramet lo vers en chantan.
> (J Rud 2/1, 29–30)

Without a letter of parchment I send the poem by singing.

These lines could indicate either that the usual way to *trametre un vers* did involve a written letter[18] or, on the contrary, that the lyric form, inscribed on the memory instead of on parchment, distinguishes itself from other kinds of permanent documents—deeds, contracts, or prose letters.

Guilhem IX complained that he had not *seen* any news:

> De lai don plus m'es bon e bel
> non vei mesager ni sagel.
>
> (Gm IX 10, 7–8)

> From the place that most pleases me, I see neither a messenger
> nor a seal.

Jeanroy, I think, is right in translating *sagel* as metonymous: "une lettre scellée," a sealed letter.

As late as the composition of some of the longer *razos*, the biographers still hesitate between depicting written exchange with literate ladies and reporting exchange via a human envoy. The *razo* of a poem by Guilhem de Balaun (P.-C. 208,1) is recounted in two manuscripts, and there is a telling discrepancy between two versions of the role of the go-between, Bernart d'Anduza, as he "transmits" to Guilhem's lady the song "Lo vers mou mercejan vas vos."[19] In *H*, Bernart carries a written copy of the poem: "Si·l portet lo vers escrit" (And he brought her the written poem). The equivalent action in *R*, however, runs to 150 words: Bernart rides to Balaun, where he interviews the poet; thence he goes to visit the lady "e comtet tota la razon de Guilhem a la dona" (and recounted the whole apology of Guilhem to the lady), whereupon he attempts to persuade her to pardon Guilhem, countering her objections. Both versions then proceed: "E la preget tan caramen . . ." (And he pleaded with her so preciously . . .). In *H*, "lo vers escrit" might itself be the *prec*, the plea; the biographer may even have considered it to be written in *rimas caras* (dear rhymes). In MS *R*, by contrast, the plea depends purely on the eloquence of Bernart d'Anduza, the go-between. The lady of *R* demands a song of apology from Guilhem, and the story requires that he deliver and perform it in person (Boutière and Schutz 1964, 328, no. 56). In this very vacillation we may find traces of the double transmission suggested by van der Werf— relying sometimes on parchment, sometimes on a memorizing carrier.[20]

The question of how commonly writing was used as an aid to composition is far from settled. A poem perhaps by Bernart Marti (its authorship is disputed by Peire d'Alvernhe, Marcabru, and Bernart de Venzac)[21] mentions a *peniers* (Hoepffner: *écritoire*, writing box) in a context that suggests the *joy* of composition and the distraction from trouble afforded by poetry:

> Non er mais drutz ni drutz no·m fenh;
> Lo peniers ni jois no m'esjau.
> ("Belha m'es la flors d'aguilen,"
> vv. 49–50, in Hoepffner 1929, 36)

I will nevermore be a lover, nor do I pretend to be one; neither the writing box nor *joy* gives me pleasure.

Since the *tornada* is one of the most frequent locations for commentary on the song—its success, its worth as a finished product, its value to the poet, its destination—the author is certainly using "the pen" in metonymy for poetic composition. If he were referring to clerical labors, he could scarcely expect *esjauzimen* (enjoyment) on a par with what *joy*, the source of inspiration that subsumes and surpasses all forms of *gaudium*, might give him (Camproux 1965). With songs occurring in few manuscripts, one must allow for the possibility that one or more *tornadas* have been edited out by the compilers of the *chansonniers* or by their performing predecessors; still, this *tornada* by itself gives the appearance of an anti-*envoi*, a defiant substitute for the increasingly usual address to a named, beloved addressee, to whom the poet expresses his modest hope that his own sense of *joy* measures the poem's worthiness of its recipient. The passage might be loosely rendered, "I have no one to send this to, so I do not enjoy composing; I don't even enjoy *joy*."

Writing may not have been a necessary step in poetic creation, however. When Bernart de Ventadorn refers explicitly to sending a written copy of a poem for private reading, he implies that if he could have sent a messenger, he would not have bothered to write the words:

> Pois messatger no·lh trametrai
> Ni a me dire no·s cove
> Negu cosselh de me no sai
> Mais d'una re me conort be:
> Ela sap letras et enten
> Et agrada·m qu'eu escria
> Los motz, e s'a leis plazia
> Legis los al meu sauvamen.
> (B Vent 17, 49–56)

Since I will not send her a messenger, and it is not fitting for me
to speak, I know no advice for myself. But of one thing I am
very glad: she knows letters and understands them, and I am
pleased that I might write the words, and if she likes, she may
read them for my salvation.

Bernart introduces the lady's literacy as if it were a great marvel, using a
whole line just to create suspense for the news. We are not meant to be
surprised that he can write, but only that her ability to read makes writing worthwhile. He implies that the written record will *follow* composition: the form of the verb (*escria,* subjunctive of *escriure*) makes the act
of writing potential rather than actual: it implies future possibility. There
is no mention of noting down the tune (*lo son*), but only the words—*los
motz* being the standard phrase used to signify "the song I am now singing." Nevertheless one manuscript (*G*) preserves a melody for the song,
indicating that at some point it *was* "transmitted" by musical performance as well. *Saber letras* (to know letters), in this context, refers to literacy in the vernacular; that he speaks of writing down this very song and
not a separate letter in Latin also finds confirmation in the fact that *entendre* nearly always has poetry as its object, whether used in the receiving sense (to comprehend) or in the creative sense (to design) (Schutz
1932). In a song whose subject is the lover's elaborate hesitation to com-
municate, the phrase *trametre mesatge* (send a message or messenger),
taken together with the position of the stanza (preceding the *tornada* in
all manuscripts that include it), spells out the motif of the *envoi:* "Go,
my song."

Elsewhere Bernart speaks again of writing to the lady: "De l'aiga que
dels olhs plor, / escriu salutz mais de cen, / que tramet a la gensor" (With
the water that I weep from my eyes, I write greetings, more than a hundred, which I send to the most noble lady; 6, 49–51). The *salut d'amor*
was at that period not an established lyric genre; Bernart calls his songs
vers or *chansos* so this is not necessarily a case of sending off a song in
writing. Nevertheless, the song is a sort of greeting. Although this is a
metaphorical use of writing, "figures of speech" usually come about
when the customs from which they derive are firmly enough established
to be taken for granted. Writing to ladies would have to be customary in
the first place before a topos about writing to them using tears for ink
could become common.

Bernart treats writing, far from essential to his song, as a novelty; thus it becomes a clever solution to the problem of the untransmittable song first posed by Guilhem IX:

> Ren per autrui non l'aus mandar
> tal paor ai c'ades s'azir,
> ni ieu mezei, tan tem faillir,
> non l'aus m'amor fort asemblar.
> (Gm IX 9, 43–46)

I dare not send anything to her through another person, so much I fear that she would immediately become angry, nor do I myself dare to demonstrate my love strongly, for fear of making a mistake.

One way or another, Guilhem's poem confesses (as its preservation attests) to its "publication," though the speaker has decided to keep his composition to himself.

The *tornadas*, for the most part, give the impression that songs are made to be sent off into the world and not hoarded. Giraut de Bornelh apparently views letters as the very antithesis of song; in despair, the speaker threatens to "turn to the profession of men of letters" if his poems continue to fail him in his personal life:

> E no·m valran una mora
> Sonet ni voltas ni lais
> Ans me sui totz acordatz
> Que viatz
> Torn'al mester dels letratz
> E·l chantar si'oblidatz.
> (Gr Bor 39, 65–70)

And they will not be worth a beet to me, melodies nor trills nor lays, but rather I have completely resolved that I would quickly turn to the occupation of lettered men, and that the song be forgotten.

The sadness of the idea that "the song be forgotten" reflects an observable antipathy toward "letters," despite a thirteenth-century biographer's implication that Giraut owned a library (Boutière and Schutz 1964, 57). For Rigaut de Berbezilh, to quit singing meant annihilation ("per tostemps lais mon chantar, / que de mi no·i a ren plus," I give up my singing forever, so that there is nothing left of me; R Berb 2, 14–15).

Arnaut Daniel shows signs of a very curious attitude toward writing. Here above all we might test the modern assumption that complex verse forms could not be composed without pen and ink—that is, we might test it if only the evidence were unambiguous. The *vida* (Provençal biography) states that Arnaut's famous style, his "maniera de trobar en caras rimas" (manner of composing in dear rhymes), is something he "took up" (*pres*) only after he "abandoned letters." This might mean that he had merely given up Latin, the better to devote himself to the enrichment of his native language; the cultivation of "letters," however, was not an obstacle to *trobar* in the first place:

> Et amparet ben letras e delectet se en trobar. Et abandonet las letras, e fet
> se joglar, e pres una maniera de trobar en caras rimas.
>
> (Boutière and Schutz 1964, 59)

> And he learned letters well and enjoyed himself by composing poetry. And
> he abandoned letters, and became a jongleur, and took up a style of com-
> posing in difficult rhymes.

However we may interpret this, Arnaut appears to have developed a reputation for giving up writing in favor of performance. The *vida* may represent an effort to synthesize two conflicting images of Arnaut—one of a brilliantly literate poet, the other of a poet so brilliant that he had no need of letters.

In one poem, Arnaut makes a statement that sounds very much like a defense of illiteracy, and may have seemed just that to his biographer:

> Ben conosc ses art d'escriure
> que es plan o que es comba.
> (Arn D 4, 41–42)

> I know well without the art of writing what is flat and what is a
> hill.

Since *plan*, in addition to its geographical sense (plain), is one of Arnaut's terms for a particular style he favors (it describes the refinement of words, their "planing" and polishing), this passage may have been understood as a boast about the poet's ability to make poetic distinctions, to *triar los motz* without writing them down. If this could be taken as an autobiographical statement (and I am not convinced that it can), then Arnaut styles himself as the exception to the rule, one who, like the lightning calculators of mathematics, dazzled his contemporaries by "doing it all in his head" while others labored with their pens.

The author of the famous anecdote introducing Arnaut's song "I've never had her but she has me" ("Anc yeu non l'aic") apparently wishes to give a similar impression. The entire *razo* creates an awesome idea of Arnaut's powers of memory: his own songs "non son leu ad aprendre" (are not easy to learn), but the song in question was made by a poet who claimed to compose "en rimas pus caras q'el" (in rhymes more precious than he [Arnaut used]; Boutière and Schutz 1964, 63). The narrator draws a humorous contrast between the difficulty experienced by the jongleur in memorizing his own song and the ease with which Arnaut "la va tota arretener, e·l son" (memorized it, including the melody).

As Arnaut's *razo* suggests, even the author of a song normally took considerable pains to memorize it, at least if he planned to perform it himself. Marcabru says, in what is probably an allusion to the poem-as-lawsuit (cf. R. H. Bloch 1977, 171–176), that he needs to practice his *affar* three times before making it public:

> E dei me tres vetz doctrinar
> Mon affar anz que si' auzit.
> (Mcb 8, 44–45)

And I have to teach myself my case three times before it may be heard.

If the jongleur competing against Arnaut made a record of his song, he certainly did not intend to rely on it on the day the king would judge it. The *razo* affords a glimpse of this process of memorization:

> Lo joglars fes son cantar leu e tost; et els non avian mas detz jorns d'espazi, e devia·s jutgar per lo rey a cap de cinc jorns. Lo joglars demandet a·N Arnaut si avia fag, e·N Arnautz respos que oc, passat a tres jorns; e no·n avia pessat. E·l joglars cantava tota nueg sa canso, per so que be la saubes. E·N Arnautz pesset co·l traysses isquern; tan que venc una nueg, e·l joglars la cantava, e·N Arnautz la va tota arretener, e·l so.
> (Boutière and Schutz 1964, 62)

The jongleur made his song easily and quickly; and they had had only the space of ten days, and [now] the king was to judge at the end of five days. The jongleur asked Arnaut if he had finished, and Arnaut answered, "Yes, three days ago"; and he had not thought of anything. And the jongleur sang his song all night long so that he would know it well. Arnaut considered how he might mock him, until there came one night, and the jongleur sang it, and Arnaut memorized the whole thing, including the melody.

Of course, here the question is not one of the ordinary troubadour versus the superior one—Arnaut's challenger is depicted as very nearly his equal, someone whose song was good enough to become a permanent part of Arnaut's repertory. We are meant to be astounded by the jongleur's speed, and then still more in awe of Arnaut's. The whole ten days allowed by the king would not ordinarily have sufficed; the five days in which the jongleur composed his song seemed "easy and quick" work to the narrator; Arnaut escalates the boast by claiming that he composed his song in two days. The jongleur practiced for long hours, perhaps every night for the remaining five nights, to assure that he would not forget his own composition; Arnaut learns it perfectly (*tota*) by ear in one night. If the jongleur's hare runs a mile in three minutes, Arnaut's ox runs it in thirty seconds.

I shall have more to say about this *razo* and its place in Gröber's theory of the autograph songbook. I believe that the *razo* makes a better case for oral, memorizing composition than for written composition. But before we address the question of *Liederbücher,* it would be well to learn as much as possible from the poets about their techniques for assuring faithful transmission without writing.

Memory and the Singer

A fascinating reference to the act of memorization occurs at the end of Peire d'Alvernhe's "Bel m'es quan la roza":

> Chantador, lo vers vos fenis:
> Aprendetz la comensansa.
> (P d'Alv 13, 36–37)

> Singers, I end for you my song: learn the beginning!

These lines do more than affirm the moral value of the *sententiae* expressed in the first stanza. Whether Peire is addressing hired singers, like the two Giraut de Bornelh reportedly brought with him to assist in performance, or simply an audience of amateur singers, he appears to be asking that they practice singing the beginning of the song immediately after they hear the end. He wants them, in short, to "take it from the top." Set next to this passage, Bernart de Ventadorn's request that Garsio "sing and carry" his song appears less redundant than it otherwise might:

> Garsio, ara·m chantat
> ma chanso, e la·m portat
> a mo Messager
> (B Vent 6, 61–63)

> Garsio, now sing my song to me, and [then] carry it for me to my Messenger

It is not at all surprising that a poet, before sending his song off to its destination by way of a jongleur, would like to know how it will sound when it gets there; he might even be expected to supervise the jongleur as he practiced until he got it right, as even Arnaut Daniel's talented competitor had to practice. The poet thus makes himself, for the first time, a part of the audience; he will hear his song in other voices many times afterward.

Peire d'Alvernhe's signal toward *la comensansa* (the beginning) may point to another key to memorization. The first stanza of a song carries with it a whole set of unspoken rules, a decorum, which the song establishes for itself and then follows. Rhyme, well known as a powerful mnemonic, makes its entrance here, and the poem's metric scheme also sets up in the *exordium* a pattern from which the rest, with greater or lesser determination, follows in a prescribed form. The dependence of the whole development of a song on its beginning was well known, for the troubadours readily applied the maxim "All's well that begins well" to their own work:

> Ab joi mou lo vers e·l comens,
> et ab joi reman e fenis;
> e sol que bona fos la fis,
> bos tenh qu'er lo comensamens.
> Per la bona comensansa
> mi ve jois et alegransa
> e per so dei la bona fi grazir,
> car totz bos faihz vei lauzar al fenir.
> (B Vent 1, 1–8)

The poem begins with *joy* and begins it, and with *joy* it stays and ends; and if only the end may be good, I hold that the beginning will be good. Through the good beginning come *joy* and happiness to me, and therefore I should praise the good end, for I see that all good actions are praised when they are finished.

Eugen Cnyrim cites dozens of examples of this motif of continuity from "comensamens . . . al fenir" (1887, 35), and in most cases the more general meaning of the proverb can appropriately be understood as a comment on songs as well. A "recreant" from the verse form he has begun will author a defective poem:

> Eu dic lo ver aissi cum dir lo solh
> Qui ben comens e poissas s'en recre
> Melhs li fora que non comenses re.
> (Cnyrim 1887, no. 329 [Peire Vidal])

> I speak the truth as I am accustomed to speak it: whoever begins well and afterward becomes disloyal to it, it would be better for him if he had begun nothing.

Theorists of the thirteenth and fourteenth centuries confirm the view that the *comensamen* was the determining element in the song, firmly establishing its decorum; however, they tend to play down the form and insist instead on thematic continuity:

> E garda be que, en axi com començaras raho en amor, que en aquella manera matexa la fins be e la seguesques.
> ("Doctrina de Compondre Dictatz," in Marshall 1972, 95)

> And be careful that in the same way as you begin the statement about love, in that same way you should finish it and follow it through.

> E si ell comensa chanson
> Deu continuar sa razon
> En aysi con le comensa
> Si ell no vol farfallensa.
> Car may mi play e agrada
> Razos ben continuada
> Que mot qan alcus los entresca
> Ab rimas e entrebesca.
> ("Doctrina d'Acort," vv. 737–
> 744, in Marshall 1972, 51)

> And if he [a poet] begins a song, he should continue his argu-
> ment just as he began it, if he does not wish to make a mistake.
> For I am more pleased and delighted by an argument with
> good continuity than by stanzas when someone braids them
> together and interweaves them with rhymes.

The troubadours of the classic period (ca. 1170) are not especially co-
operative in this rule of thematic continuity, and Bernart de Ventadorn
provides Raimon Vidal with an example of "razons mal continuadas ni
mal seguidas" (an argument with poor continuity and in poor sequence;
Las razos de trobar, in Marshall 1972, 22).

Yet whether one emphasizes the form or the material, it is clear from
all this that once one obeys the order "Aprendetz la comensansa" (Learn
the beginning), the task of memorization is half done: "La meitat del fait
tenc per faita / qui de be comensar se traita" (I hold that half the deed is
done if a man takes care to begin well; Cnyrim 1887, no. 320). At least,
as long as the *cantador* sings something in the same form as the first
stanza, no one can tell whether he has forgotten the exact words he was
taught, or whether the song is "improving" or "worsening" (*si melhura/
si pejura*).

The certainty that the rhyme scheme makes all the difference in the
aptitude of a song for memorization can be illustrated with an extreme,
almost contrary, case. Peire Vidal challenges Alfonso II of Aragon to
memorize a poem with seventy-four rhymes in -*atz:*

> Tant me platz jois e solatz
> D'omes onratz, per qu'ieu fatz
> Tal chanso viatz,
> Bons reis, que prec qu'aprendatz.
> E si·m demandatz:
> "Tan soven per que chantatz?"—
> "Quar es enuegz als malvatz
> E gaugz a nos envezatz."
>   (P Vid 4, 1–8)

I am so pleased with *joy* and the conversation of landed men—
that is why I make such a fast song, good king, which I beg
you to memorize. And if you ask me, "Why do you sing so
often?"—"Because it is an annoyance to the wicked, and a
pleasure to us enviable people."

Unless the king had a far more prodigious memory than his status as part-time troubadour would imply, Peire's request that he learn such a song might appear to be a joke. How could the king possibly remember in what order the stanzas came? Knowing well Alfonso's fondness for his songs, Peire pretends to anticipate annoyance on the king's part: "What! Are *you* singing again?" But the poet's reply forestalls any expression of displeasure with his tongue twister: "Only bad people dislike my songs."

Learning the *comensansa* may have been a great aid to memory, but sustaining the pattern it set, at least one poet admitted, could overtax the memories of those destined to learn it. Berenguer de Palazol, who comes close to belittling the musical and literary talents of those to whom he has dedicated his song, makes us appreciate by contrast the compliment Peire Vidal's poem in *-atz* paid to Alfonso's capacities. Berenguer takes it for granted that Count Jaufre and his wife will want to learn his song, and therefore he attempts to accommodate it to them, cutting it short before it becomes too cumbersome for them to learn:

> Aissi fenira ma chanso
> E no vuelh pus longa sia
> que pus greu la·n apenria
> mo senher, e siey companho
> lo coms Jaufres, que Dieus ampar.
> (B Pal 6, 33–37)

Thus my song will end, and I do not want it to be longer, for my lord would learn it with more difficulty, and [so would] her companion the Count Jaufre—may God protect him.

The presence of the word *greu* (heavy, difficult) here—really far more frequent than *clus* (closed) as an opposite to *leu* (light, easy) in stylistic programs—may serve to remind us of the vital importance of audience, and of transmission by members of the audience, in shaping this body of poetry. The danger, all too evident in Berenguer's compliment to his sponsors, is that the poet may limit himself unreasonably, never allowing himself to surpass the amateur.

Berenguer was not proposing an unusual task to the Count Jaufre. It is fairly common, in the final lines of poems of the period, for poets to recommend that the addressee learn their songs—and they do so, for the most part, without exhibiting quite so awkwardly any fears about the recipient's power of memory. Peire Rogier makes the request explicitly in two of his eight preserved songs. In "Tan no plou ni venta," he imposes a time limit (like the ten-day limit imposed for Arnaut Daniel's contest), asking in two *tornadas* that the lady learn his poem before Christmas:

> Peir Rogier per bona fe
> tramet lo vers denant nadal
> a sidons que·l fai vivre.
> Clama li per gran merce
> qu'aprenda·l vers denant nadal
> s'ab joy de lui vol vivre.
> (P Rog 2, 64–69)

Peire Rogier in good faith sends the poem before Christmas to his lady, who makes it live. He begs her as a great favor that she learn the poem before Christmas if she wishes to live with the *joy* of it.

An addressee who could double as a performer, and hence as a re-transmitter, would indeed "make a song live," since she would expand its renown by the number of her acquaintances, who might in turn learn the song from her.

In "Ges non puesc. . . ," Peire makes a slightly greater demand on the recipient's sense of responsibility toward the song: he asks that she first learn it and then send it on ("have it conveyed") to a second lady:

> Mon Tort-n'avetz mant, s'a lieys platz
> qu'aprenda lo vers, s'el es bos
> e puois vol que sia trames
> mon Dreit-n'avetz lai en Saves:
> Dieu sal e guart lo cors de liey.
> (P Rog 6, 57–61)

To my You're-wrong I send instructions that if she likes [and] if it is good, she might learn the song, and then I wish it to be sent to my You're-right there in Savès: may God save and keep her.

Peire is not the only poet to cultivate the idea of transmission as a sort of relay, with the poem passed from hand to hand (or voice to voice) like the Olympic flame. Guilhem IX introduced the relay, as (at least for us) he introduced so many things:

Fait ai lo vers, no say de cui;
e trametrai lo a celui
que lo·m trametra per autrui
enves Peitau,
que·m tramezes del sieu estui
la contraclau.
(Gm IX 4, 43–48)

I have made the song, about I don't know whom, and I will
send it to someone who will send it for me through another
person over to Poitou there, so that he can send me from his
box the counterkey.

The possibility that the addressee in Poitou (MS *E*, Anjou MS *C*) in sending *la contraclau* would be sending another poem is supported by the fact
that many of the *senhals* naming poems' recipients have been shown to
designate other poets. A skilled poet, in fact, would be a likely choice for
a retransmitter in the process of relay. Poems sent via a first jongleur to
a recipient named *Joglar* (performer) or *Messager* (messenger) or *Drogoman* (interpreter) are almost certainly expected to be sung again, until
the song is publicly known.

Invitations to learn songs by heart can often be detected even when
they are not phrased quite so boldly as Peire Rogiers's. Rigaut de Berbezilh, famous for his shyness,[22] softens the practical, professional request—that Miels-de-dompna memorize and perform "Lo nous mes
d'abril"—by weaving it into a subtle comparison:

e li ausel son chantador,
qu'atendut an en parvensa
lo pascor.
Miels de dompna, atretal entendensa
aten de vos . . .
(R Berb 6, 3–7)

and the birds are singers, for they have awaited, it seems, the
springtime. Miels-de-dompna, I await/expect from you a comparable understanding . . .

It is Rigaut's special invention, the forerunner of the Italian conceit,
that he introduces the vehicle of his metaphor in an extensive, descriptive
sweep and then modulates it. In some poems he gives the vehicle an un-

expected twist, changing the proverbial to the original—like his lion, which, by its roar alone, wakes its cub from death. In the present case, he splits a single vehicle between two tenors: himself and the lady. The fact that the poet compares himself to the birds as well, using the same verb, *atendre*, does not interfere with the first comparison; instead, it gives the sequence of words *atretal entendensa / aten de vos* an uncanny compactness. The speaker waits, like the birds, for the lady to show *entendensa* like that of the birds. Other troubadours' frequent efforts to involve the addressee directly in the diffusion of their songs, some of which have been brought forward here, make it plausible that Rigaut might like to share the role of *chantador* with Miels-de-dompna.

THREE

Song Sheets and Song Books

Arnaut, Gioglaret, and Individual Song Sheets

The troubadours' own comments have given us a picture of the first phase of transmission that differs sharply from Gustav Gröber's hypothesis that troubadour songs were first "published" in the form of *Liederblätter*—individual song sheets. In order to reevaluate this traditional theory of written transmission, I would like to return to the story (*razo*) that recounts how Arnaut Daniel "got possession of" the song "Anc yeu non l'aic . . ." (see above, pp. 47–48) and to examine Gröber's analysis of it (1887, 337–338).

This *razo* has long been considered key evidence to be accounted for in any hypothesis on how the troubadours composed, learned, and performed their works. It is central to Gröber's theory of transmission, too, since for him it verifies the use of writing in composition and so substantiates his idea of autograph *Liederblätter* as the original components of later anthologies. Since this theory still shapes modern scholars' assumptions, both in editing troubadour "texts" and in interpreting them, his treatment of the *razo* is well worth examining in some depth.

Gröber concludes, in his discussion of the *razo*, that Arnaut and the jongleur were expected to write their poems on a *carta*. Weak links in his argument, however, reveal that the evidence in fact favors the opposite inference. First, Gröber asks what would be the good of locking the poets into separate rooms, if they meant to compose in their heads. More pertinent, I think, is to ask what would be the good of separate rooms if they meant to compose silently. One can conceal "little strips of parchment covered over" more easily than one can muffle a voice that tests its rhymes aloud.

56

Second, Gröber claims that the song could not have been "given" to Arnaut, unless we assume that the king "gave" some tangible object, namely "a sheet of parchment" (*ein Pergamentblatt*). Yet the inclusion of the song in Arnaut's canon suggests that, for the author of the *razo* at least, Arnaut was awarded authorship of the poem and was not merely given a copy. He had no need of a parchment copy in any case, since he knew the song by heart already.

Third, and most important, we should reexamine the anonymous stanza Gröber adduces to show the troubadours' awareness of the usefulness of writing. Actually preserved in two stanzas, the song "Gioglaret, when you pass by" (P.-C. 461,142) tends to sabotage rather than corroborate the idea of poets' reliance on written records. I cite both preserved *coblas,* which are found only in MS *P:*

> Gioglaret quant passarez
> Garda no moill ta cappa uerz
> Qe fols fora si noi lai derz
> Ceu darre un moi descle
> Sen carta qen teregle
> Poi scriver una tal cobla
> Sun daqist moti non si dubla.
>
> Ben es sauis e sel e serz
> Qe son castel bast dinz e derz
> Sqe dedinz nol prenda en grez
> El sera belle el dintegle
> Si qe nuils non lintegle
> Qieu non prez una carobla
> Terra qi dauol genz pobla.
>
> (Stengel 1872, 282)

Gioglaret, when you pass by, be careful not to get your green cape wet, for you would be crazy not to elevate it in that place; I would give a barrel [*muid;* dry measure, 1,872 livres] of rye if, on a page which in you I rule, I could write such a stanza that not one of these rhymes is duplicated.

That man is very wise and discreet and certain who builds his castle thick and strong so that the violent do not capture him within, and [builds] the buttresses beautifully, and the battlements, so that no one may carve into it. For I do not think it

is worth a carob bean, a piece of land which is populated with
poor society.

The *carta* (page) mentioned here may have been brought into the literal
from the metaphorical realm by Gröber's emendation alone. Line 5, "S'en
carta q'en te regle," makes sense as it stands in the manuscript; Gröber's
"S'en carta qu'eu te regle" (on the page which I rule *for you*) implies that
the jongleur, despite his difficulties in keeping his cape out of the mud,
can carry safely with him on his travels a sheet of neatly lined parchment
from which to read during his performances. I see no reason to reject the
line in the manuscript, which means with its context, "if I can write, on a
page which *in you* I mark with lines, such a *cobla* that not one of these
rhymes will be duplicated." It makes sense as a conceit, the jongleur's
memory being compared to a blank page, freshly ruled and ready for a
neat "inscription." If writing alone sufficed to prevent "doubling," then
why "such a cobla" (*tal cobla*)? It would make no difference *qualis est*,
unless some danger that the jongleur might "double the rhymes" lay in
certain kinds of composition. The monumentalist metaphor of the second
stanza, then—describing the poem as a fortress—specifies a program for
"tal cobla": he envisions a *kind* of verse that can, through inherently
sturdy "construction," withstand the assaults of the common throng.

The poet's doubt of his ability to write such a cobla in the *carta* of the
jongleur's mind may be justified by the topos of the jongleur's ineptitude
as a diplomat, representing the poet: he gets his clothes dirty, abuses the
host's hospitality by eating and drinking too much, and then, when the
time comes for him to perform, he bungles his lines.[1] *Carta* is also a
measure of capacity, and the poet may be hinting at the jongleur's prodigious thirst, with all his talk of barrels and quarts (*moi*, Fr. *muid*, v. 3;
carta, v. 4).

Neither the metaphorical *carta* of Gioglaret nor the "transfer of
ownership" of a song to Arnaut Daniel provides very substantial evidence
for the existence of the autograph parchment song sheets that Gröber
supposed to be the original components from which derive all copies preserved in the anthologies. The next step in Gröber's theory maintains that
some poets collected these *Liederblätter* containing their own individual
poems and compiled autograph songbooks, the better to preserve their
work for posterity. Again, the evidence for these individual authors'
manuscripts should be reevaluated in the light of new knowledge about
the transmission of troubadour poetry.

At least one poet made a private collection of his own works. Giraut Riquer, significantly the "last of the troubadours," left a "book" of poems recorded in chronological order, noting the dates of their composition—perhaps even the explanatory notes are his own. Even in such a book, the written record bows to the sung performance: there are detailed instructions for joining the words to the tune when the poet's plan departs from normal practice.

Canson redonda & encadenada de motz e de son d'en Gr.' Riquier, facha l'an m.cc.lxxx.ij. en abril. E·l sos de la segonda cobla pren se el mieg de la primeira e sec tro en la fin, pueys torna la comensamen de la primeira e fenis en la mieija de la primeira aissi quon es senhat; pueys tota la cansos canta se aissij: la primeira e la tersa e la quinta d'una maneira, e la quarta e la sexta d'autra maneira. *Ez* aquesta cansos es la xxiiij. (MS C)[2]

A song by En Giraut Riquer that is both round and enchained both in words and in music, composed in the year 1282 in April. And the music of the second stanza takes up in the middle of the first stanza and follows through to the end, then returns to the beginning of the first and ends in the middle of the first, just as it is notated; then the whole song is sung thus: the first and the third and the fifth in one way, and the fourth and the sixth another way. And this song is number twenty-four.

We also have evidence of poets making anthologies of the works of others—Ferrari de Ferrara, Uc de St-Circ, and Miquel de la Tor all at least tried their hand at composing original verse. But all of these writers lived in the second half of the thirteenth century, and efforts to trace "authors' manuscripts" for poets composing before 1250 have relied heavily on Gröber's theoretical model for the compilation of anthologies, for lack of more straightforward evidence.

Raimbaut d'Aurenga makes one allusion to "his book," assuring us at least that a collection of poetry like his was not inconceivable:

> Mas aura ni plueja ni gel
> no·m tengran plus que·l gen temps nou
> s'auzes desplejar mos libres
> de fagz d'amor ab digz escurs.
>
> (R d'Aur 10, 10–14)

But neither wind nor rain nor ice will hold me more than the fine spring weather, if I dared unfold my book of deeds of love in obscure language.[3]

In the context of the poem, the passage serves as an announcement that Raimbaut does not intend to sing of love. To "unfold his book" would be to bring out his repertory of the topoi suited to love, the furled book holding in storage the resources of his artistic imagination. Since "digz escurs" is a stylistic term from a poetics Raimbaut sometimes supported, its presence lessens the likelihood that the poet meant us to imagine a "book of amorous deeds" in another genre—a romance, for example, or "the book that never lies," Ovid's *Ars amatoria*.[4] Rather, in "*desplejar mos libres / de fagz d'amor ab digz escurs*" Raimbaut envisions an alternative, erotic development for this poem: its *Natureingang*, full of dreary weather, does not preclude a love poem. A *libres* would be a scroll, like the ones on which the poets wrote in the miniatures, and it is remarkable that Raimbaut conceives of the *déroulement* of a song as analogous to the unrolling of a scroll: the metaphor makes a striking identification of the verse itself and its parchment record. Nevertheless, Walter T. Pattison (1969), Raimbaut's modern editor, shows that even when one uses Gustav Gröber's method to analyze the sequence of Raimbaut's poetry in the *chansonniers*, one finds no trace of an author's collection.

Because it would be so exciting to discover traces of an "author's manuscript," more than one claim has been put forward that does not hold up. For example, François Zufferey (1987, 232–233) deflates the hypothesis offered by Martín de Riquer that *chansonnier* V included an authorial *Liederbuch* assembled by Pons de la Guardia. The Catalan manuscript contains a section copied by R. de Capellades, whose name designates a place only three kilometers from where Pons's patroness made her home at Cabrera.

Peire Vidal's "Book": Sequence by Chance or by Design?

D'Arco Silvio Avalle (1960) has concluded that for Peire Vidal's surviving works, one branch of the manuscript tradition derives from the author's own collection. To reach this theory, Avalle analyzes the relationships among manuscripts largely by the method invented by Gröber: by comparing the sequences of songs in the *chansonniers*, one finds series and pairs of songs grouped in similar or "scrambled" order in two or more manuscripts. Such similarities among pairs of manuscripts form networks of latent "similarities" among several manuscripts; on this basis, Gröber's method permits Avalle to speculate about the written descent of song collections and to reconstruct an "original" grouping of Peire's poems. Avalle then brings evidence from textual criticism, the comparison of variants, to support his reconstruction.

One problem with this method is that the groups of manuscripts found to present the poems in similar orders do not correspond to the stemmata constructed for individual poems; furthermore, the stemmata vary from poem to poem within a single poet's work.

If Avalle is right, then writing offered little safety from the transposition of stanzas in transmission: 56 percent of Peire Vidal's songs show stanzaic transposition. But the evidence for Peire's songbook is much more subtle than the evidence for Giraut Riquer's, and can be elicited only by means of very complicated editorial procedures.[5] Traditional textual criticism presupposes a single original, which the editor must try to reconstruct as nearly as possible; in effect, the method itself assumes that an author's manuscript once existed.[6] Since no geometry can prove its own postulates, we should examine the validity of using textual criticism to reconstruct and *then* attest the existence of "il libro del Vidal."

Available methods for identifying *Liederbücher* take too much for granted. To accept the use of Gröber's method to "reconstruct" an individual songbook, we must assume a high degree of literalism in copying. Surely a literalist principle strong enough to leave clear marks of manuscript filiation should have tended to stabilize the works of poets who compiled their own collections. Medieval scribes knew how to copy one word after the other; they generally maintained verbatim fidelity to sacred texts. If they could just as reverently preserve a sequence of vernacular poems, why not a sequence of stanzas or of lines?

The traces of an "authorized collection" discovered by Avalle in the works of Peire Vidal do not correspond to outstanding textual stability. If we assume a purely written transmission, so literal that nineteen of Peire's poems were copied mechanically enough to mark the lineage not only of individual texts but of sequences from an authorized canon as well, then how do we explain the high rate of version production in Peire's corpus?[7] Why would the *codice antico* contain two poems *not* by Peire Vidal (P.-C. 344,4 and 70,3)?[8] Would an "authorized" source of written descent give immunity from stanzaic transposition to the nineteen poems of the *codice antico?* If writing were viewed as a way to stabilize one's poems, why would Peire, seeing the opportunity to immortalize his words and desiring to do so, limit his selection to sixteen poems in the archetype? Could he, if he collected fewer than half of the surviving songs attributed to him, have intended to monumentalize one group of poems and still allow others to be transferred during his lifetime?

A count of the variations among manuscripts in their order of strophes, for the sixteen poems of the "archetipo" (i–xvi in Avalle's edition), shows that fewer than half resisted stanzaic transposition, and only one escaped both transposition and abridgment:

Song No.	Versions with Transposition	Versions with Transposition, Abridgment, or Both	Song No.	Versions with Transposition	Versions with Transposition, Abridgment, or Both
i	5	6	ix	1	1
ii	1	2	x	2	2
iii	5	7	xi	3	4
iv	5	7	xii	1	4
v	1	5	xiii	2	2
vi	3	4	xiv	1	6
vii	3	4	xv	3	3
viii	3	3	xvi	1	2

The "author's manuscript," if one existed, clearly failed to stabilize the order of stanzas. Still less did it guarantee that all of the stanzas of a given poem would be included in all manuscript versions (nor did it control which stanzas would be omitted in abridgments).

Several branches of Avalle's stemma must have gone back much earlier than the *codice antico*,[9] and rival versions may have been known to Peire Vidal; the poet died sometime after 1204, his late travels taking him to some of the countries where manuscripts were made (i.e., Italy and Spain). Avalle's stemma postulates five written "editions" prior to MSS *I* and *K*, copied in the mid–thirteenth century.[10] Yet there may not have been time for Peire's "authorized text" to erode gradually through the inadvertent errors of the scriptorium. We may conjecture about the time it took to prepare and execute an anthology (analogous to the modern book's time "in press") from the making of the Catalan *chansonnier* of Venice (*V*): the original collection contains no poem composed much later than 1200, since the compiler includes nothing newer than Arnaut Daniel's works, and yet the *explicit* is dated May 31, 1268 (Frank 1949, 234–237). If the compiler had been interested in updating the texts of the poems he had selected, he would probably also have updated the selection itself, including more recent work.

The five "manuscripts" predating *I* and *K* in Avalle's stemmata might easily have been people and not *Liederblätter* or *Liedersammlungen:* a jongleur with his repertory is much more mobile, more susceptible to local influence and style, freer to experiment with the interplay of words and music, than is the sedentary scribe with his quill and ink and *issemple.*

The system Avalle uses for tracking down "il libro del Vidal" places great faith in coincidence. When one compares even random selections of poems, the laws of probability strongly favor the occurrence of matching pairs, triplets, and longer series—particularly if series with gaps or substitutions are considered to "match."[11] This fact tends to discount the method invented by Gustav Gröber for establishing genetic relationships among manuscripts that share such sequences: although two long, identical series of numbers will rarely be drawn by chance from a limited pool, the chances are extremely high for "scrambled series" or groups sharing several inverted pairs.

Avalle's application of textual criticism to describe the manuscript tradition of Peire Vidal's poetry and to guess its history is so cohesive and minutely detailed that it can be extremely convincing: the evidence from Gröber's method supports the evidence from Lachmann's, and vice versa. Still, even with such an impressive work of scholarship, we should be cautious. In order to demonstrate the applicability of this type of textual criticism, Avalle must apply it extensively, and along with this circular reasoning there is also great danger of selecting the evidence to fit the model.

For example, Avalle's principal reason for believing that Peire Vidal himself compiled the original book from which the archetype would derive is that the manuscripts' sequences tend to suggest a chronological order of presentation for poems in the archetype. Textual criticism had isolated several common errors which indicated that the archetype was copied from a copy "contraddistinto in alcuni luoghi da un *ductus* fortemente individualizzato, non calligrafico" (counterdistinguished in certain places by a strongly individualized, noncalligraphic *ductus;* p. xxxvii). One may well ask what Avalle means by "a noncalligraphic ductus"—a written source such as a jongleur's copy, or "foul papers" of some sort, or an oral source? Avalle continues:

> For this reason one may justly ask oneself if this copy were not in fact edited by the poet himself with the intention of grouping in chronological order a part of his production. How else can one explain the indisputably

exceptional fact that a lover of Provençal poetry was capable of arranging, with such chronological exactness, such a substantial number of songs, especially when we consider that the medieval lyric anthologies were put together on the basis of criteria of a strictly formal type. (p. xxxvii)

Avalle's Table VI (p. xxxvi) shows that of the first sixteen poems in his edition, MS A presents ten in the roughly chronological order chosen by the editor—though not without intermediate poems that disrupt the chronology. If we discount the undatable poems from the sequence, A has only seven poems in this chronological order:[12]

Song No.	A	Date
iii	268	before October 3, 1187
iv	274	1188–1192
v	276	1188–1192
viii	279	before 1194
xii	287	1201–1202
xiv	289	after 1196
xvi	292	from the poet's old age

The main Peire Vidal collection in *chansonnier A*, nos. 268–292, could easily have placed certain of its poems in chronological order simply by chance. But Avalle sees strong circumstantial evidence: "Obvious is the conclusion that the results which obtain impose themselves, so to speak, in a peremptory manner: the original order in which these songs were arranged in the 'archetype' is that, well or badly preserved, of A" (pp. xxxvi– xxxvii). The conclusion that A reflects even dimly an original order is not so obvious if we consider not only the tenuous basis on which these poems are dated but also the fact that other *chansonniers* may give the poems in orders that, by coincidence, are also well within the bounds of establishable chronological order and yet contradict the chronology A would lead us to suppose. Compare, for example, the placement of poems viii and iv in A and in N:[13]

Song No.	A	N	Date
xxviii	278	97	before 1176–1181
viii	279	99	before 1194
xxxviii	270	100	Oct. 1187–Sept. 1189
iii	268	104	before Oct. 3, 1187
xxxi	275	105	1187–1188
iv	274	106	1188–1192
xxi	615	107	spring 1188–Sept. 3, 1189
xii	287	109	1201–1202
xix	—	111	1201–1202
xxxv	614	113	1201–1207

We look for authenticity of all kinds in MS *A* because it is an "excellent" manuscript: it is old, neat, and ample, and Karl Bartsch (who first assigned the *sigla*) had cause to give it primacy in his alphabetical rating. But is its chronology really more "exact" and "conspicuous" than that of *N*? We find coincidence where we seek it. The above table shows that *N* may be credited with having preserved a chronological sequence that could not have derived from the hypothetical *codice antico*. Since its sequence includes poems outside the sixteen singled out by Avalle as an "author's book," the chronology in *N* challenges two of Avalle's assumptions. First, it must make us doubt that *only an author* could be "capable of arranging, with such chronological exactness, such a substantial number of songs." Second, it must make us doubt that *A*'s superior chronology can lend support to Avalle's reconstruction of a manuscript lineage descending from an autograph copy that consisted only of poems numbered i–xvi in his edition.

The evidence for Thibaut de Champagne having compiled his own author's anthology includes the fact that his songs "appear in almost exactly the same order in nearly every manuscript" (Huot 1987, 66). This trouvère, as king of Navarre and a descendent of Guilhem IX, had both the resources and the motivation from "family pride" to preserve his poems in a book. We are a long way from this degree of stability with Peire Vidal.

The Songbook as Literary Property

When Walter T. Pattison determined that there was no trace of an autograph songbook in the manuscript sequences of Raimbaut d'Aurenga's poetry, he took Gröber's method as a point of departure. In his view, his findings support Gröber's theory of the individual songbook by helping to establish a *terminus a quo* for the presumed chronological trend toward writing. Pattison also suggests that Raimbaut's neglect of writing may reflect on the probable social standing and wealth, as well as on the literary self-consciousness and "carefulness," of poets who would be likely to collect their own works:

> Gröber believes that the custom of preparing individual songbooks was prevalent toward the end of the period in which the troubadour art flourished, when the poets had become more self-conscious with respect to their fame. The first two generations of troubadours, especially those of noble

rank, were much more careless about their literary reputation and the preservation of their works. The evidence from Raimbaut's works seems to prove that there was no individual songbook in his case. (1969, 232)

For several reasons, the default of evidence for Raimbaut's writing a song-book does not work constructively to show that later, poorer, or more "careful" poets did write songbooks. That prestige and wealth make people "careless," like F. Scott Fitzgerald's Daisy, is a novelistic rather than a historical principle. Nor can we safely conclude that the failure to make an autograph songbook, as evidenced by the diversity of the manu-script tradition, reflects disregard for "their literary reputation and the preservation of their works." Few poets were more self-conscious than Raimbaut, and he seems if anything to exercise closer control over the distribution of his songs than did his humbler contemporaries.[14] Finally, as the evidence discussed in the next chapter will indicate, it is not true that the poets gradually became more successful in preserving their works.

To associate the author's proprietary interest in his creation with the manufacture of books is too modern an impulse: must Raimbaut, as a "man of property," therefore have had no need to secure "literary prop-erty"? Raimbaut's castles were almost all pawned, in any case. Most troubadours were *not* men of property (Köhler 1962); moreover, the per-sona of the poet/lover in troubadour poetry identifies itself strongly with the artisan rather than with the landlord.

And what might the troubadours' conception of literary property have been? Could the written document alone have constituted a "product" convertible into income for the literary artisan, as Gröber's analysis of Arnaut Daniel's *razo* suggests? We might also ask seriously to what type of landed property the troubadours might have compared "literary prop-erty," should the analogy occur to them at all: was a poem a fief or an *allodium*? Was it an inalienable possession or merely an *honor* entrusted to one's temporary care? The symbolic "territory" of authorship seems to have been as transferable as a fief, or even more so, since the troubadours witnessed a rapid expansion in the use of money, "the mobile form of property *par excellence*" (R. H. Bloch 1981, 956). The poets' compari-son of poetry with currency becomes explicit in discussions of *trobar clus* (see Chapter 6).

Whether or not they made literary castles for lack of the real thing, poets of humble rank are even less likely than noblemen to have made songbooks; even having acquired the luxury of an alphabet and the leisure to apply it, poor poets would still face the high cost of parchment. Granted, among "the first two generations of troubadours," Marcabru did succeed in leaving a large body of work compared with the small poetic legacy of the Counts of Poitou and Blaye. Yet his contemporary, Cercamon, who must also have depended on his literary reputation to make a living (if we can trust the *vida* and speculate on his use of a professional name), seems to have been no more "careful" than titled poets: only seven poems remain to attest to any reputation at all.[15]

Rigaut de Berbezilh had no noble title: he belonged to a family of overseers during the decline of its prestige and fortune (Lejeune 1957, 1962). If he tried to preserve his songs by making a book, then writing did him little good—six of his nine surviving songs show transposition of stanzas. Further, in the case of the song "Si co·l solilhs per sa nobla clardat . . ." (337,1), imitation shades into adaptation so subtly that one wonders whether a transfer of literary property took place. Attributed by C and α to Peire de Cols, and by f to Rigaut, the poem is so like Rigaut's work that the best argument against his authorship is the improbability of self-imitation. Várvaro speculates that perhaps a song of Rigaut's, "with a few modifications, might have been made the property of some jongleur, who might have been Peire de Cols" (1960, 244). It is conceivable that Rigaut made the song and then gave it away—perhaps not as finished verse but in its "skeletal form": a conception, a scheme, rhymed ideas and images recognizable as Rigaut's, a few perfect lines, the rest perfectible. The very idea is unsettling to modern readers accustomed to copyright and the sanctity of the poet's original text. But whether the song was given, sold, or stolen, the "deed and title" to it appear to have changed hands.

As I have shown, the theory of the writing troubadour has its firmest adherents among modern scholars. The troubadours themselves discuss composition and circulation as a matter for the memory, the intelligence, and the voice. When they speak of writing, they treat it as a curiosity or as a metaphor, not as a necessity for the transmission of their songs.

The evidence I have brought forth thus far, both from the transmitters and from the poets, depends on the interpretation of the poets' own words—texts made doubtful by the very process of transmission they describe. The poets' statements about poetry also have to be considered within their rhetorical contexts: when a poet commends his song to a jongleur, for example, there is always the possibility that said jongleur is there for fictive or conventional reasons and not because, at the historical moment of composition, the poet needed a jongleur. Bernart de Ventadorn's tornada beginning "Garsio, now sing my song for me . . ." could even, conceivably, have been the jongleur's *own* "signature" to his performance, rather than the poet's "original" instructions to him. The modern reader will feel the need for some way of gauging the degree to which the transmitters, singing or writing, changed songs. How *much* of a given song, as the text(s) come down to us, can be attributed to "the poet"? Unfortunately, performers and scribes masquerading as "the poet" can easily blur the distinction between their contributions and the "original." Even the painstaking discernment of various dialect traits in a work can be misleading: once we have discovered several contributors, which one is the poet? Is it not typical of medieval scribes (and perhaps of performers as well) to mix dialectal variants within a single work? By throwing out variants from dialects not the poet's own, we risk throwing out the poet's "original" words as preserved in another dialect in favor of "revisions" created by someone else in the poet's own dialect. Furthermore, the poets' own frequent acceptance of variants created by performers other than themselves helps to defeat, by rendering pointless within a twelfth-century context, the search for "the original."

In Part Two of this book I will approach the questions treated here from a very different perspective, to see what can be learned from the external "facts" about the way songs have actually come down to us. How many copies? Attributed to whom? In what metrical form? In what variety of stanzaic sequences? These are the physical results, the circumstantial evidence in which the mode of transmission has left its traces. The conclusions reached here—that twelfth-century troubadours did not produce "author's manuscripts"; that their songs were reproduced and circulated in performance rather than on "parchment leaves"; and that if some troubadours were more likely than others to regard their work as "literary property" or as "fixed texts," it was neither their social class nor their ability to write that made them so—can thus be tested against an objective analysis of the "end products" of transmission.

PART TWO

The View from Without

PERFORMANCE AND POETICS

REFLECTED IN THE

CHANSONNIERS

FOUR

Mouvance in the Manuscripts

"High-fidelity reproduction" of troubadour lyric, then, may not necessarily have meant verbatim replay of an original. The customary fidelity, as both poets and transmitters inform us, relies most upon *bona fe* and *drechura,* "good faith" and "rightness": a singer or writer is true to the song when realizing it in its best form. The singer acts as the poet's representative in more than one way, assuming some of the duties of the maker along with the maker's persona. The variety of transmitters mentioned by the poets—not only trained performers hired to reproduce the master's voice, but also friends, patrons and their courts, village boys from the jongleurs' home towns [1]—makes *mouvance* appear the natural result of many years' *melhuramen* (improvement), some for the better and some for the worse.

Under these circumstances, the greatest wonder is that many of the troubadours' songs remain essentially unchanged, often in more than one manuscript tradition. *Mouvance* operates selectively: it leaves certain poems almost untouched no matter how far they travel, while it alters others so drastically that even the most Lachmannian of editors must sometimes print more than one version. The purpose of Part Two is to uncover some of the principles that govern this selectivity.

Of particular interest in the search for those principles are the disturbances in stanzaic sequence that characterize the troubadour *chansonniers.* Here is *mouvance* on a large scale: a single poem comes down to us with its stanzas in nine different arrangements, another with nineteen; the transposition (or, to borrow a term from mathematics, "permutation")[2] of stanzas offers large-scale variants of a type that has generally been ignored in stemmatic reconstructions of "original" texts, yet obviously affects the meaning and structure of each text in a profound way. Since most of the conscientious editions of troubadour poems indicate the various stanzaic sequences preserved in the manuscripts, the degree of stanzaic transposition undergone by poets' works can be quantified, studied, and compared more simply than can other kinds of variants. The study of this type of large-scale variant has the advantage of independence from the stemmatic system (which is based on comparison of word and phrase variants) of establishing "authentic texts": manuscripts with shared word and phrase variants do not necessarily share a stanzaic sequence.[3]

That stanzaic transposition is distributed unevenly among the Occitan poets has been documented, but the reasons for this unevenness have not. William D. Paden delineates three areas of investigation that might explain the variance among poets in the stability of their texts; he suggests that "permutation" might correlate with the period of time in which a poet produced his work, with his degree of stylistic difficulty, or with his ability to write and thus to produce a written archetype for future manuscripts. Toward this last question Paden contributes much, including a substantial study of Guilhem IX's literacy. He concludes tentatively that the count could not write. These findings have meaning for the study of other troubadours in at least two ways: first, an illiterate Guilhem would not have established the author's manuscript as the first step in transmitting a kind of poetry for which he set so many other precedents; second, unless Guilhem wrote, the remarkably low rate of stanzaic transposition in his songs (22 percent; see Appendix A) cannot be explained as the effect of an autograph copy on the manuscript tradition.[4]

Paden also argues that sung transmission grew less popular as time went on. His study of the occurrence of the names of jongleurs in poetry, as a function of the date, shows a clear historical trend in the poets' use of a device that includes the transmitter in the message itself: naming the jongleur within the poem (1979, 4–7; 1984). Mention of jongleurs declines gradually—not in the number of occurrences but in the percentage of known troubadours who name jongleurs—especially between A.D. 1220 and 1340. Since many of the jongleurs named have been documented as living near the poets or in their households (e.g., Raimbaut d'Aurenga's Levet in 1173), it is safe to assume that the named jongleur is not merely a writer's affectation. The decline in the practice of naming the jongleur within the poem proves first of all that *mention* of jongleurs had gone out of fashion, and only secondarily that writing had overtaken singing as the primary mode of transmission. But clearly the weight of evidence points to a rise in writing, and a decline in sung transmission, from about 1250 onward. If we conclude, with Paden, that the increasing scarcity of troubadours who name jongleurs in the thirteenth and fourteenth centuries[5] reflects "a gradual shift from oral to written transmission" and, concurrently, "elevation of the vernacular from the status of low language into competition for that of high language in the culture of Occitania," then we also observe that, along with the decline of the *joglar*, "the lyric pulse weakened" (Paden 1984, 13–14). The present study concentrates on the troubadours of the twelfth and early thirteenth centuries, when the "lyric pulse" still beat unabated.

One caution to drawing conclusions from the incidence of jongleurs' names: there are many loopholes in the criteria for determining what is the name of a jongleur and what is not. I have shown in preceding chapters that the recipient of a poem is often asked to memorize it, so that he or she—without losing class status—partakes of the jongleur's role in repeating the song. Both types of names—the *senhals* and the jongleurs' professional names—include fanciful, descriptive nicknames as well as ordinary given names. A *tornada* may contain several names and *senhals*. Might the "Joglar" of Azalais de Portcairagues, or one of Guilhem de St-Didier's three "Bertrands," or Rigaut de Berbezilh's "Bels Bericles," ever have performed as a jongleur? These poets are merely the first three to come to mind; there may be many more such cases. None of these three poets, nor others addressing potential transmitters whose names have traditionally been taken as *senhals* for a nonperforming addressee, were counted as having "named joglars." Yet their inclusion might change the percentages—and thus the appearance of a trend—rather dramatically, since the percentages are based on numerically small samples.[6]

The third issue, that of stylistic difficulty as a control on the mutability of lyric texts, will receive careful attention here. Friedrich Diez observed the function of elaborate rhyme schemes as a mnemonic aid not only in fixing the internal structure of each stanza but also, for some poems, in fixing the order of their stanzas.[7] Martín de Riquer, in his introduction to *Los trovadores*, explains the development of many of the metrical forms that draw rhymes from one stanza into the scheme of the next— *coblas doblas, alternadas, capcaudadas, capfinidas*, and so on—as the result of a deliberate effort on the poets' part to bring transposition under control.[8] The recent recognition that some poets both acknowledged and defied the tendency of lyrics to alter in circulation has led to the further claim that poets conceived complex versification as, among other things, a safeguard for textual integrity: "Some troubadours came up with the idea that a complicated metrical structure, a complex word arrangement might be appropriate in order to protect the composition of the poem from outside influence. Indeed, a public of literary experts could be expected to detect the mutilations of the *avol chantador* right away and denounce them as such" (Mölk 1979, 5).

That complex verse forms were developed expressly "to protect the composition of the poem from outside influences" is very plausible, but it requires verification.[9] Mölk's statement assumes the drive to textual integrity, the perception of rhythmic and rhyming structures as potential tools for this purpose; it also assumes that "outside influence" would be perceived as undesirable, as *worsening* the songs it changed. Finally, though time increased the number of complex metrical forms that had been *invented,* we cannot say that time brought an increase in their *use.* On the contrary, the use of certain kinds of complex forms actually declined between 1100 and 1250 (see Appendix A, Fig. A-9).

Taken as a hypothesis, Mölk's notion is well worth testing: we cannot understate the importance of such a discovery, should it prove true. This would indeed be, as Mölk calls it, an "obviously significant moment in literary history": the moment when poets in a performing tradition, where outside influence could be expected, began to look on their works as artifacts; the moment when they rebelled against the instability of their medium, when they idealized a verbatim textual integrity beyond the capability of available means of publication. It would be an exceptional development, in the midst of medieval tradition favoring anonymity and adaptation, if the idea of authorship suddenly became applicable to contemporary lyric when authority had heretofore been reserved for the ancients.

Did the troubadours really view metrical complexity as a possible remedy for *mouvance?* The texts indicate that some did. Yet the story is not that simple. Complex verse forms do stabilize the order of stanzas; but the poets do not increasingly use them. Only 19 percent of the 552 poems in my survey avail themselves of one type of stabilizing device studied: stanzaic linkage, that is, connecting one stanza to the next by establishing a pattern in the rhyme scheme that requires their contiguity.

What is more, the use of this type of device drops to an all-time low among the very poets who perfected it (see Fig. A-9, poets 13–16). Clearly, something is wrong with this theory that the poets, relating stylistic complexity to textual integrity, "tried" to use complex verse forms as a protective measure.

The "solution" of stylistic complexity proves to have been effective in practice, but its use responded to the "problem" only intermittently, whether deliberately or accidentally. The relation of "problem and solution" finally depends on evidence that elaborate metrics were *perceived* as a guard against outside influence, and that at least some troubadours both knew transposition to be a problem and believed stylistic complexity capable of solving it. Some poets show very little awareness of textual change in their works; some openly welcome "outside influence" while still using certain kinds of "stylistic complexity" that promote textual stability (for example, Jaufre Rudel uses stanzaic linkage). More disconcerting, in view of the historical movement around 1180–1195 to abandon stanzaic linkage, is the need to face the distinct possibility that certain poets *chose not to* "solve" the "problem."

The opinions of the poets on the subject of "textual integrity" vary widely. Some apparently believe, for instance, that only inept tampering with a poem qualified the singer as an *avols chantaire*, whereas skillful tampering that actually improved the song could earn the singer the praise of its original author as well as of the audience. Nearly all troubadours take a stand against bad renderings of their works, but few object openly to "outside influence" in itself. Part Three will probe more deeply the vocabulary, the imagery, and the cast of characters with which the poets illustrate "textual integrity" and its alternatives; for now, then, I will only sketch out some of the questions behind my statistical survey.

The external evidence presented here and in Appendix A offers a way of looking at *mouvance* from a point of view not available to the troubadours themselves. It can tell us what actually happened in transmission, regardless of whether the typical processes were known or viewed as problematic by the poets, and regardless of any intention they might have conceived, whether to subvert those processes or to encourage them. This evidence will tell us which poems—when, by what poet, using which techniques of rhyme and meter—were most *likely* to produce versions with variation in the sequence and array of stanzas. It will also tell us which variables made no difference to that likelihood.

Instability in Transmission: Popularity and Repertories

Since some poets say that their songs will improve or appreciate with repetition, I decided to test the hypothesis that their poems might have ful-
filled this forecast in the *chansonniers*—that is, that the more often a
song was repeated, the greater its chances of being recast by transmitters.
Because of the special character of this manuscript tradition and its apparent status as the last step in a much longer process of transmission—
its status, perhaps, as the result of translation from a "fluid" medium to a
"monumental" one—the rate of survival in written copies probably reflects not only popularity with copyists but also frequency of performance. Based on my survey, the "average" troubadour song (extant in
more than one copy) survives in 8.8 manuscripts, with its stanzas in 2.1
sequences and 3.2 different stanzaic arrays (including abridgments and
fracturings).[10] Deviations from the norm in the rate of manuscript survival can serve as a rough index to popularity in the jongleurs' repertories. Paden believes that jongleurs had very small repertories (1984, 93).
If this is so, one might expect jongleurs to be very selective in composing
those repertories, favoring songs that not only suited their voices and
stage personalities but also consistently pleased audiences (and brought
coins to the cap).

I am assuming that essentially self-supporting jongleurs, both those
mentioned by the poets and later arrivals, performed the songs. Even if it
is true that certain jongleurs, those mentioned in the poetry, "worked
with only one poet" (Paden 1984, 94), it does not necessarily follow that
every jongleur *had* a partner-poet who consistently provided his songs.
Mailolis, who approaches Bertran de Born requesting a song, is described
by Bertran as a stranger to him, and an obnoxious one at that; he gives
him a song ostensibly designed to reward its singer with a rain of overripe
tomatoes rather than of kudos and coins (B Born 27 [P.-C. 80,24]). Since
the jongleur apparently received his payment not from the composing
poet but from the addressee or audience, we may expect that jongleurs
chose to perform certain "successful" songs more often than others. It
would be naïve to suppose that a popular favorite song like "Can vei la
lauzeta mover" ("When I see the lark move") was performed *only* by a
single jongleur whom Bernart de Ventadorn designated as his partner and
then consigned exclusively to parchment on the retirement or death of
that lucky jongleur. Certain poems inevitably "pay" better than others—
as the poets were well aware, given the tenor of their discussions of "clo-

sure" and "integrity" (treated in Part Three). The kind of "exclusive franchise" involved in the supposed one-to-one relationship of poets to jongleurs would conform to a concept of literary property, exclusivity in performance, and authenticity that was shared by some poets in the school of Marcabru but denied by Jaufre Rudel, Bernart de Ventadorn, and Giraut de Bornelh.

My interpretation of the indices of manuscript survival (M and MS) therefore supposes that popularity with copyists can be traced to popularity with jongleurs and ultimately with audiences. We recall that Bernart Amoros compiled poems that he had "seen *and heard*" in their native lands. I arrived at an index of the rate of retransmission (manuscript survival, M) by very mundane means: by counting the total number of copies of a given poet's works. To get MS (manuscripts per poem), I divide M by the number of different poems copied. These popularity indices, rating each poet as to his work's survival in manuscript copies, were then measured against several different indices of susceptibility to stanzaic transposition.

Rate of transposition versus year, when plotted on a graph, shows "clouds" of thoroughly random "scatter" reflecting the wide variation in stability among poets composing at the same time; the correlation of date and percent-with-transposition is virtually nonexistent up through 1250 (Fig. A-6). Thus, chronology cannot explain why some poets keep a larger *percentage* of their poems intact—at least in regard to the arrangement of stanzas—than do others. We still need an explanation of these variations (index TR). Did some poets deliberately fix the ordering of stanzas in their works, while others—not from artlessness but by choice—give free rein to stanzaic transposition? Or do the unvarying poems reflect sheer luck with transmission? The proportions of unvarying songs were doubtless influenced by poets' expressed intentions, by the formal properties of individual poems, by trends in performance or in copying, and by transmitters' reverence for certain poets. Manuscript survival—a finger on the pulse of the transmitters rather than of the poets—proved by far the single most important factor in *all* measures of stability or instability.

Popularity Correlates with Rate of Transposition

The rate of transposition (TR) can be explained as a very close correlative of popularity (MS). When the question to be answered is, "Why do the poets vary in the proportion of their work that manifests stanzaic transposition?"[11] we can say confidently that it covaries regularly with the number of manuscripts per poem. Nothing else correlates so strongly with rate of transposition. The number of manuscripts per poem is the key factor in predicting the degree to which a poet's work will manifest stanzaic transposition (Fig. A-5). With a correlation coefficient of .62 between TR and MS, even the conservative analyst can say that popularity "explains" about 40 percent (r^2) of the differences among poets in their rates of transposition. This is considered quite a strong correlation for statistics involving social phenomena, since the activities of human beings are always too complex to be accounted for by only two variables. The significance level for this correlation confirms its importance: the probability that these data could have come from a "no-slope population," that is, from a sample with no real trend, is .0018, or eighteen in ten thousand.

Stepping back to look at the relationships among primary data, however, we find that "percent transposed" (= T/P) versus "manuscripts per poem" (= M/P) is not the whole story. These two derived indices, both filtered through the number of poems (P), register as a kind of shadow of an impressively regular interrelationship between transpositions and manuscripts. The *number* of poems showing transposition (T) is directly proportional to the number of manuscripts surviving (M), as Figure A-3 in Appendix A illustrates. The odds of *this* correlation coming from a no-slope population are only one in ten thousand.

The close relationship between manuscript survival and transposition rate shows that, to a great extent, stanzaic transposition is a phenomenon of the transmitting culture. It also indicates that authorial interference (rewriting and republication of poems) was clearly not the only source of new versions. The alternative (that the number of poems showing transposition, T, "causes" M, the number of extant copies) is improbable: it would mean that the number of songs a poet revised and reissued after "first drafts" had been placed in circulation somehow tended to make him popular with his own and later generations or increased the tendency of his poems to survive in many copies.

Time—the period in which a poet composed his songs—is again somewhat discounted as a significant factor in determining the rate of transposition. Guilhem IX and Guilhem de Montagnagol, the earliest and latest poets in my survey, appear close together on the graph (Fig. A-6). The distribution of transpositions in proportion to manuscripts does not discriminate between earlier and later poets.

If popularity were the only factor in determining rate of transposition, the graph mapping the relation of TR and MS (Fig. A-5) would show a fine line and not a wide band. The popularity distribution makes it possible to see the transposition rates in perspective and suggests further ways to explore the reasons for great differences in transmission among poets productive within the same span of time. It filters out, for example, the proliferation of manuscripts of Bernart de Ventadorn's poems when we compare him with his contemporary, Raimbaut d'Aurenga: even considering their respective popularity ratings, Raimbaut's lyrics are significantly more stable than Bernart's. Yet the spread between them is not as wide as the transposition figures alone might suggest.

In drawing the trend line for manuscript survival versus rate of transposition, one notices that poets on either side share certain stylistic tendencies: Bernart de Ventadorn, Peire Rogier, and Jaufre Rudel may not be equally popular or equally mutable, yet they all fall well above the trend line, requiring fewer manuscripts than the others to produce transpositions; none of them has been accused of practicing *trobar clus*. Peire Rogier is famous for warning Raimbaut d'Aurenga not to be so learned but to play the fool if he wished to please audiences. On the other side of the line, among poets whose songs change less than the number of copies warrants, we find Raimbaut d'Aurenga, Guilhem de St-Didier, Giraut de Bornelh, and Arnaut Daniel—all of them innovators in versification, most of them identified as the heirs of Marcabru and Guilhem IX rather than of Jaufre Rudel. This pattern confirms Paden's idea, arrived at on the basis of transposition figures alone, that "stylistic difficulty correlates with low permutation in Marcabru, Raimbaut d'Aurenga, and Giraut de Bornelh, all poets associated with *trobar clus*—although the case of Arnaut Daniel, with higher permutation, tests the rule" (1979, 3).

When we take into account his popularity, Arnaut Daniel's above-average rate of transposition still places him well below the trend line, since a higher percentage of his poems remain stable than one would expect from the number of extant copies. Thus, the popularity/transposition distribution, as it divides the troubadours roughly into two fields, supports Paden's tentative rule about the effects of stylistic difficulty, especially since it makes it unnecessary to except Arnaut Daniel from the general pattern.

With regard to the number of poems with transposition versus the number of manuscript copies (Fig. A-3), only a few poets do not conform to a very regular statistical pattern. "Out of line" on the unstable side (with an excess of transpositions per manuscript) are Bertran de Born, Bernart de Ventadorn, Raimon de Miraval, and Peire Vidal. Who among us would be willing to declare Bertran and Peire incapable of "stylistic difficulty"? On the stable side (with an unusually high proportion of manuscripts to transposed poems) are Guilhem de St-Didier, Raimbaut d'Aurenga, Giraut de Bornelh, and Folquet de Marselha. Coincidentally, the first three of these were contemporaries in close literary contact; could they have shared some "secret weapon" against transposition? Raimbaut's poems tended to be abridged more than average but transposed less (Fig. A-4). Conversely, Bernart de Ventadorn's were transposed more than average but abridged less!

What constitutes stylistic difficulty has been partially explained, though not completely captured, by quantification of the two elements studied here: the length and "linkage" of stanzas. Songs with what I call "linked stanzas" have rhyme schemes that join together two or more stanzas in such a way that their sequence cannot be disrupted without a noticeable breach of pattern. These rhyme schemes and their stabilizing effects will be discussed in detail further on; at this point, it suffices to know that stanzaic linkage, by itself, stabilizes *poems* but not *poets*. For each poet, I found the percentage of poems with linked stanzas and observed its influence on other elements of stability. This percentage of poems with linked stanzas (abbreviated LK+) can be taken into account when we try to explain variations of stability.

Stanza Length and Version Production

An unexpected result of my statistical survey is that the length of stanzas probably did affect the stability of troubadour songs. The longer the poet's average stanza length, the more manuscripts it took to produce a transposition (Fig. A-10). Stanza length also correlates strongly with version production, when we define "version" as any alternate array, be it an abridgment or a transposition.

The stabilizing power of longer stanzas may partly explain Giraut de Bornelh's success in "evading" *mouvance*—if one can say he "evades" it without implying that he *tried* to evade it. He rarely uses the fancy rhyme schemes that discourage transposition, yet by any index his work is extremely stable. Among the twenty-three poets I surveyed, he holds the record for the longest stanzas, averaging eleven to twelve lines per stanza (11.48). His rate of version production is among the lowest. Likewise,

Arnaut Daniel uses very long stanzas (averaging 10.83 lines), rarely with stanzaic linkage. His version production is unusually low, and even his rate of transposition is low when we consider his popularity. "L'aur'amara," with its seventeen-lines-long stanzas, comes down in only two sequences in nine manuscripts (*CDHNU* and *IKN²a*); the frequency of its rhymes certainly qualifies as a kind of stylistic difficulty.

There was also, as scholars have long observed, a chronological trend to compose more and more lines per stanza (Fig. A-8). Although the trend to longer stanzas could be viewed as "progress" toward an identifiable "goal" of creating stable poetry, there are two major drawbacks to this view. First, on the average, stanza length increased by only two lines per hundred years. Such a slow trend cannot have been the reaction to a "problem" viewed as urgently important. Second, long stanzas did not imply the creation of fixed texts. They stabilized, they perhaps reduced the number of possible combinations and permutations, but they did not absolutely or effectively dictate the sequence of stanzas.

As a very slight trend among the poets surveyed, linked stanzas and long stanzas occur in inverse proportion: the longer a poet's stanzas tend to be, the less often he is likely to use stanzaic linkage.[12] As we shall see, though, combining both devices tended to help stabilize troubadour poetry.

Instability and Chronology

If it were widely agreed among the troubadours that jongleurs habitually scrambled stanzaic sequence, that complex rhyme schemes would help to combat this tendency, and that such combat was desirable, then we might expect to see overall "progress" toward textual stability and an increase, over time, in the use of devices that promote stability. That is, we should see a chronological trend. My study examines how the factor of time (using the assumed midpoint of each poet's lifespan) was related to the other two elements in question—sequential stability and poetic form. The results do not confirm the notion of a widely accepted need to "remedy" the vicissitudes of transmission, because they offer only qualified support to its underlying assumption that "progress was made."

Versions per Manuscript and Chronology

How can one suppose a chronological trend and still explain the remarkable stability of Raimbaut d'Aurenga's songs (only 16 percent show transposition), when his contemporary Bernart de Ventadorn has a high proportion of unstable songs (76 percent show transposition)? At least one measure of variation in the stability of twelfth-century poets' works—the percentage of poems showing stanzaic transpositions—follows no historical trend at all (Fig. A-6). It seems even less likely that the *causes* of this variation are related to chronological progress.

There was no chronological trend toward altering stanzaic sequence in fewer and fewer troubadour songs, or toward producing fewer versions per song. In my original survey, which included only one thirteenth-century poet, Raimon de Miraval, I found no chronological "progress" in any area, except toward an increase in stanza length. Yet when I extended the data, adding thirteenth-century poets up to Guilhem de Montanhagol, with an assumed midpoint of life in the year 1250, a weak chronological trend toward conservatism in version production came to light. This was not a trend to alter fewer songs, but to produce fewer versions per manuscript. Version production for both transpositions and abridgments correlated significantly with time.[13] As time went on, it took more manuscript copies to produce either a rearrangement of stanzaic sequence or an abridgment.[14] Either performances or copyings slowly and intermittently became more rigid. That this trend manifests itself only when thirteenth-century poets are included suggests that it may be related to the rise of the book culture and its accompanying model of the text as a fixed document, an entity capable of verbatim inscription whether encountered as a written object or not (Stock 1983). It may point toward the kinds of changes Paden suggests in his work on the jongleurs (1984).

Our broader definition of version production, including abridgments as well as stanzaic transposition, covaries more closely with time than does the strict definition by stanzaic transposition. In fact, more generally, the definition of "version" that includes abridgment follows all the same trends, but with greater predictability, than does the definition using stanzaic transposition as its criterion. This suggests that the two phenomena arose from the same causes and that "versions showing transposition" are actually a subset of a more general and predictable set of "versions." The broader criteria for "versions" (I refer to them below as "stanzaic arrays") thus seem most useful for discovering what element of transmission may have decreased "version production" over time.[15]

Many will hasten to conclude, based on the clear trend toward fewer versions per manuscript among later poets, that it must have been an "improvement" in the poets' ability to write down their compositions that tended to stabilize their works. But we can explain most of the trend by examining measurable variables of poetic form, without resorting to speculation about the poets' ability to write.

If we partition the graph of stanzaic arrays per manuscript versus year (WM vs. Y; Fig. A-7) into quadrants, we begin to see within them meaningful clusters of poets. This schema illustrates what each cluster has in common:

Quadrant 1	*Quadrant 3*
Early poets	Later poets
Unstable	Unstable
High use of linked stanzas	Low use of linked stanzas
Short stanza length	Average stanza length
Quadrant 2	*Quadrant 4*
Early poets	Later poets
Stable	Stable
High stanzaic linkage	Moderate stanzaic linkage
Average/long stanzas	Average/long stanzas

I extract the following conclusions.

Mnemonic rhyme schemes did not make early poets stable. Early poets with a high ratio of versions to manuscripts (quadrant 1) tend to be low in stanza length (seven lines or fewer) and high in stanzaic linkage (30–50 percent). Most of these also have a numerically small body of MS copies ($M = 53$ or fewer, where the mean M of poets surveyed is 188).

Poet	Year	WM	LK+	Z	M	
2. JRud	1125	.641	.40	7.0	53	
4. BMar	1150	.649	.33	6.9	20	
11. PonsG	1171	.415	.50	7.0	22	
1. GmIX	1098	.500	.22	5.09	34	
3. Mcb	1139	.465	.35	8.48	168	(MS = 4.1)

Jaufre Rudel and Pons de la Guardia both invite their addressees to reperform the text. Bernart Marti speaks out against Peire d'Alvernhe's pretensions to textual integrity in his boasts of making *vers entiers* (see Chapter 7 for full discussion). Thus, these three early poets are openly uncommitted to the concept of the fixed text. Guilhem IX and Marcabru, though relatively "early and unstable" and therefore appearing in quadrant 1 of the schema, lie close to the trend line, so they are "average" in stability when their early dates are taken into account. They are stabler than the others in their quadrant. While they use stanzaic linkage less often than do Jaufre Rudel and Pons de la Guardia, their kind of "stylistic complexity" does include unusual or coined rhyme words. Marcabru also begins to use the longer stanzas that significantly improve stability. His statements on poetics suggest he believed in literary property and the original version, at least for his own works (see Chapter 6, pp. 150–60).

Bernart de Ventadorn is a special case, an early poet appearing relatively "stable" as regards stanzaic transposition but relatively "unstable" if abridgments as well as transpositions are considered.[16] His overwhelming popularity surely contributed to the creation of new versions in his poetry.

Some earlier poets using mnemonic rhyme schemes were especially "stable." Early poets with a low ratio of versions to manuscripts (quadrant 2) tend to have high stanzaic linkage (30–50 percent) and moderate or high stanza length. These are the best "survivors." Their works passed the maximum of time with the minimum of "damage" before being solidified by the book culture that brought us existing manuscripts.

Poet	Year	WM	LK+	Z	M
5. RBerb	1151	.360	.30	9.33	123
8. Rd'Aur	1160	.375	.30	7.47	195
12. GmSt-D	1179	.304	.46	8.0	112

For these poets, we can say that despite the mnemonic device supposedly offered by stanzaic linkage, their poems were "difficult." These three make use of such fancy devices as derivative rhymes, coined rhyme words, and fixed or pivotal "refrain words."[17]

Abandoning stanzaic linkage made poets' stability reliant on stanza length. Of those "middle poets" around 1180–1196 who rejected stanzaic linkage—though all of them showed that they *could* do it, and brilliantly, if they wanted to—the best "survivors" (lowest in abridgment *and* transposition) were those who elected to use very long stanzas.

Poet	Year	WM	LK+	Z
13. GrBor	1180	.330	.10	11.48
14. ArnD	1187	.254	.11	10.83
15. BBorn	1193	.474	.15	8.34
16. PVid	1195	.456	.09	9.09
17. ArnM	1195	.310	.05	8.2

An exception, Arnaut de Mareuil, has stability comparable to Arnaut's and Giraut's, though he uses the shorter stanzas typical of less stable poets. For *transposed* versions per manuscript (VM), though, he is less stable than Arnaut Daniel and more stable than Peire Vidal.

Complex and sophisticated poetry without mnemonics produces frequent transposition. The later poets of quadrant 3, with high ratios of versions to manuscripts, have very low stanzaic linkage (less than 15 percent) and merely average stanza length (eight to nine lines per stanza):

Poet	Year	WM	LK+	Z
15. BBorn	1193	.474	.15	8.34
16. PVid	1195	.456	.09	9.09
23. GmMon	1250	.392	.00	8.36

Moderate complexity with some mnemonics and with temporal proximity to the advent of book culture promoted stability best. Later poets with low versions per manuscript (quadrant 4) tend to have moderately high stanzaic linkage *and* moderately high stanza length:

Poet	Year	WM	LK+	Z
18. FMars	1205	.181	.22	9.5
20. JsPcb	1225	.344	.23	10.2
22. DPrad	1248	.277	.20	8.76

Thus, seeing the drop in version production over time, we need not assume it was caused because poets were slowly learning to write. Part of the trend can be ascribed to tendencies toward stabilizing formal properties in poetry. Two "unsuccessful" strategies, if the poets are assumed to be deliberately fighting change in stanzaic arrays, were (1) to put all one's energy into stanzaic linkage using short stanzas, as the early poets like Jaufre Rudel did, and (2) to abandon stanzaic linkage *and* use short stanzas, as some of the unstable middle poets did. Stanzaic linkage did help poets who participated in the movement toward longer stanzas. And it did help poets who already had "time on their side" because the *chansonniers* began to be compiled during or soon after their lifetimes. But it did not produce stability for early poets using short stanzas, whose work had to weather a hundred years or more before it was copied into MSS *I*, *K*, or *V*—and much longer before it reached late manuscripts such as *a*.

Time, although irrelevant to the number of versions per *poem*, was somewhat relevant to the number of versions per *manuscript*. This supports the theory that there was no movement toward authorial revision (which would have created more variation in "versions per poem" to start from and, hence, would have multiplied the variation in "versions per poem" in transmission). It also confirms that, except for stanza-linked poems, which defy the trend, the formal features of the poems themselves, or of particular poets and their reputations, only partly determined the likelihood of version production. Rather, there must have been change (though slight and gradual) in the practices of the transmitting culture—whether in its media or simply in its attitudes regarding textual integrity. As we reconstruct the forces for and against textual stability, we revisit a struggle between stabilizing formal properties or attitudes toward poetry, and the transmitters' steady, usually victorious, process of destabilization.

Rhyme as a Means of Fixing Stanzaic Sequence

One type of "stylistic difficulty" that significantly reduces transposition is the use of rhyme schemes that link one stanza to another or that by some system of alternation dictate the placement of each stanza within the whole poem. Because the motifs of *fin'amors* can follow in almost any order without disturbing convention, an abrupt contradiction is usually required to betray a *frachura* in the *razo,* a "breakage" in the "line of argument." When the versification is inconsistent, however, breakage becomes much more obvious. With *coblas unissonans* (uniform stanzas, each obeying the same structure and using the same rhyme sounds) and *singulars* (in which each stanza has an independent set of rhyme sounds), some errors within a single stanza can easily be detected: the mismatched rhyme, the incomplete stanza, or the line with too many or too few syllables. Such errors can signal either a failure of the poet's control or a deterioration through transmitters' imperfect grasp of the poem's requirements. The versification can also alert the hearer to displacement of entire stanzas, but only when it groups or links them in some way.

In my quantitative study of the effects of linking rhymes on the rate of transposition, I found it necessary to treat all types of "poems with linked stanzas" as a group because of the rarity of individual schemata other than the pairing of "twin" stanzas, *coblas doblas.* Under the heading of "poems with linked stanzas" came *coblas doblas* (stanzas matched in pairs), *coblas ternas* and *quaternas* (stanzas matched in groups of three and of four), *coblas alternadas* (alternating stanzas), *coblas capcaudadas* and *capfinidas* (stanzas linked by head-and-tail rhymes or repetitions), *coblas redondas* (stanzas paired by a ring structure), and songs with any system of rotating rhyme or alternating refrain words (see Appendix B).

An illustrated discussion of each of these types of rhyme scheme can be found in Chapter 5. Only about 19 percent of the 552 songs surveyed used linked stanzas (104/552), and nearly half of these were composed in simple *coblas doblas* (46/104, or 44 percent).

As a group, poems with linked stanzas resisted transposition much better than did those composed with uniform or unmatched strophes in *coblas unissonans* and *singulars;* they were much more likely to be preserved in only one strophic sequence. Among poems preserved in more than one manuscript, resistance to transposition is strongly related to stanza linkage: 51 percent (198/390) of *coblas unissonans* and *singulars* show transposition; among poems with linked stanzas the rate drops to 23 percent, or almost one in four (22/94). In terms of version production, linked-stanza poems also fare well: while the average unlinked poem produces 2.2 different stanzaic sequences (863/390), the average linked-stanza poem yields only 1.6 (146/94).[18]

Poems with linked stanzas were not, overall, much more frequently copied than unlinked poems. Linked-stanza poems average 7.7 mss./poem, whereas poems without stanzaic linkage average 7.9 mss./poem. Yet a poem with linked stanzas was slightly more likely, if preserved at all, to be preserved in more than one manuscript: linked-stanza poems make up 19 percent of all poems surveyed but only 15 percent of unique-manuscript songs.

These findings present a serious challenge to the theory that the troubadours wished to stabilize their "texts" and therefore invented complex verse forms, using them deliberately to inhibit change in transmission. If the troubadours developed these linked-stanza forms for the purpose of protecting their works from outside influence, why did they use them so seldom? Of all the linked-stanza forms, why did they rely most heavily on *coblas doblas?* (In view of the possibilities for rearrangement without disrupting the formal requirements, *coblas doblas* seem to provide the least sequential security of all the linked-stanza forms. Any poet who wanted to use linked-stanza forms to stabilize sequence should, in principle, have favored schemes with stronger interlocking of strophes. Conversely, *coblas doblas* are the simplest mnemonic device, with no potentially self-defeating complexity; thus, their prevalance could still be used to argue in favor of purposeful preventive use.) We cannot expect the troubadours to have foreseen how the centuries of transmission, both oral and written, would treat their works. But the theory that complex verse forms were intended as a "solution" to "problems" of transmission depends on the idea that they tried, to some extent, to second-guess the transmitter and to use forms that seemed sturdiest based on their own experience with jongleurs or with scribes.

Since poems with linked stanzas were comparatively stable, as a group, I expected to find that poets who used them most frequently would score lower in their rates of transposition. Not so: the percentage of stanza-linked songs (LK) among a poet's works did not correlate with his rate of transposition (TR). Frequency of stanzaic linkage as measured by LK+ (an index limited to poems in more than one manuscript) actually tends to *increase* slightly with versions per manuscript (Fig. A-12). Habitual use of linked stanzas therefore did not by itself persuade a poet's retransmitters to preserve the stanzaic arrangement in his whole body of poetry. In other words, it did not create "reputations for fixity" that particularly inspired reverence for a given poet's exact, "authorial" array of stanzas. One might expect the opposite in a written tradition: that the more usually a poet organized his rhyme scheme in ways that dictate stanzaic sequence, the more precision in sequential copying would seem to be called for in all his works.

Other indices also teach us something about the behavior in transmission of poems with linked stanzas: poems with unlinked stanzas behave much more predictably. When I subdivided the versions-per-manuscript index into separate categories of "linked" and "unlinked" poems, the songs with linked stanzas resisted nearly every trend. The very existence of these correlations signifies predictability, dependence on known factors in transmission or poetic form. Poems with linked stanzas generally refuse to fit neatly into the patterns obeyed by their unlinked counterparts.

Thus, poems with linked stanzas protected themselves from transposition, but the habit of using them did not particularly improve a given poet's chances of stabilizing his opus—except perhaps when combined with other kinds of "stylistic difficulty." So few poets use them more than 20 percent of the time that their variations in stability must be explained as resulting from other causes. The most telling factor was circulation. The poet's appeal, his success with audiences, encouraged transposition more consistently than other influences discouraged it.

Nevertheless, the finding that stanza length and stanzaic linkage affect stability proves that the formal properties of each song could influence whether or not performers and scribes rearranged the song. Although a preference for linked stanzas seems to be mildly associated with *instability* (so that stanzaic linkage, if conceived as a purposeful "solution," sometimes backfired), poems with linked stanzas do fare better as a group than do songs constructed without a built-in mandate for stanzaic sequence.

The concept of the fixed text evidently did come to light in troubadour poetry. Many poets did connect textual fixity with stylistic complexity and elaborate rhyme schemes. But textual fixity was an idea before its time. The transmitting culture overwhelmed and appropriated whatever most appealed to it. It relentlessly altered whatever it chose to, no matter how strongly safeguarded. No doubt the troubadours observed the ultimate power of the transmitters within their own lifetimes. True, they seem to have envisioned an ideal of the fixed text, worked out grand ways and aesthetically impressive devices to safeguard it, and produced prototypes of the "incorruptible text." But the ideal of the fixed text was impractical within their transmitting culture. The same poets who most dramatically proved the possibility of fixing the text through monosequential rhyme schemes—Peire Vidal, Arnaut Daniel, Rigaut de Berbezilh, Giraut de Bornelh—were ultimately the poets who relied least on stanzaic linkage for their poems' stability. These poets earned their stability (or, in Peire Vidal's case, instability) through a combination of factors of "stylistic difficulty." Some of these factors, unmeasured here, could prove revealing in some future study: for example, lexical rarity might account for some variation. My investigation isolates only two factors of stylistic complexity—stanza length and stanzaic linkage—both of which contribute measurably to the stability of troubadour poetry.

Many poets who took part in exploring the concept of the fixed text seem, ultimately, uncommitted to its practice. Arnaut Daniel uses stanzaic linkage in only two of his eighteen or nineteen songs; he pokes fun at "the firm intention" (the ideal of incorruptibility) in his sestina. Giraut de Bornelh was said to have undergone a conversion from *trobar clus* to *trobar leu*. I suspect he tried the fixed text and then abandoned it, since he knew the only truly effective way to preserve textual integrity was to limit the song's circulation—and what good is an unchanged song if it is unheard?

The reasons for the unpredictability of songs with linked stanzas will be partly explained by a closer look at individual metrical forms: those for which the poets claimed superior stabilizing powers and those which we might expect to stabilize the sequence of stanzas. In the next chapter, the manuscript tradition of exemplary poems in each type of rhyme scheme will give us much information about the advantages and short-comings of such inventions as *coblas capfinidas* as safeguards against amateur revision. At the same time, this study will allow us, in some cases, to compare the poet's apparent expectations regarding textual stability with the actual outcome of manuscript transmission.

FIVE

Rhyme and *Razo*

CASE STUDIES

Uniform Strophes: *Coblas Unissonans*

Poets' boasts that their songs cannot be dismantled often occur in songs that lack formal safeguards for preserving stanzaic sequence. That is, the notion of textual fixity precedes—anticipates, but does not by itself attain—the capability to fix texts. Peire d'Alvernhe's "Be m'es plazens" with its "locked and closed words" boasts of fixity in *coblas singulars* (an "early" type where each stanza has its own set of rhyme sounds) preserved with as many sequences as there are manuscripts. Marcabru connects his veto on altering his poem with the song's workmanship, but the stanzaic structure within which he claims to "lassar la razon e·l vers" provides no clear bond between one stanza and the next, or even between half-stanzas:

> Aujatz de chan, com'enans'e meillura
> E Marcabrus, segon s'entensa pura,
> sap la razon   e·l vers lassar e faire
> si que autr'om   no l'en pot un mot traire.[1]
> (Roncaglia 1957, 23, vv. 1–4)

> Hear how the song advances and improves; and Marcabru, in accordance with his pure intention, knows how to bind up the argument in the versification so that another man cannot remove one word from it.

Marcabru appears to believe he has devised a way to stabilize the poem, to ensure its integrity: the term *lassar* clearly refers to precautions he has taken to prevent others from damaging his song. The reference to "advancement" (*s'enansa*) claims sequentiality, especially when combined with the notion that "intention" remains "pure."

Retrospect over the manuscript tradition, however, proves this boast to have been over optimistic. Marcabru may dream of a sequential *razo*, but here at least he does not compose accordingly. The relationships among the stanzas are still flexible, both in their development of an argument and in their fulfillment of the versification. *AIK* and *E* give the stanzas in two different sequences, and the version of *AIK* is two stanzas shorter. Furthermore, the two versions do not even give the same stanzas: the transmitters take advantage of the two-part stanzaic form (10a′ 10a′ / 4b 6c 4b 6c) to construct new stanzas from available parts. This "fracturing" occurs within nearly every stanza. Dejeanne's 1909 edition invented yet a third sequence, reshuffling half-strophes to create stanzas that existed in neither written tradition and suppressing stanzas that existed in both. Roncaglia points out that scholars have long considered it one of Marcabru's most obscure poems. The obscurity vanishes, he claims, when the proper sequence of stanzas is restored (1957, 20). I intend to argue that, though the 1909 version may be "obscure," clarity and logical continuity characterize the stanzaic sequences of both *AIK* and *E*.

If *razo* means "argument" or "line of thought" here, its "bonding" to the versification is not apparent. Nothing in the poem's construction dictates a single necessary, continuous sequence of reasoning: these are *coblas unissonans* (uniform strophes), meaning that each stanza repeats the same pattern of rhyme sounds throughout. Each of two sequentially distinct versions develops a defensible logical progression of its own.

The half-stanzas are syntactically independent: only in the exordium does the subject-verb connection bridge the natural breaking point at midstanza. This sirventes proceeds by amplification, such that sequential relations between motifs remain flexible. The first half-strophe makes an assertion related to the central idea, "Evil and dishonesty are on the rise; society is going to the dogs." The second half-strophe usually does one of three things: (1) provides a cause or reason to support the first half, (2) presents a descriptive appositive to the first half, or (3) offers a supporting, secondary assertion with its own causal clause. Because of the half-strophes' syntactic independence and because each half-strophe gives an amplification closely related to the poem's theme, both versions (each with its own sequence of half-strophes) maintain logical continuity. Let us look, for example, at both versions of stanza two:

A: Per so sospir, car mouta gens ahura
   de malvestat c'ades creis e pejura:
   so m'en somon   qu'ieu sia guerrejaire,
   c'a lieis sap bon   quan m'au cridar ni braire.

Therefore I sigh, because much of society augurs an evil that is soon increasing and worsening. Thus they summon me to be a warrior, for it pleases them when they hear me cry out and sing.

E: Pero sospir, car tota gens aura
   de malvestat que creis e pejura:
   C'aquist baron   an comensat estraire
   e passat   per un pertus taraire.

But I sigh, because all society augurs an evil that is increasing and worsening. For these barons have begun to take [instead of give], and they've passed through a very small aperture.

In both versions, the poet begins with a statement that his complaining song ("sighing") was prompted by a forecast of the decline of morals in society; he then gives an explanatory clause. In A, the explanatory clause amplifies *sospir* (I sigh) as a vocalization, by expanding on the reasons for singing: "mouta gen," foretelling decline, has asked him to fight "the evil." In E, the second half-strophe amplifies instead the decline of morals, pointing accusingly at "these barons" and specifying that generosity, in particular, has lost ground. In A Marcabru supports an aristocratic class in its battle against moral decline; in E, "tota gen" includes specific barons in moral decline. A's version thus shows more literary self-consciousness and awareness of the audience, while E's version moves quickly to the *object* of critique rather than dwelling on the speaker or its audience. Each version combines two half-strophes to make a "logical" strophe, and each offers a "logical" sequel to the opening stanza.

Again, for their third and fourth stanzas, both versions can be said to "follow a reasoned progression." Having devoted two strophes to the poet's qualifications and reasons for singing, A now narrows down the general theme of "social decline" to "decline among the youth."

A3: No·i a conort en joven, mas trop surra,
   ni contra mort ressort ni cobertura,
   pos ist baron   an comensat l'estraire
   e passat don   per pertuis de taraire.

There is no hope among the youth—instead they become very
corrupt—nor is there any resource or shelter against death.
For these barons have begun to take [instead of give], and
they've passed "giving" through a very small aperture.

Both *A* and *E* follow this comment on the decline of generosity with another division of society into two classes, this time "the worst and the
best," both greedy. The strophe is roughly the same in both versions, but
in *A* it is the fourth and in *E* the third.[2]

> A4/E3: Li sordeior ant del dar l'aventura
>   e li meillor badon a la peintura:
>   la retraisso·n   fatz trist e sospiraire,
>   c'a rebuzon   fant li ric lor afaire.

The worst run the risk of giving, while the best merely ogle the
illusion: the story of it makes one sad and sighing, for the rich
do their business backwards.

The sequence of *AIK* now develops this criticism of "the rich" by con-
templating the corrupting effects of wealth. This version personifies moral
qualities, using in its fifth stanza the image of the embattled fortress. As in
war, justice is abandoned when money conquers, "when, because of
wealth, a child is made emperor." For its sixth stanza, the *AIK* version
continues the list of virtues lost through avarice; he who loses his virtues
in this way is no better than a beast or a thief:

> AIK5: Proeza·is franh e avoleza·is mura
>   e no vol gaug cuillir dinz sa clauzura;
>   dreit ni razon   no vei mantener gaire
>   que d'un garson   fai avers emperaire.

Courage shatters, and greed walls itself up and refuses to accept pleasure into its enclosure; neither right nor reason do I
see maintained in the slightest, for wealth makes a boy the
emperor.

> AIK6: Qui per aver pert vergonh'e mezura
>   e giet' honor e valor a noncura
>   segon faisson   es del semblan confraire
>   a l'erisson   e al gos e al laire.

He who, for money, loses his sense of shame and measure and casts honor and worth into indifference is to all appearances the brother of the hedgehog, the bitch, and the thief.

Meanwhile *E*, for its fourth and fifth stanzas, uses many of the same parts to construct a similar, but not identical poem. *E* returns its focus to "youth," which, like the rich, "does its business backwards" by falling prematurely under the shadow of death; *E* delays pursuing the motif of avarice until its fifth stanza, where it again ties together "greed and youth" through the image of the rich boy emperor.

> *E*4:   Non a conort en joven, mas trop fura,
> ni contra mort ressort ni cobertura,
> Qu'ist acrupit   l'an gitat de son aire
> e de cami,   per colpa de la maire.

There is no hope among the youth—instead they sweep it quite away—nor is there any resource or shelter against death. For these abased men[3] have cast it [youth] out from its lineage and from the road, because of a blow struck by the mother.

> *E*5:   Qui per argen pert vergonh'e mezura
> e giet'honor e valor a noncura
> Pretz ni valor   no vezem tener
> quan per aver   es un gartz emperaire.

If someone for silver loses his sense of shame and measure, he also casts honor and valor into indifference. We do not see worth and valor upheld, when through wealth a boy is made emperor.

With these two strophes the version of *E*, while still "logical," begins to show flaws. In the second half-strophe of each, this version strays from the required rhymes (*-on* and *-aire*). Some of *E*'s lines are hypometric. In *E*4, the proximity of the verbal adjective *acrupit* to the noun *camin* sounds, to my ear, so echoic of one of Marcabru's famous coinages, *crup-en-cami* (croucher-in-the-road), that it suggests the work of a disciple. But poets sometimes do reuse their inventions.

The continuity remains smooth and thoughtful. *E*'s strophe 4 elaborates on "youth" to speak of family, lineage, and legitimacy (if the "blow struck by the mother" refers, as seems likely given Marcabrunian misogyny, to a betrayal of the father leading to illegitimate offspring). While a "lost generation" of decaying youth is dispossessed in $E4$, the "rich boy" triumphs in $E5$.

Thus, it is a flaw of versification rather than of *razo* that announces alteration. The two versions equally possess a "logical progression," each with different emphases and continuities. Only when the transmitter allows formal requirements to lapse can we be sure, with Mölk, that "a public of literary experts could be expected to detect the mutilations of the *avol chantador* right away and denounce them as such" (1979, 5).

Do these poorly rhymed half-strophes mean we should reject the version of E as completely "inauthentic," while embracing *AIK* as the "authentic" version? If we do, we have to sacrifice more than two whole strophes, nine lines that address specific men in powerful political positions and that establish the poet's relationship with several addressees: Guilhem X, Duke of Aquitaine, perhaps Marcabru's patron (Roncaglia 1957, 44); Alfonse Jordan, Count of Toulouse; and Alfonso VII of Castile and Léon. The configuration of "names named" in E is consistent with composition in 1133–1134 by a poet staying at Toulouse in the court of Alfonse Jordan (Roncaglia 1957, 46–47)—in turn not *in*consistent with what we know of Marcabru. The lines about the boy who through wealth becomes emperor, present in both versions, allude to an actual event of June 4, 1133.[4] Dating through the poem's political allusions thus rules out long-term wear and tear as an explanation for the corrupt rhyme scheme of E's version. We can detect errors without being able to distinguish the errors of the original poet from the errors of a reviser. Who is to say that Marcabru never sang a false rhyme? Roncaglia accepts both versions as authentic: he is "surprised" to encounter "probable authors' variants: more exactly, residues of an earlier draft" (1957, 20–21). In the terms of my interpretation, these are "residues" of two performances, not necessarily both given by the original poet but both equally "authentic."

Marcabru may have believed that since *coblas unissonans* were difficult to compose, they would also be difficult to alter. To some extent, they can expose imposture, though they do not prevent rearrangement. The enlacement within the stanza does permit us to recognize "false rhymes." The scheme of repeated rhymes, more difficult to "find" with each stanza, might tend to prohibit adding to the poem, but it puts no barrier in the way of those who would like to subtract from it. Marcabru does not ask that the poem remain in a single order; he asks only that nothing be removed. Neither kind of stability ensued.

With *coblas unissonans,* the security of the poet's original composition, at least in regard to stanzaic sequence, has nothing to bolster it unless it can depend on the coherence of a necessary sequence of ideas in the *razo,* the "argument," whether narrative or meditative. Given the circumstances of transmission, the troubadours could not expect to depend on continuity as part of the poem's entirety until they had developed the means to secure it. Bernart de Ventadorn's "When I See the Lark Move" would have failed through its very success if it had been planned as yielding its message, and its *joi d'entendre,* only to the keepers of the MSS *Q* and *U.* Yet this version has been defended as cohering in a necessary sequence of stanzas, on the assumption that Moshe Lazar's edition represented a fixed text, a "poem" in the modern sense. In fact, Lazar merely follows Appel's choice from among eleven different sequential arrangements. This underscores that one cannot safely perform the kind of literary analysis that relies on linear development without first ascertaining that a particular linear development is part of what constitutes "the text." Only the exceptional troubadour poem develops with an *inevitable* thematic continuity. After all, it would have been foolhardy for a poet to compose, in *coblas unissonans* as easy to fracture and rearrange as those in Marcabru's "Aujatz de chan," a song whose capacity to make sense would be destroyed if a few stanzas should come, in time, to be transposed.

Doubled and Alternated Rhyme Patterns: *Coblas Doblas* and *Coblas Alternadas*

The "problem" of the jongleurs' tendency to rearrange the order of stanzas (and not all poets viewed it as a "problem") was far from "solved" by the invention of systems for grouping stanzas, whether in pairs with *coblas doblas* and *alternadas* or in series of three or four with *coblas ternas* and *quaternas.* Numerous poems have survived, apparently, as seriously damaged *coblas doblas.* Peire Rogier's "Dous'amiga, no·n puesc mais," described by Nicholson as "six coblas singulars (plus three which are missing)" (1976, 125),[5] could not have given a sure sign of deficiency without the fact that two of its stanzas match: either the poem was once entirely in *coblas doblas,* or else Peire Rogier committed the ineptitude of trying *coblas doblas* and then giving up. Many more songs survive in an indecisive form of *coblas doblas,* with one or more unmatched *coblas* intruding after the system of pairs has been established.

Raimon de Miraval's *sirventes joglaresc* "A Dieu mi coman, Bajona"

(Topsfield 1971, 316–320, song 39) appears to have consisted, at one time, of paired strophes also linked by a sort of rotation in the rhyme:

i	-ona, -ut
ii	-ona, -ier
iii	-anta, -os
iv	-orna, -ier
v	-orna, -ieu
vi	-anta, -os
tornada	-anta, -os

The poem (preserved only in *CR* and presenting no alternate structures in these manuscripts) passes for *coblas singulars* (where each stanza has its own rhyme sounds), but stanzas ii and iv, iii and vi, and iv and v *nearly* follow the rules for constructing paired stanzas. Did Raimon de Miraval compose this poem with a system, only part of which is now visible? And if so, what sort of system was it? Did the paired stanzas follow each other consecutively, as in *coblas doblas* (as AABB etc.), or did they alternate (ABAB or ABCABC etc.)? The MSS *C* and *R* agree, as they often do, too closely in phrasing and strophic order to make us suppose that they represent separate traditions. Their agreement is more likely to affirm the vitality of a variant (flawed) version than to authenticate their version as "original."[6]

A weakness of *coblas doblas,* as well as of *coblas alternadas,* is that one can adapt the same material to either system. In transmitting a poem of Guilhem de St-Didier (324, 5: "Bel m'es oimais qu'eu retraja"), in which the pairing of *coblas alternadas* is dictated by a system of derivative rhymes in retrograde order, the transmitter of *C* has inverted *coblas* ii and iii. As a result, the form of the poem appears in *C* as two sets of *coblas doblas* followed by one set of *coblas alternadas* and one set of *tornadas.*[7] One of Jaufre Rudel's poems in *coblas doblas,* "Quan lo rius de la fontana," generated some confusion: what if the version known to the compiler does not have an even number of stanzas? The system of doubling breaks down. Some versions begin with two initial *coblas* whose first line rhymes on *-ana,* and then follow the pair with three more *coblas* beginning with a rhyme on *-ina;* version 2b settles for a compromise, with two *coblas* in *-ana,* two in *-ina,* and then one each in *-ana* and *-ina.*[8] Although *coblas* in *-ina* appear to have been remembered in abundance, there were not enough *coblas* in *-ana* to make up a second double stanza. In version 2b, then, Jaufre's poem manifests the same hesitation we saw in

MS *C*'s version of Guilhem de St-Didier's *coblas alternadas*. Likewise, for Marcabru's "Puois la fuoilla revirola," the manuscripts *AEIKa* give a version in *coblas doblas* with one unmatched stanza; the longer versions of *C* and *R*, however, arrange the stanzas as *coblas alternadas*.[9]

Despite these failings, the use of *coblas doblas* did inhibit transposition, reducing it to 25–30 percent (compared with almost 50 percent transposition in poems with unlinked stanzas).[10] Were it not for the transmitters' freedom to reverse the order of two matching stanzas, we might explain the success of *coblas doblas* very simply: they check stanzaic transposition by reducing the number of movable units.

Mathematically, the number of permutations increases with the number of stanzas at an alarming rate. Only seven stanzas could, in theory, produce more than five thousand different sequences. Consider the values of factorial n (i.e., $n!$), representing the number of different possible stanzaic sequences, where n is the number of stanzas:

n	$n!$
1	1
2	2
3	6
4	24
5	120
6	720
7	5,040

The first stanza of any troubadour poem is stable in its position, so in practice we have $(n - 1)!$ as the number of possible sequences. If the linkage among stanzas effectively divides in half the number of movable units, with the first *two* stanzas stable in their position, then the number of permutations drops to $([n - 2] / 2)!$, a substantial improvement. When we allow for inversion within pairs, then this figure is multiplied by the number of ways we can arrange the invertible pairs.[11] Six stanzas in *coblas doblas*, then, could be arranged in only 2 different ways, assuming a rule that the pairs must not be inverted, or in 8 ways without that rule; the same number of *coblas unissonans* can be arranged in 120 different ways, given a stable first stanza.

Coblas ternas and *quaternas* should, in theory, work the same way by reducing the value of $n!$. These forms, however, are rare, and the sequences are not as stable as one might expect: as the movable unit lengthens, it becomes increasingly difficult to control inversion *within* the unit.

Paired *coblas* (i.e., *doblas* or *alternadas*) with controls built into the rhyme scheme to prevent inversion of pairs should, then, be nearly invulnerable to permutation. Guilhem de St-Didier's "Bel m'es oimais qu'eu retraja," mentioned earlier (at note 7), simultaneously arranges its strophes in contiguous pairs and discourages their inversion. It does this through a system of derivative rhymes in inverse order (*rimas retrogradadas*). Two strophes, in this system, comprise as close-knit a unit as a single strophe:

I. Bel m'es oimais qu'eu *retraja*
    Ab leugieira razon *plana*
    Tal chanson que cil l'*entenda*
    A cui totz mos cors s'*aclina*
    Q'en la soa des*mesura*
    Mi part de si e·m des*loigna;*
    Tant m'es de merce *estraigna*
    Que no·l platz que Jois m'en *veigna*

II. Non sai si·m muor o viu o *veing*
    o vau, c'a mal seignor *estraing*
    serv que no·m met neus terme *loing*
    Que ja jorn vas me s'a*mesur.*
    Et on ieu plus ll'estau cap*cli.*
    Negun de mos precs non *enten.*
    Ans sai qe m'aucirant de *pla*
    Li ben c'om de lieis mi *retrai*

III. Trop si feing vas mi *veraja.*
     Car una promessa *vana*
     No·m fai . . .

                (Gm St-D 4, 1–19)[12]

I. It pleases me henceforth to *repeat* a song with such an easy *flat* argument that she toward whom my whole heart *bends* may *understand* it. For in her *intemperance* she divides herself from me and *distances* me. She is such a *stranger* to mercy on me that she is not pleased when joy *comes* to me from it.

II. I know not whether I am dying or living or *coming* or going, for I serve a *strange* lord who does not set me a date, even a *distant* one, when she might someday treat me *temperately*. And the more I *bend* my head, the more she *understands* not one of my pleas. But instead, I know I will be killed *flat out* by the good things *repeated* to me about her.

III. She pretends to be very *true* to me, for she does not make me an *empty* promise . . .

Out of ten manuscripts, only C disrupts the sequence of paired stanzas by inverting strophes 2 and 3. The poem thus "shows permutation" but still protects itself very well from sequential change. Guilhem's poem carries further the schematic idea introduced in Raimbaut d'Aurenga's "Cars, douz e fehnz," which uses derivative rhymes in inverse order within each of its *coblas unissonans*. Raimbaut's rhyme scheme echoes the content, which "comes back on itself": the male wren's low song makes the singer arise; the cricket's voice comes light as cork from the heavy stone wall and becomes, like the square stones in the wall, aligned and "squared." The singer in turn is raised high, rivaled in exaltation only by the cricket and the female wren. Ascribing to the voice such properties as weight and geometry, while at the same time vividly painting the scene of a summer's evening when the poet is wonder-struck by affinities between nature's singing and his own, Raimbaut "squares off" the masonry of his rhyme scheme. Each stanza is indivisible within itself because of its self-reinforcing construction:

> Cars, douz e fenhz   del *bederesc*
> M'es sos bas chans,   per cui m'*aerc*;
> C'ab joi s'espan   viu e noire
> El tems que·lh grill   pres del *siure*
> Chantan el mur   jos lo *caire;*
> Que·s compassa e s'*escaira*
> Sa vos, qu'a plus leu de *siura*
> E ja uns non s'i *aderga*
> Mas grils e la *bederesca.*
>
> (R d'Aur 1, 1–18)

The low song of the wren, on account of which I am exalted, is dear, sweet, and fictitious to me, for it spreads abroad, exists, and grows with joy at the time when the crickets, near the cork tree, sing in the wall under the block of stone; so that their voices, which are lighter than cork, are aligned and squared; and let no one exalt himself so high except the cricket and the female wren.

(trans. Pattison 1952, 65)

Raimbaut's system—with each stanza part of a *coblas unissonans* scheme—produces extremely self-contained, autonomous *coblas*: solid "bricks" in a well-aligned wall. Guilhem's, going further, makes each *cobla* dependent on the next. In regard to transmission, we might say that "Cars, douz e fehnz" protects itself only against fracturing and transposition within the stanza (in six manuscripts it produced only one sequence), while "Bel m'es oimais . . ." protects itself from transposition within each pair of stanzas. One could also say that Guilhem is merely working with a longer (double-length) stanza; however, the melody generally marks the beginning of a new stanza.[13] Guilhem's method, then, bridges two repetitions of the melody.

Head-and-Tail Linked Stanzas: *Coblas Capcaudadas* and *Coblas Capfinidas*

An easier way to forestall inversion in *coblas doblas* might be to join them by repeating the final word of each stanza in the first line of the next, thereby making them *coblas capfinidas*. This would strengthen the hearer's sense of continuity, both in sound and in meaning. Pons de la Guardia's "Be·m cujava que no chantes oguan" (Frank 1949, no. 7) uses these two techniques together. The poet claims to have composed the song expressly for Marqueza (de Cabrera, according to Frank) and her entourage, hoping that through them it "will be sung and learned in many a good place." Perhaps Pons believed that a song with its stanzas both paired and linked head-to-tail would be *leu ad aprendre* (easy to learn) and so used this form in deference to noble, but amateurish, transmitters. The manuscripts offer no evidence of either difficulty or ease for transmitters, however, since such information cannot be drawn from agreement between *C* and *R*, the only manuscripts in which the song survives.

Supposing that one has chosen *coblas capfinidas* as one's method for stabilizing *coblas doblas*, one might decide to discard the system of doubling as a redundant safeguard. *Coblas capfinidas* dictate the sequence of stanzas intended by the poet and might be expected to remain stable without the aid of other devices. An overview of the transmission of *coblas capfinidas* does show that the device was extremely effective in preventing transposition but that it was rarely used. The surviving works of the twenty-three poets in my survey (552 songs in total) include only eleven songs in *coblas capfinidas*, four of them by Guilhem de St-Didier. Only two have transposed stanzas: Arnaut Daniel's "Chansson do·ill mot son plan e prim," and Peire Vidal's "Nulhs hom non pot d'amor gandir"—the latter barely qualifying as *capfinidas*, with only four links extant among eight stanzas. Defective *coblas capfinidas*, however, are likely either to become unrecognizable as such or to lose their attribution to famous poets such as those in my survey.

Close scrutiny of the manuscript variants in Arnaut's "Chansson do·ill mot son plan e prim" will demonstrate both the value and the potential fallibility of "redundant safeguards" on stanzaic sequence. The song illustrates how the technique of *coblas capfinidas*, even when reinforced by a system of pairing *and* a system of rotation among the rhymes, can fail as a guard for stanzaic order.[14]

I.   Chansson *do·ill* mot son plan e prim   1
farai puois que botono·ill vim
e l'aussor cim
son de color
de mainta flor   5
e verdeia la fuoilla,
chan e·il braill
son a l'ombraill
dels auzels per la *bruoilla*

II.   Per *bruoill* aug lo chan e·l refrim   10
e per q'om no m'en fassa crim
obre e lim
motz de valor
ab art d'Amor
don non ai cor qe·m tuoilla;   15
ans si be·m faill
la sec a traill
on plus vas mi s'*orguoilla*.

III.   Val *orguoill* petit d'amador
que leu trabucha son seignor   20
del luoc aussor

      ius al teraill
      per tal trebaill
      que de ioi lo despuoilla;
      dreitz es lagrim   25
      et ard' e rim
      qi·n contr'amor *ianguoilla.*

IV. Per *ianguoill* ges no·m vir aillor,
      bona dompna, ves cui ador;
      mas per paor   30
      del devinaill,
      don iois trassaill,
      fatz semblan que no·us vuoilla;
      c'anc nos gauzim
      de lor noirim: 35
      mal m'es que lor *acuoilla.*

V.   Si ben m'*acuoill* tot a esdaill
      mos pessamens lai vos assaill;
      q'ieu chant e vaill
      pel ioi qe·ns fim   40
      lai o·ns partim;
      dont sovens l'uoills mi muoilla
      d'ir' e de plor
      e de doussor
      car per ioi ai qe·m *duoilla.*   45

VI. Ges no·m *duoill* d'amor don badaill
      ni non sec mesura ni taill;
      sol m'o egaill
      que anc no vim
      del temps Caym   50
      amador meins acuoilla
      cor trichador
      ni bauzador,
      per que mos iois *capduoilla.*

      Bella, qui qe·is destuoilla   55
      Arnautz dreich cor
      lai o·us honor
      car vostre pretz *capduoilla.*

I. A song whose words are smooth and supreme I will make now that the willows [*osiers*] are budding, and the highest peaks are the color of many flowers, and the leaf turns green, and the songs and birds' cries are in the shadow *across the woods.*

II. *Through the woods* I hear the song and re-echo it, and so that no one may make this a crime by me, I work and polish words of worth with the art of love, from which I have no will to part; rather, although I slip, I follow its path, all the more though it raises its *pride* against me.

III. The *pride* of a lover is worth little, for it easily trips up its master from the highest place down to the ground, through such trouble that it strips him of joy; it is right that he should weep and burn and rhyme [burn], whoever *chatters* against love.

IV. I do not turn elsewhere for the sake of *chattering,* good lady toward whom I make adoration; but for fear of riddling which makes joy tremble, I make the appearance of not wanting you; for we never rejoiced from their lineage; it is unlucky that I *met* them.

V. Though it *comes to meet* me all haphazardly, my thought attacks you there, that I may sing and have worth through the joy we made there where we separated; because of which my eye is often wet with anger and with tears and with sweetness, for through joy I have that which *grieves* me.

VI. I do not *grieve* for the love I yearn for, nor do I follow moderation or measure; I alone am equal to this, for never have I seen since the time of Cain a lover who less accepted a trickster or capricious heart, and therefore my joy *reaches its crown.*

Fair one, whoever [else] might turn away, Arnaut runs straight to where he can honor you, for your worth *reaches its crown.*

For this song, incontestably, there is one and only one "correct" stanzaic sequence. Arnaut has created, by building sequence into this rhyme scheme, the capability to incorporate a linear movement, a progression in the *razo,* into the "integrity" of his song. In this case, linearity is part of the theme as well as of the formal structure.

Like Raimbaut d'Aurenga, Arnaut uses geometric figures as imagery—and here, the straight-line path represents the "right road" for the faithful lover and the faithful poet. From the first stanza, the poet makes us conscious of the extremes; he moves our line of vision from the "aussor cim" (highest peaks) to the shadowy forest floor, where vision is restricted and sounds, instead, mark the way. With a hunting metaphor he speaks of following the track of love along the slippery path, which he does not wish to leave, though he does lose his footing, and where the pride of lovers makes them fall also: "del luoc aussor / ius al teraill" (from the highest place down to the ground). He passes judgment in terms of what is "straight" or "right": "dreitz es lagrim . . . qi·n contr'amor ianguoilla" (it is right that he should weep . . . who chatters against love). He does not turn from this path ("ges no·m vir aillor"), though gossip makes *joi* unsteady ("don iois trassaill"). Although he follows the path of love, he does not follow that of moderation, "ni non sec mesura ni taill," for he recognizes no counterpart, as a lover unreceptive to trickery, since biblical times. The idea of linearity and "straight" progression follows through all the way to the *tornada,* where the speaker contrasts himself with those who swerve: "qui qe·is destuoilla / Arnautz dreich cor" (Whoever else might turn away, Arnaut runs straight).

Yet in eighteen manuscripts, only half preserve the correct order of strophes (*ABGIKN²QSg* and *c*), while the other nine invert strophes 5 and 6 (*CDEHLNPRS*). The thematic progression, the sequence of ideas, did not hold together by itself: strophe 5 presents a memory of past *joi* that makes the speaker weep, while strophe 6 describes the lover's immoderate fidelity by way of the rather sinister biblical figure of Cain. It may be that some performers or copyists chose to end the song not with Cain but with the remembrance of joy and the lover's tears: nine of the manuscripts make the poignant note of past joy their concluding stanza, and four of those nine end on that note by omitting the *tornada.* Arnaut evidently intended to contrast the "trembling" of joy in strophe 4, where it was shown as vulnerable to gossip, with the powerful joy of the speaker's memory (str. 5). With this "correct, original" sequence, the strong memory of joy brings tears (str. 5), but it also leads to a boast of the lover's immoderate fidelity (str. 6), in turn leading into the *tornada,* which signs the name Arnaut to a second boast of faithfulness.

Why was the stylistic device of *coblas capfinidas* not strong enough to prevent this transposition? Apparently what happened is that the linking mechanism, which should derive the *cap* of one stanza from the *fin* of the preceding stanza, began to weaken after the third *cobla*. Thirteen manuscripts invert lines 28–29, exclaiming "Bona dompna!" at the head of the fourth stanza and thereby dropping its formal linkage (with *ianguoilla/ianguoill*) to the third stanza. At that point, the "redundant safeguard" of *coblas doblas* probably helped prevent transposition: the form dictated a matching stanza with the same rhymes as those preceding.

The device of the linking word weakens as the song progresses. Lines 36–37, the meeting of stanzas 4 and 5, appear in Toja's edition as follows:

> mal m'es que lor *acuoilla*.
> Si ben *m'acuoill* tot a esdaill

> Woe is me that I met them. Although it meets me all haphazardly, . . .

Although no manuscript inverts the stanzas at this point, memory does weaken here. *R* lacks lines 37–45 entirely, and even the manuscripts that do follow strophe 5 with strophe 6 lack the linking rhyme word in *-uoill:* the manuscripts instead give "Si be·m vau (vai)" or "Si tot val(s)," and it was only a lucky conjecture of Lavaud that restored the linking word *acuoill* in line 37.[15]

At the next bridge between stanzas, the loss of linking words leads to an actual alteration of stanza order. Where in Toja's edition stanzas 5 and 6 are joined with *duoilla/duoill* (vv. 45–46: "car per ioi ai qe·m duoilla. / Ges no·m duoill d'amor don badaill," Through joy I have that which *grieves* me. I do not *grieve* for the love I await), the transmitters again have difficulty in "remembering" the grammatical derivative of the final rhyme in *-uoilla*. Only three manuscripts retain a rhyme in *-oill* in the first half of line 46: *P* has *doill,* while *LS* have *toill.* A remarkable thing thus occurs in the manuscript *S,* which displaces lines 37–45: strophes 4 and 6 become properly linked *coblas capfinidas:*

*S*36:	Cor ai queu lor o *toilla*
S"37"(46):	Ges no·m *toill* d'amor dun badaill

> I have desire to *take* it *away* from them. I do not *take* myself *away* from love for which I wait in vain.

All other manuscripts abandon the idea of *coblas capfinidas* at line 46, where a bridge with *duoill* is needed:

ABCDEGHIKNN²QSgc: Er *ai fam* d'amor don badaill (Now I am
  hungry for the love I long await)
R: Er *ai fag* d'amor un badaill (Now I have made of love a long awaiting)

In general, scribes or performers "remembered" the linking word well
enough in its position as the final rhyme word in a stanza but easily "for-
got" it in its unrhymed position at the beginning of the next line. Without
these linking words, stanzas 5 and 6 become free-floating *coblas doblas,*
prone to inversion within the pair. The poem's system of rotating rhymes
also proves useless in preventing the inversion of *coblas doblas,* since it
dictates only the sequence of pairs and not the sequence of stanzas. The
combination of devices was probably responsible for delaying until late in
the poem the disruption of sequence and for minimizing the production
of versions. The beginning of a song is the most stable, and its stability
weakens progressively. By the time the weakening linkage finally broke,
only two different sequences were possible: 123456 and 123465.

Transmitters were often unobservant of *coblas capfinidas,* and only
rarely did they attempt to restore an apparently lost set of linking words.
A song of Rigaut de Berbezilh, "Tot atressi con la clartatz del dia"
(Várvaro 1960, song 8), comes down in nine copies (*HIKLL'NTa¹d*) as
imperfect *coblas capfinidas:* of the four "links" needed to join five
strophes, only the first two survive, and not a trace of lost linking words
persists among the variants. It would have been easy for a writing redactor to create such bridges between the strophes, since the final rhyme of
the *cauda* is the most common verb ending, -*ar.* Here is the way Rigaut's
pattern works in the first two "bridging rhymes":

  strs. 1–2: *desviar/desvia*
  strs. 2–3: *servir esforzar/servia*

One could easily continue this pattern by deriving common verbs from
the initial lines of strophes 4 and 5:

  str. 4, v. 28: Domn'es de mi, qu'eu non auz *dir amia*
  str. 5, v. 37: Mas ieu consir si *merces m'en valria*

to compose stanzaic links for lines 27 and 36:

  str. 3, v. 27: Per far de mi zo c'om del sieu deu far
  hypothetical redaction: *Per far de mi zo c'om *disses amar*
  str. 4, v. 36: De que ia·m puosca Amors ochaizonar
  hypothetical redaction: *De que Amors ia·m puosca *mercejar.*

But no copyist, no redactor, attempts this in nine manuscripts. Perhaps they were accustomed to unfinished *coblas capfinidas* and could untroubled allow such inconsistencies to pass; or perhaps, like Bernart Amoros, they had scruples about emending passages they did not understand. In any case, this poem does not show permutation. Its first three strophes are fixed in their position by the surviving linkage, and only two remain vulnerable to transposition. Thus, only two different sequences are possible (12345 and 12354).

Similar to *coblas capfinidas,* and about equally rare, is the device of *coblas capcaudadas.* Here the rhyme sound rather than a refrain word links the end of one stanza to the beginning of the next. Only twelve poems in my sample used this system of linkage, and it was almost always supported by some form of alternation or rotation among the rhymes— partly because the technique itself assumes that a single rhyme will shift in position from one stanza to the next. Thus, the apparent success of *coblas capcaudadas* (of eleven songs in more than one manuscript, only three show stanzaic transposition) may be attributable rather to the accompanying patterns of shifting rhyme than to the rhyming "heads" and "tails" of adjacent stanzas.

Raimbaut d'Aurenga's "Joglar, fe qed eu dei" (Pattison 1952, song 33) illustrates the simplest form of *coblas capcaudadas:* each stanza takes up a different monorhyme, except in its last line, which foretells the rhyme of the next stanza: aaaaab / bbbbbc / cccccd and so on. Since linkage is confined to a single line, a slight error could lead to transposition; moreover, a writing transmitter (working without the aid of the melody), might easily mistake such a form for *coblas singulars.* Because the poem is preserved in only one manuscript, though, the stability of its form remains untested.

The next more complicated use of *coblas capcaudadas* is in conjunction with *coblas alternadas:* the two poems in my sample that use this method alternate only the "head" and "tail" rhymes (producing *rimas dissolutas*). The manuscripts' treatment of Bernart de Ventadorn's "Non es meravelha s'eu chan" (Appel 1915, song 31) creates the impression that transmitters eagerly took advantage of every flexibility in the poem to individualize their versions, within the bounds of acceptable form. Each, evidently, wanted to sing it "melhs de nul autre chantador." The song was extremely popular; excluding the fragmentary version of *F,* it is preserved in nineteen manuscripts, with eleven different sequential arrangements. Despite this amazing variety, almost all manuscripts preserve the alternation of odd and even stanzas and thus preserve the rhyme link of *coblas capcaudadas* between adjacent stanzas. The sequences of strophes, as summarized by Appel (1915, 187), illustrate the remarkable strength of the "head-and-tail rhyme," despite transposition:

ADIKO	1 2 3 4 5 6 7
U	1 2 3 4 7 6 5
CMa	1 2 3 6 7 4 5 (8t)
V	1 2 3 6 7 5
R	1 3 2 6 7 5
Q	1 2 3 7 4 5 6
N	1 2 6 3 7 4 5
W	1 2 5 6 3 7
L²PS	1 2 5 6 7 4 3
L¹	1 4 3 6 5 2 7
G	1 4 3 6 5 7 8t
F	3 5 6

There are only a few deviations from the pattern that alternates odd and even stanzas. Manuscript *R* presents the poem as *coblas doblas* (two odd, two even, two odd); so does *N*, which leaves the first and last strophes unmatched (one odd, two even, two odd, one odd, one even). *V* begins with *coblas alternadas* but ends up with an extra odd strophe. The only others to disrupt the pattern of *coblas alternadas e capcaudadas* are *G* and *Q*, the "nonidentical twins," both of which place strophe 7 after another odd strophe. In *G*, however, strophe 7 and the *tornada* (half-strophe 8) follow in a logical sequence: having offered the *bona domna* his services, Bernart allays his fears about such submission by contrasting her with ferocious carnivores: "ors ni lion non etz vos ges, / que·m aucizatz, s'a vos me ren" (you're not at all a lion or a bear, who would kill me if I yielded myself to you; vv. 55–56). In *G*, thereupon, Bernart sends his poem "A ma tortre" (To my Turtledove) (in *C*, "A Mo Cortes," To My Courtly One). The lady is not a lion or a bear, but a turtledove; the connection of the first two animals with the *tornada*, as *G* has it, might have made it undesirable to omit strophe 7 even though it does add an extra odd stanza.

Let us stand back for a moment from the abstract evaluation of particular rhyme schemes to see how the meaning of a song like "Non es meravelha" is affected by sequential changes in transmission. It is interesting to see to what extent the mode of composition gives the poem flexibility and actually accommodates sequential changes. In order to make this kind of analysis practicable, I can cite the poem only once in a complete form, and I will subsequently work with synopses of each stanza to show how the rearrangement of topoi affects meaning. First, here is the song as edited by Appel (1915, song 31):

I.   Non es meravelha s'eu chan   1
melhs de nul autre chantador,
que plus me tra·l cors vas amor
e melhs sui faihz a so coman.
cor e cors e saber e sen   5
e fors'e poder i ai mes;
si·m tira vas amor lo fres
que vas autra part no·m aten.

II.   Ben es mortz qui d'amor no sen
al cor cal que dousa sabor;   10
e que val viure ses valor
mas per enoi far a la gen?
ja Domnedeus no·m azir tan
qu'eu ja pois viva jorn ni mes,
pois que d'enoi serai mespres   15
ni d'amor non aurai talan.

III.   Per bona fe e ses enjan
am la plus bel'e la melhor
del cor sospir e dels olhs plor,
car tan l'am eu, per que i ai dan.   20
eu que·n posc mais, s'Amors me pren
e las charcers en que m'a mes
no pot claus obrir mas merces,
e de merce no·i trop nien.

IV.   Aquest'amors me fer tan gen   25
al cor d'una dousa sabor:
cen vetz mor lo jorn de dolor
e reviu de joi autras cen.
ben es mos mals de bel semblan,

que mais val mos mals qu'autre bes;   30
e pois mos mals aitan bos m'es,
bos er lo bes apres l'afan.

V.   Ai Deus! car se fosson trian
d'entrels faus li fin amador
e·lh lauzenger e·lh trichador   35
portesson corns el fron denan!
tot l'aur del mon e tot l'argen
i volgr'aver dat, s'eu l'agues
sol que ma domna conogues
aissi com eu l'am finamen.   40

VI.   Cant eu la vei, be m'es parven
als olhs, al vis, a la color,
car aissi tremble de paor
com fa la folha contra·l ven.
non ai de sen per un enfan,   45
aissi sui d'amor entrepres;
e d'ome qu'es aissi conques,
pot domn'aver almorna gran.

VII.   Bona domna, re no·us deman
mas que·m prendatz per servidor,   50
qu'e·us servirai com bo senhor,
cossi que del gazardo m'an.
ve·us m'al vostre comandamen,
francs cors umils, gais e cortes!
ors ni leos non etz vos ges,   55
que·m aucizatz, s'a vos me ren.

VIII.   A Mo Cortes, lai on ilh es,
tramet lo vers, e ja no·lh pes
car n'ai estat tan lonjamen.

I. It is no wonder if I sing better than any other singer, for the more my heart/body draws me toward love, the better I am suited to its bidding. Heart and body and knowledge and sense and strength and power I have devoted to it, and the rein draws me so hard toward love, that I pay attention to nothing else.

II. He is truly dead who does not feel from love some sweet taste at the heart, and what value has living without value, except to annoy people. May God never hate me so much as to let me live a day or a month longer, if ever I should be guilty of annoyance or have no wish for love.

III. In good faith and without trickery, I love the fairest and best woman. From the heart I sigh and from the eyes I weep, because I love her so much, and on this account I suffer harm. What more can I do if love takes me, and the prison in which she has placed me no key can open but mercy, and I find no mercy there?

IV. This love strikes me so softly at the heart with a sweet taste: a hundred times a day I die of pain, and I revive again from joy another hundred times. My ills are truly of fair appearance, so that my ills are worth more than another's good, and since my ills are so good to me, the good will indeed be good after the pain is gone.

V. Ah, God, if only true lovers were distinguished from the false, and slanderers and tricksters wore horns on their foreheads! All the gold in the world, and all the silver, I would like to have given, if I had had it, if only my lady could have known how perfectly I love her.

VI. When I see her, it is very apparent in my eyes, my face, and my complexion, for I tremble with fear, just as the leaf trembles against the wind. I have not enough sense for a child, I am so encumbered by love; and a lady may have great pity for a man who is thus conquered.

VII. Good lady, I ask nothing of you but that you take me as servant, for I will serve you as a good lord, just as if recompense were coming to me. Here I am at your command, you honest and modest person, so gay and courtly! You are neither a bear nor a lion who would kill me if I offer myself to you.

VIII. To My Courtly One, there where she is, I send the poem, and let it not trouble her because I have not been [there] for such a long time.

The greatest number of manuscripts, *ADIKO,* supports the sequence just given, but *without the tornada.* The opening sequence of stanzas 1 and 2, where the second stanza justifies devoting oneself completely to love, by equating love with life and nonlove with death, is used by sixteen manuscripts: (1) "I sing better than other singers because I put all my energy

into love"; (2) "And what is the good of living without love?" As a second
stanza, (2) sounds like idealism, but as a final stanza it would sound like
an admission of defeat, or even a suicide threat. Eleven of these sixteen
follow with (3) "I love the best woman in the world; I am in a prison,
merce is the only key and there is no *merce*." The sequence 1–2–3, then,
moves from the singer's claim of superiority (1) justified by his absolute
placement of value in love as life (2) to more conventional topoi of the
lover's preferring death to loss of love (2) and the motif of love as a prison
(3). The prison of love and the "pleasant pain of love" are closely associated, so *ADIKO* and *U* follow with (4) "This love wounds me sweetly; I
die and revive daily; this harm is better than another good."

At this point *ADIKO* move to a topic that is characteristically Bernart's, as well as a typically Ventadornian way of envisioning an impossible world: (5) "If only true lovers were distinguished from false! If only
liars and cheats had to wear horns on their heads! I'd give all the gold in
the world if she could know how well I love her." True love, then, does
not give a visible outward sign, or at least not a sign blatant enough to let
his lady understand him. He is misunderstood, then. He does not have all
the gold in the world, nor do tricksters wear horns, so it seems unlikely
that the lady will understand his love. In this medial position, the stanza
(5) does not contain a strong self-reference to the *canso* itself.

Yet his love *is* visible, and does carry outward signs—how could the
lady not have noticed? (6) "Whenever I see her, I show physical symptoms of love; I tremble like a leaf and have less sense than a child—a lady
can pity a man so overtaken." Following on stanza 5, the argument is that
though cheats do not wear horns, true lovers visibly love, and in general
such a case calls for pity. The sixth stanza, then, in *ADIKO* serves as a
generalized prelude to the lover's personal request: (7) "I ask only that
you take me for your servant: don't be cruel like a bear or lion if I give
myself to you." Thus *ADIKO* end with the lover offering himself up to
what *may* be a hungry lion. The speaker hopes she is not, but the final
lines of the poem (in this version) voice that possibility.

The sequence of *Q* is just like that of *ADIKO* except that it places
strophe 7 in the middle (1237456) as if to avoid ending on the line
"Que·m aucizatz, s'a vos me ren" (That you might kill me if I give myself
to you). Or perhaps *Q* merely wants to run through the conventional topoi: why *not* follow "the prison of love" (3) with "the vassalage of love"
(7) and then the "pleasant pain of love" (4)? *Q* disrupts the alternation of
coblas alternadas in presenting this sequence. It ends with the pair 5-6,

which first voice the wish that lovers and nonlovers were clearly marked, then points out that this lover *is* openly symptomatic and asks, indirectly, for pity.

Manuscript *U* (1234765) also follows the mainstream up to a point. After stanza 4 and "the pleasant pain of love," however, it makes the lover surrender: the speaker offers himself to the lady as her servant (7), though he fears her so much that he has to remind her (and himself) that she is not a lion or a bear. His subsequent descriptions of his love symptoms (6) seem to stem from this fear; even though his physical and mental weakness are quite outwardly visible signs of love (6), he still fears misunderstanding (5), wishing that false lovers were obliged to wear horns.

At midpoem, stanza 5 does not insist on the poem's self-reference. "Would that false lovers and true were clearly marked—would that tricksters wore horns on their heads. I would give all the gold and silver in the world if my lady could know how well I love her." When (5) appears as a final stanza, however (as it does in eight manuscripts), it draws from the convention of poetic self-reference in the *tornada* and closing stanzas and from the expectation that the poem will create a bridge between the speaker and the addressee. By giving persuasive testimony to the speaker's fidelity, it does "let her know how well he loves her," and it is therefore perhaps worth "all the gold in the world." As a final and self-reflecting stanza, then, stanza 5 is a request for payment to the performer. Six manuscripts have this as a final stanza (*CMRUVa*), and three (*RUV*) have it as their ending.

The sequence in *CMa* (12367458t) sharply challenges the kindness and goodness of the lady herself. We cannot say it is "unlike Bernart" to be so critical, since he is forever using the courtly conventions to undercut one another. The first two stanzas establish the superior devotion of the lover; the third claims superiority for the lady; yet meanwhile he is in a hopeless prison of love and there is no *merce*. By moving directly to (6), the symptoms of love and the generalization that such a man should be pitied, the poet raises the question, If she is the best of ladies, why isn't she unlocking his prisonhouse with her *merce*? This question is reinforced when the speaker offers himself as her vassal (7) and then has to plead with her not to act like a lion or a bear. In making such a bond of fealty, the lord should know how to do his part as a civilized human being, without having to be told by his prospective vassal. Thus far the poet has kept the question of the lady's cruelty or kindness uppermost in our mind. Now when he speaks of the sweet wounds of love (4) he lets the hearer imagine the savage lady-lion-bear inflicting them. By using (5) as a final stanza, the speaker drives home the idea that, although he loves perfectly, he is after all misunderstood. It would take all the gold and silver in the world to make her understand: she is not only cruel, but insensitive as well. The *tornada* of C addressed "To My Cortes," makes one wonder if "My Cortes" can possibly be the lady in question; if it is, it is no wonder that he has "been away so long."

Manuscript G (1436578t), which like C defuses the danger of the lady, this time by addressing the song "To My Turtledove," follows the singer's initial boast with "the sweet pains of love." The sequence 1−4 highlights the verbal play in (4), where the meanings of the words *good* and *bad* are altered through love: now *both* refer to "good." This stresses the power of song to "enchant" reality, as much as the power of love. Stanza 2, the "suicide threat," is completely absent from this version: nothing so realistic as death intrudes on this world made of words. Next comes "the prison of love" (3) and the "visible symptoms of love" (6), both of which end with a request for pity (*merce, almornas*). Having already stated the visibility of his own love symptoms, the singer now wishes that false lovers were more clearly marked (5). To clearly express his love would be worth all the gold in the world—gold that he pointedly does not have, and expression which he manifestly has accomplished. Thus in G, the singer (7) offers himself as the lady's servant, "*as if* he were to be recompensed." Since "Ma Tortre" is gentler than the lion or the bear, perhaps she will also be more generous.

The preceding sketch of a multiple reading of one poem in its many sequential versions has demonstrated that sequence remains essential to a given performance's meaning: every moment depends on moments that have gone before. At the same time, songs constructed with the stanza as the movable unit lend themselves well to a number of different sequences. Just as all the topoi of *canso* convention are interrelated, just so any given sequence of the topoi will yield a network of interrelations. Each stanza is syntactically autonomous, yet each is potentially linked to the others by a common ground in *fin'amors* convention. The integrity of the song, "It is no wonder if I sing . . . ," is not harmed by alteration; on the contrary, through the many versions it realizes more fully its potential as a multifaceted song. The song both celebrates the performer's uniqueness and allows him artistic leeway in presentation. By contrast, Arnaut Daniel's "Song whose words are polished . . ." claimed a particular sequence, a linear progression in time, as part of its integrity. The manuscript tradition of Arnaut's song shows that performers who had lost parts of the "original" entity attempted nonetheless (by forging new "bridges" between linked stanzas) to reinstate the continuity and sequentiality of the form. The contrast between their two apparent claims to stability is much sharper than the contrast between the two rhyme schemes. All else being equal, Arnaut's *coblas capfinidas* and Bernart's *coblas alternadas e capcaudadas* could have had comparable stabilizing effects.

Far less variety is possible when, with *coblas capcaudadas,* the system of rotating rhyme groups the stanzas in *threes* instead of in pairs. Bernart de Ventadorn's "Can vei la flor, l'erba vert e la folha" ("When I see the flower, green grass, and leaf," Appel 1915, song 42) suffers transposition in only two (*CQ*) out of thirteen manuscripts. The rhyme scheme dictates the sequence of strophes, provided that the transmitter can distinguish between introductory strophes and concluding strophes, and can discern the pattern in the first three:

strophes	1, 4, 7	2, 5	3, 6
a	-olha	-eya	-atge
b	-atge	-olha	-eya
c	-eya	-atge	-olha

Manuscript C, with its usual waywardness, reorganizes the strophes into a ring structure: 12365478t. The only disturbances this might create for the listener would be the loss of *coblas capcaudadas* at the juncture of strophes 3 and 6 and the crowding of strophes in *-olha* near the end. The sequence of Q, 123475, suggests poor transmission (where stanza 6 was not available) rather than deliberate revision. This version weakens toward the end.

Although in his extant poems of secure attribution Bernart de Ventadorn seems to rely mainly on simple *coblas doblas* for stanzaic linkage, the compilers of *chansonniers* apparently characterized him as a composer of *coblas capcaudadas* and *capfinidas*. Among the uncertain or erroneous attributions to Bernart edited by Appel, nearly half have linked stanzas—there are four with *coblas capcaudadas,* two with *coblas capfinidas,* and two with *coblas doblas* (one of them incorporating rotating rhyme).[16]

One poet whose extant work is dominated by *coblas capcaudadas* is Pons de la Guardia: three of his nine songs take this form. All employ some form of simple rotation in the rhyme, and none shows transposition. Unfortunately, each of these songs has come down in only two manuscripts (*CV*, *EV*, and *CR*), so very little can be concluded about their stability. The agreement of *V* with other manuscripts is, however, more meaningful than agreement between *C* and *R*: *V* is early, somewhat isolated, and (like Pons himself) of Catalan origin.

Systems of Rotating Rhyme

Marcabru seems to have developed simple forms of rotation in the rhyme scheme as a variation on *coblas alternadas*. Instead of two rhyme sounds alternating in every other strophe, song 2, "A l'alena del vent doussa," has three rhyme sounds that shift their position in each stanza, returning to their original positions in every third stanza. If we compare the schema for this song as reconstructed in István Frank's *Répertoire métrique* (1953, 733:1) with other types of *coblas alternadas*, we can see a progression in the complexity of stanzaic interdependence, and in the interlocking of lines:

Mcb 35	a	-i / -es
	b	-o / -on
Mcb 34	c	-ina / -ana
	d	-ana / -ina
Mcb 14	a	-ansa / -alh
	b	-alh / -ansa
	c	-ans / -alha
	d	-alha / -ans
	e	-esc / -esca
	f	-esca / -esc
Mcb 2		"A l'alena del vent doussa"

	1, 4, 7	2, 5, 8(?)	3, 6
a	-an	-on	(-or)
b	-on	(-or)	-an
c	(-or)	-an	-on

As if to tantalize us, "A l'alena del vent doussa" comes down only in manuscript *C*. The transmitters have not preserved any of the presumed rhymes in *-or* but have replaced them all with rhymes in *-um*, *-an*, and *-on*. This shows that *C*, at least, reflects a certain resistance to the increase in complexity brought on by the addition of a third element to *coblas alternadas*:

strophe	line	
1	4	Contra la doussor del *frescum* (frescor)
2	7	E l'auzel desotz la *verdon* (verdor)
	8	Mesclon lur critz ab lo *chanton* (chantor?)
3	11	De sai sen un pauc de *feton* (fetor)
4	19	Qu'ilh van a clardat *e ses lum* (ses lumor)
5	22	Que ves luy no van *cobeitan* (cobeitor)
	23	Li guandilh vil e *revolum* (revolor?)
6	26	Greu cug mais que *ja lor don* (. . . lor?)
7	34	Cist fan la malvestatz *rebon* (?)

We have no way of knowing how the rhyme scheme might have protected this song in other manuscript families. The version in C, however, suggests that early corruption in the rhyme scheme might have discouraged other compilers from including this song in their collections.

The trio of rotating rhymes is by far the most common kind of rotation. Sometimes it appears as *coblas capfinidas* or *capcaudadas;* it stabilizes songs by linking stanzas in groups of three, each group having its sequence fixed by some pattern of progression.

Bernart de Ventadorn's "Tant ai mon cor ple de joya" (song 44) displays a simple yet effective system of rotation, combined with a somewhat longer stanza than is usual for Bernart. Only two rhymes change; the rest remain *unissonans:*

	1	2	3	4	5	6
a	-oya	-ura	-iza	-ansa	-onda	-aire
b	-ura	-iza	-ansa	-onda	-aire	-ire

Each stanza converts the old "b" rhyme into the new "a" rhyme and introduces a new "b" rhyme that will in turn carry over into the next stanza. If the singer knows the stanzas, he knows in what sequence they are intended to be sung.

In eleven manuscripts, the song undergoes no stanzaic transposition, although as Appel's edition shows, there is a great deal of transposition of individual words in unrhymed positions:

	MS A	*MS V*
vv. 7–8	Per que mos *chans* monta e poia	Per que mos *pretz* mont'e poia
	E mos *pretz* meillura	E mon *chant* meillura

	MS A	MS V
	(Wherefore my song rises and climbs and my worth improves)	(Wherefore my worth rises and climbs and my song improves)
v. 63	*S'ieu aug de lieis ben* retraire (If I hear good said of her)	*Can de leis aug ren* retraire (When I hear anything said of her)

	MS A	MS M
vv. 11–12	Que *l'iverns* mi sembla flor e *la neus* verdura (For winter seems to me a flower and snow [seems] greenery)	Qe *la nieus* me sembla flor e *l'inuertz* verdura (For snow seems to me a flower and the winter [seems] greenery)

Some variants offer a similar idea in different words:

	MS A	MS V
v. 4	Mi *par la* freidura (Appears cold to me)	Mi *sembla* freidura (Seems cold to me)
v. 57	*dompna,* vas vostr'amor (lady, toward your love)	*bela,* per vostr'amor (fair one, for your love)
v. 59	*bels* cors ab fresca color (beautiful body with fresh color)	*gen* cors ab fresca color (noble body with fresh color)
vv. 45–47	Tant trac pena d'amor c'a Tristan l'amador non avenc tant de dolor (So much pain of love I bear that to Tristan the lover not so much pain befell)	puix trac pena d'amor de Tristan l'amador que·n sofri manta dolor (More pain of love I bear than did Tristan the lover who suffered from it many a pain)

· Others change the meaning entirely, yet remain true to the rhyme sound:

	MS A	MS V
vv. 24–25	no vuoill aver *Frisa* de s'amistat m'*enräisa* (I would not want Friesland. In her friendship I root myself)	no vuill aver *Pisa* de s'amistat me *resissa* [R: *tenc assiza*] (I would not want Pisa. In her friendship I seat myself) [R: I keep her seated]
v. 49	Dieus, *car mi sembles* yronda (God, make me resemble a lark!)	Dieus, *car no fui* ironda (God, why wasn't I a lark?)

Substantial variation of this kind is the rule rather than the exception in very popular troubadour songs, even those that do not show transposition in the stanza order.

An interesting feature of this song, a device not uncommon in the songs surveyed, is the fixed word *amor* that appears at the end of each stanza's ninth line. While other rhymes are shifting and changing one word stays in its place, serving as a steady axis around which other rhyme sounds pivot. The fixed word gives unity (as it did in Marcabru's "Vers del lavador"); it also doubtless compounded the difficulty of composition.

Some poets increased the number of these fixed rhymes. Raimbaut d'Aurenga's "Ar resplan la flor enversa," which uses eight rhyme words and their derivatives alternately in retrograde order, seems to reach the extreme limits of this technique and to proclaim itself the ultimate—and thus the last—of its kind. The song (which, in effect, is linked only as *coblas alternadas*) survives in eight manuscripts and in only one sequence. Its *tornada* suggests that Raimbaut did want the song to be protected from outside influence. He has in mind a particular addressee, whose musical ability qualifies her as a worthy retransmitter:

> A midons lo chant e·l siscle
> clar, qu'el cor l'en entro·l giscle,
> selh que sap gen chantar ab joy
> que no tanh a chantador croy.
> (R d'Aur 39, 45–48)

> To my lady (so that the shoots of it will enter her heart) let him sing and warble it clearly who knows how to sing well and joyfully, for it is not fitting for a bad singer.
> (trans. Pattison 1952)

As the "shoots" of the song "enter the lady's heart," she learns it *par coeur* in her turn. Raimbaut specifies that it should enter the heart of a competent singer, "que sap gen chantar ab joy," and not a bad one, "chantador croy." He then sends the song to two people: "doussa dona" and "Jocglar"—the latter perhaps the *trobairitz* Azalais de Portcairagues, who had the skill to maintain or improve the song rather than damage it (Sakari 1949).

The ultimate in difficulty is to integrate these *mots-refrain* into a pattern of rotating rhyme. Giraut de Bornelh does this so sparingly that it is hardly noticeable: in two songs, he uses one or two refrain words that shift their positions in alternate stanzas.

At the opposite extreme is Arnaut Daniel's sestina, with six refrain words "rotating" through six stanzas. Each stanza dictates the sequence of rhymes in the next. The song opens with a boast of superior textual stability:

> Lo ferm volers q'el cor m'intra
> no·m pot ies becs escoissendre ni ongla
> de lausengier, qui pert per mal dir s'arma.
>
> (Arn D 18, 1–3)

> The firm intention which enters my heart, neither the beak nor the claw of an evil-speaker can break into fragments—an evil-speaker who by speaking ill loses his soul.

Neither "orally" nor "manually" (not by beak or by nail) can an ill-speaking *lausengier* "fragment" Arnaut's "firm intention." It was true: although Toja calls the manuscript tradition of the sestina "confusa e contaminata" (1960, 378), the strophic order remains stable in all twenty-four manuscripts. Only one (V) omits the *tornada*. The sestina attributed to Bertran de Born (P.-C. 233,2), preserved in only three manuscripts, suffers no transposition; however, two of the three (D^aH) give only the first five stanzas (Paden, Sankovitch, and Stäblein 1986, 403).

The sestina is the most famous scheme with rotating refrain words, but it is neither the first nor the most elaborate. Rigaut de Berbezilh's "Pauc sap d'amor qui merce non aten" (song 7) both alternates and inverts its refrain rhymes to create an extremely complex rotation using eight shifting refrain words:

> Pauc sap d'Amor qui merce non *aten,*
> des qu'el *consen*
> qu'om suffra e *atenda,*
> qu'en pauc d'ora restaura et *esmenda*
> totz los **mals traigz** qu'a faigz lonc temps *suffrir;*
> per qu'eu voll mais ab fin'amor *murir*
> que senz amor aver lo cor *iauzen,*
> qu'aissi·m fadet Amors *primeiramen.*
>
> (R Berb 7, 1–8)

> Little he knows of love who does not expect grace, after he consents to suffer and wait, for in a short time she restores and

amends all the ill treatments she has made him suffer for a long time; that is why I would rather die of perfect love than to have a joyous heart without love, for in this way love enchanted me at the start.

The thematic words of the song create a balance of sadness and happiness, completion and expectation, harm and restoration. The collocation *mal traig* appears in stanzas 1, 2, 5, and the *tornada*, so it functions as a sort of sporadic internal refrain. It may well be that the range of meaning in the pair *mal traig/esmenda* includes the idea of transmitters' errors and emendation. Translating the terms of love into the terms of poetry, one finds here a song that complains bitterly of "the mutilations of the *avol chantador*," accepts them as inseparable from poetry, and begs for "amendment" that will restore the *joi* of the poem. The *tornada* asks the lady to "know" the poet's account of the ill treatment that comes to one who waits (or "expects it"):

> Miels de domna, no mi laissatz murir
> quar mais non es maltraigz mas de suffrir,
> per qu'eu volgra, s'Amors vos o cossen,
> que'n saubeses qual mal trai qui aten.
>
> (R Berb 7, 41–44)

Better-than-Lady, do not let me die, for there is no ill treatment worse than to endure; therefore I wish, if Love permits you this, that you should know what pain he who waits endures.

"Pauc sap d'amor" is preserved only in *AIKa,* and thus their agreement on the order of stanzas probably owes as much to close manuscript filiation as to the song's built-in controls. Although he anticipates the sestina, and even outdoes it in the sheer number of recurring rhyme words, Rigaut still did not carry the system to its limits. Peire Vidal won that distinction.

As the *ne plus ultra* of "rotating rhyme," Peire Vidal's "Mout m'es bon e bel" (P.-C. 364,29), with sixteen rhyme words rotating systematically in eight 12-line stanzas, cinches up its already incorruptible sequence by linking the stanzas head-and-tail (for *coblas capcaudadas*). As a further complication, in strophes 2–7 some of the refrain rhymes move in pairs: even if the rhymes were not refrain words, we would have two sets of four stanzas with rotation where, from one stanza to the next,

$a \rightarrow d$ $b \rightarrow a$ $c \rightarrow b$ $d \rightarrow c.$

Although the rhyme scheme nearly requires advanced mathematics to schematize, the positional shifting of refrain words is so intricately regular that the pattern of the first strophe would predictably reappear, having come full circle, in a hypothetical seventeenth strophe (Carroll 1970, 345; see also Chambers 1985, 144–145). At that point, the sequence of positions (indicating the line in which a particular rhyme word appears as it moves from stanza to stanza), and the sequence of rhyme words (indicating which of the sixteen rhyme words appears in the first line of the stanza) coincide, returning simultaneously to "1."

The poem can be read as the elaborate offering of a speaker who proves his devotion as lover by his achievement as poet. He identifies himself with the song, which "renews itself" (by its principles of rhyme renewal) through the *joi de trobar:*

> Qu'ab joi lonjamen
> viu e renovel
> Co·l fruitz el ramel
> Quan chanton l'auzel.

> Because for a long time, with *joi,* I live in renewal [or: I live
> and renew] like the fruit in the branches when the birds sing.

This renewal's association with bird song affirms its reference to the pattern of rhyme. In this context, the "wholeness" of the speaker's enjoyment, and the assertion that "everything seems easy," recalls the vocabulary of textual integrity and of "difficult poetry":

> Qu'e mon cor ai folh' e flor
> Que·m ten tot l'an en verdor
> Et en gaug entier, per qu'eu
> No sen re que·m sia greu.

> For in my heart I have leaves and flowers that keep me in
> greenery all year, and in entire enjoyment; therefore I feel
> nothing that might be hard for me.

The speaker's insensitivity to physical reality, achieved through his absorption in the poem ("en gaug entier," where "integrity," "wholeness," characterizes the pleasure of composition), is associated with difficult poetry, with *trobar natural,* and thus with the primacy of the original version (see Chapter 6). It is the lady's *sen,* her understanding of social and poetic conventions, that explains her ability to appropriate something that was once difficult (*greu*) for her. If the poet speaks for the poem, then her native rank and intelligence have fitted her to overcome the problems of learning a complex poem and to "make it her own":

> Quora que·lh fos greu,
> Ara·m te per seu
> La genser sotz Deu
> E del melhor sen.

No matter when I was difficult for her, now she keeps me for her own, the most noble woman under God, and of the best intelligence.

Several times he subordinates his love for the bird song to his fulfillment of the lady's will:

> Mes ai lonjamen
> Mon cor e mon sen
> En far son talen
> Plus qu'en chan d'auzel.

I have for a long time set my heart and my intelligence on doing her will, more than on bird song.

Clearly, he has made a serious pursuit, both intellectual (*sen*) and emotional (*cor*) of bird song—that is, of his poetry. The claim, then, is that he has applied himself more assiduously to this song than to the songs of those others, the birds, whose music is not dedicated especially to his addressee.

The poet's *talen* (motivation) to make a song merges with the recipient's *talen* (will), so that the words realize a mutual desire. The personal will of both parties is transformed into an intent to perfect the song: the poet's steadiness is the song's steadiness; its unswerving fulfillment of its own inner mandate—insofar as it embodies a speaking *amador*—demonstrates and in fact fully constitutes the speaker's unswerving obedience. Twice he boasts that he is "hard to change," and this applies both to *talen* (desire) and to the self as *amador:*

> Qu'anc non camjai mon talen
> Ni anc amador
> No vitz qui·s camjes plus greu.

> For I never changed my intention, nor have you ever seen a
> lover who changes with more difficulty.

The boast of superlative stability applies not only to the speaker as lover but to the poem itself; *greu* (heavy, difficult), by itself a dark attribute on the continuum from sadness to happiness, is transformed in each of its eight systematic repetitions into a benefit: the poem's very difficulty ensures its (and, depicted within it, the lover's) constancy.

If *maltrag* does refer to the song's potential mistreatment by singers—the structural isomorph of the lover's ill treatment by the lady—then the last four lines of the exordium can be read as a protest against the usual course of transmission. That this protest is an active one is confirmed by the song's very form:

> Amaire sui e drutz sui ieu,
> Mas tan son li maltrag grieu
> qu'ieu n'ai suffert longamen,
> qu'a pauc n'ai camjat mon sen.

> A man who loves and a lover am I, but so severe are the mis-
> treatments that I have suffered from it a long time, that I have
> all but changed my sense.

With *maltrag* the lover almost "goes mad," the poet almost changes his "meaning." To literary *maltrag,* moreover, this poem is almost immune: it cannot change its *sen* (direction). Yet its means of preventing transposition of lines or stanzas, through schematic intricacy, has one drawback: it also cannot be duplicated. Peire has guaranteed the uniqueness of his song forever. Its form solves the problem of tampering for itself as a single song, but it does nothing to solve the problem for the rest of troubadour lyric.[17]

Conclusions to Part Two: Sequence and *Razo*

The outward features of troubadour song, as they come down to us written in the *chansonniers,* have provided new and specific information about the conditions of performance and transmission, both oral and written. This is particularly true for the ways in which the technical form of the rhyme scheme could act—and sometimes conspicuously did not act—to stabilize stanzaic sequence.

Since stanzaic transposition is a phenomenon of the transmitting culture, whereas rhyme scheme is a matter of the poet's particular art, we can observe in poems where transposed stanzas clearly violate the rhyme scheme an indirect clash between poet and later performer (or scribe). On the one hand the poet asserts a specific strophic order (or a limited range of acceptable orders); on the other the transmitter persists in habits of revision and rearrangement that had caused no trouble when applied to poems in which each strophe was an independent unit.

Judging by the claims Marcabru and Peire d'Alvernhe made for *coblas unissonans,* the poets could not fully anticipate which verse forms would prevent transmitters from "taking words out." Many of them seem to have begun to form the ideal of "textual integrity," without actually having considered that the sequence of stanzas might be a desirable thing to protect. A few, who may have tried to work with a logically sequential *razo* (tropeic development [Ghil 1979]), looked to linked-stanza forms for its protection only sporadically. Poems like Arnaut Daniel's sestina, Rigaut de Berbezilh's "Pauc sap d'amor qui merce non aten," and Peire Vidal's "Mout m'es bon e bel" seem to reduce to absurdity the idea of protecting a song's sequence by interlocking the rhymes. Such intricate and muscle-bound schemata produce their own peculiar harmony, but despite their individual success they could never have become standard for all poets who wished to compose fixed texts.

If the "fixed text" did become an ideal for certain troubadours, then that ideal came before its time. It was at least impracticable.

Stanzaic transposition brings a crisis in the literary interpretation of troubadour poetry. One cannot deny *mouvance,* so the question is, What does one make of it? The Gandensian formalist response to "*mouvance* in the manuscripts" and stanzaic transposition potentially disenfranchises literary interpretation by making the lyric *not a work of art,* not "a text in the modern sense":

> Can the song be a unique work of art, a *text* in the modern sense? An important objection has been raised by Dragonetti and Zumthor: that in the manuscripts we find versions of the same piece in which stanzas appear in different and varying order. According to these scholars, 1) the order in which the strophes are arranged is of no esthetic importance; 2) the song is made up of an arbitrary juxtaposition of strophes, without continuity, without a sense of narrative or duration; therefore 3) the stanza itself and not the poem plays a central role in poetic composition, is the basic unit, the kernel so to speak, of courtly discourse. (Calin 1983, 76)

Seeking to refute these three points—which, stated this way, bereave traditional literary criticism of its dearest "fundamentals of poetry" (from the French *explication de texte*, which requires the student to identify the "movement" or progress in a poem, to New Criticism, which desires continuity, unity, and the possibility of justifying the poet's choice and positioning of each word within his text)—Calin argues from modern reception theory: "When these poems were sung aloud by a trouvère or minstrel to a court public, the order in which the strophes were sung is crucial to our own and the audience's interpretation of the text" (ibid.). Extending Zumthor's quasi-mathematical formulation of stanzaic sequence, Calin argues:

> In a series "n" plus "x," the audience's interpretation of "x" will be shaped by having heard "n" previously. . . . Each stanza should unleash an esthetic reaction, at its best a shock that would enlarge the horizon left by the preceding stanza. Therefore, the reception of the song, the audience perception, recreation, and response to it, will be totally different depending upon whether "n" comes before "x" or "x" before "n." (p. 77)

Clearly, a song expressing suicidal despair in strophe 2 and hope in strophe 6, with courtly topoi intervening, will impress the audience as gradually mending the speaker's state of mind, while in the same poem, performed with the hopeful stanza first and the suicide threat at the end, the intervening courtly topoi (the sickness of love, the wish to be a bird, the lady's silence, etc.) will have seemed gradually to destroy the speaker's strength and sanity. A competent performer could decide which of two such versions best suited his audience and his own disposition.

Even given my findings about the likelihood of transposition and the poets' means to control it, I would be the last to argue that "the order in which the strophes are arranged" is "of no aesthetic importance." The juxtaposition of strophes is not "arbitrary," not "without a sense of narrative or duration." Obviously, from the point of view of performance and reception, sequence is central to the character of each realization of a particular song. Yet sequence *is* "arbitrary" in the sense that the particular path and direction "of narrative or duration" is left to the *libre arbitre* of the performer or scribe. As I have shown in my study of their manuscript transmission, poems in *coblas unissonans* and *coblas singulars* come equipped with a high degree of flexibility as to their realization.

This flexibility, problematic and challenging as it is for the modern reader of troubadour verse, has proven indispensable to our purposes of conceptualizing medieval poetic creation. Given that, however, we need not abandon sequentiality as an "essential element" in interpreting troubadour lyric. The sequence of stanzas in a particular *version* will still constitute the "movement" of that version; the critic should merely take the additional step of distinguishing between "a version" and "a song" as poetic entities—bearing in mind that the song itself may embody plural movements. Finally—and Part Three is largely given over to detailed studies of this alternative—the "flexible poem" may not have been the only model for lyric known to the troubadours. Even if they could not successfully "swim against the tide" of transmitters' insistent habits, some poets apparently did conceive of the "firm lyric" as a desirable product of their poetic creation.

In Part Three, I will examine some of the stylistic ideals debated by the troubadours circa 1170 and relevant to the idea of a fixed text. *Trobar clus* will be the first considered (Chapter 6); the poets' discussion of other elements of "textual integrity" will be treated in Chapter 7.

PART THREE

Poetics and the Medium

———

SIX

Nature Enclosed

THE "CLOSED" STYLE AND THE

"NATURAL" POETICS

I have shown in Part One that *leu*, as a stylistic term, often stands as an abbreviation for *leu ad aprendre*, "easy to learn." Long believed to be the master categories from which all other troubadour styles formed, *trobar leu* and *trobar clus* have remained an enigmatic pair, so that specific knowledge about one term demands application to the supposed antonym. Can *trobar clus*, then, also take one of its meanings from the process of memorization and transmission? Is *vers clus* "hard to learn"? One of Raimbaut d'Aurenga's most complex songs announces itself as *chanson leu*, and the poet apologizes for his choice of style as a concession to his audience. *Greu* (heavy, difficult) is the usual antonym for *leu*, but in a variant the term *clus* appears:

> *IKNN²d* and *ψ*:   pos vers plus greu
> son fer al faz

since more difficult poems are hard for the fool

> *A:*   pos vers clus greu
> fan sorz dels fatz
> (R d'Aur 18, 5–6)[1]

since difficult, closed poems make deaf men of fools

Fools are deaf to "hard" verses, and especially to "closed" ones. What they do not hear, they can neither understand nor memorize; thus, al-

133

though the passage does situate the opposition *leu*/*clus* within the context of performance, it specifies the most fundamental level of "closure," precluding reception itself.

When we think of "closed poetry" in the context of transmission, we might expect something that "excludes" part of its potential audience by restricting who may hear it, who can understand it, or who can learn and retransmit it. Or a poem might "close itself" by "drawing to a close," declaring itself "entire" or "complete" and admitting no further lines of verse, no new strophes. Its lines might interlock, shutting out revisions: in this case, poems whose stanzas are linked would be more "closed" than *coblas unissonans,* since linked stanzas restrict transposition. And yet, because they serve as a mnemonic aid, linked stanzas make a song *plus leu ad aprendre,* "easier to learn."

Without the *tenso* between Giraut de Bornelh and Raimbaut d'Aurenga, the most famous discussion of the term *trobar clus,* scholars would never have supposed that there was, around 1170, an important "controversy" on the subject. The term is much rarer than other stylistic terms such as *ric, car, prim,* and *plan*; even the *tenso* itself appears to abandon the subject, ending apparently with *trobar natural* and *trobar ric.*[2] Yet if we follow where the concept of "closure" leads Giraut and "Linhaure" (Rambaut's nickname, "Golden Line") as they circle around the concept and apply it in various ways, their dialogue shows that it can stand for some of the major obsessions and unsolved problems of their developing art.[3] The *tenso* does not debate *trobar clus* as a technical "style"; rather, it debates the value of closure, and its stylistic implications, within the system of "publication" available in 1170.

The word *prezatz* (valued, prized) occupies the same pivotal position in each poet's opening statement (vv. 5 and 12); the poets concur in choosing as their issue the question of where poetry gets its value. Does its worth come from the poem's making or from what the public makes of it? Is aesthetic *valor* inherent, or can it be acquired? The poets first set the issue in a political context (strs. 1–2); the resulting opposition forms the basis for their dispute about the rewards of song (strs. 3–4) and the poet's right to restrict transmission (strs. 5–6); each poet then proposes a standard for the legitimation of style (strs. 7–8). Raimbaut plays the reactionary. *Trobar clus,* the feudal style, must defend its birthright of hierarchical value against the rising threat of a style that Raimbaut calls "comunal": when all are equal, there will be no "good" poems because no poems will be called "bad":

aisso·m digatz
si tan prezatz
so que es a totz comunal
car adonc tut seran egual.
(R d'Aur 31, 4–7)

Tell me why, if you value so highly that which is common to
all—for then all will be equal.

For Raimbaut, communality meant abolishing the stratification that
creates value by comparison. The structure he attacks in these first lines
bears some resemblance to the communes, the beginning of organization
among bourgeois tradesmen: "In feudal society the oath of aid and 'friendship' had figured from the beginning as one of the main elements of the
system. But it was an engagement between inferior and superior, which
made one the subject of the other. The distinctive feature of the communal oath, on the other hand, was that it united *equals*" (M. Bloch 1961,
355). Raimbaut—who had been paying homage to the count of Toulouse
since the age of ten (1154), receiving homage since the age of thirteen
(1157), and pawning castles since the age of seventeen (1161) for the cash
he needed to fulfill his lordly obligations—was in no position to approve
of anything "communal," whether in property or in poetry.[4] Pattison
indicates the communes as a probable source of distress to Raimbaut, citing more than a dozen of these "independent city corporations" organized between 1109 and 1157 in Avignon, Arles, Nice, the region of
Béziers, and, closest of all to home, in Montpellier, near Raimbaut's
cloth-producing domains of Miraval and Omelas: "The commune of
Montpellier revolted against its lord in 1142 and sustained a two years'
war," according to Pattison (1952, 16–17).[5] Raimbaut's titles and re-
sponsibilities commit him to social inequality; in poetry, recognizing a
parallel inequality, he distinguishes between those "good at" judging poetry and those who trample it underfoot.[6] This inequality of good sense,
independent of social rank, favors "good people, both great and small":

Giraut, non voill q'en tal trepeil
Torn mos trobars, que ja oguan
Lo lauzo·l bo e·l pauc e·l gran.
(R d'Aur 31, 15–17)

Giraut, I do not want my poetry turned to such noise, for
never again would good people, both great and small, praise it.

Guilhem IX was able to joke about such "equality," attributing it to his rhymes, as if the "goods" he manufactured had a social order of their own; in this way he converted the guildsman's "fighting words" into the literary man's harmless metrical terms:

> Del vers vos dic que mais ne vau
> qui be l'enten ni plus l'esgau
> que·l mot son faitz *tug per egau*
> *comunalmens.*
>
> (Gm IX 7, 37–40)

Concerning the poem, I tell you that it is worth more to him who understands it well and enjoys it better, for the rhymes are all created equal, communally.

Guilhem confidently entrusts his poem to performers and audiences who will "increase its value" by "understanding" and "enjoying" it; both *entendre* and *esgauzir* may describe the activity of a recreating performer as well as of an appreciative public.[7] Guilhem's confidence in his song derives from its structure. Its strength in organization, the words formed like a community unto themselves, will ensure that its worth improves in proportion to the abilities of its hearers.

Although Raimbaut values an understanding audience, he sees the worth of the poem as independent from its reception. Audiences are either "good" or "foolish," without intermediate ratings; "the good" would withdraw their praise if the poet made any concession to *los fatz* (the fools), who will never praise his poems or, if poetry were subject to common vote, "approve them."[8]

Giraut sees the absurdity in making laws for poetry, and denies any wish for a uniform aesthetics that effaces individual style:

> . . . no·m coreill
> si qecs s'i trob' a son talan.
>
> (R d'Aur 31, 8–9)

I do not object if each man composes according to his wish.

Giraut argues, then, that his aesthetic democracy does not prescribe equality among poets, or sameness in composition; it merely places all *audiences* on an equal footing. Giraut's own judgment cedes to the public evaluation:

> Mas eu son jujaire d'aitan
> Qu'es mais amatz
> E plus prezatz
> Qui·l fa levet e venarsal.
> (R d'Aur 31, 10–13)

But I am a judge to this extent: that it is better loved and more
highly valued if one composes it to be light and popular.

To enforce the contrast in their views, Giraut describes the style he favors
with a word that would in many contexts condemn it: *venarsal,* usually
translated as "low, common," is a drawn-out form of *venal* and suggests
availability in the marketplace as well as, perhaps, indiscreet loquacity.[9]
Taking the stance of the bourgeois artisan or merchant to counter Raimbaut's advocacy of poetic feudalism, Giraut affirms that poetry "must
have a market." The poet may compose as he wishes, but the value of his
work is determined by public acclaim.

What is more, according to Giraut, poetry must be available indiscrimi-
nately both to distributors and to their "market" of willing audiences, if
it is to be "rewarding." Riquer glosses *capital* as "remuneration" in this
passage:

> A que trobatz
> si non vos platz
> c'ades o sapchon tal e cal?
> Que chans non port'altre cabtal.
> (R d'Aur 31, 25–28)

Why do you compose if it does not please you that any So-and-
so can learn it quickly? For song carries no other reward.

> Giraut, sol que·l miels appareil
> e·l dig'ades e·l trag'enan,
> mi non cal sitot no s'espan.
> C'anc granz viutatz
> non fon denhtatz
> per so prez'om plus aur que sal
> e de tot chant es atretal.
> (R d'Aur 31, 29–35)

Giraut, as long as I prepare it as well as possible, and recite it
without hesitation and bring it forward [to public attention], I

do not care if it does not spread. For great baseness was never deemed valuable: for this reason people value gold more than salt, and it is the same with all songs.

The poet's "reward" is the sole possession of a song that he has prepared to the best of his ability (*miels aparelhar*) and has performed before an audience (*dir, tragar enan*). When Raimbaut claims to be indifferent "if the song does not spread," he takes an extreme stance advocating "closed" performance; a song that "non s'espan" (literally, "does not spread") may never be heard again. "Expansion" refers to the widening influence of a song in public circulation and to its "amplification" by other performers. According to Raimbaut, these effects of popularity can never increase the original quality of composition. Raimbaut deprecates the term *amatz* (loved) with which Giraut had set the standard for *pretz* (value), by making *viutatz* (commonness) its abstract counterpart; Giraut's aesthetics, he implies, depends on the subjective judgment of the *vilain* rather than on intrinsic excellence. He replaces Giraut's equation of *amatz* and *prezatz* with the equation of *prezatz* (valued) and *denhtatz* (dignified): to "judge a song worthwhile" is better praise than "to love" it.

Giraut's reply, in the sixth strophe, has been read as an "admission of defeat," which might be paraphrased, "Linhaure, you are the expert; my own songs are fit only for hoarse singers and not for noblemen." In fact, Giraut continues to defend *amor* as the criterion of aesthetic value and mocks the "dignity" of Raimbaut's closed circuit. He exaggerates his alarm: "Etz fis amans contrarian, / e per o si n'ai mais d'affan" (You are an argumentative perfect lover, and for that reason I am even more shocked; vv. 37–38). In calling Raimbaut "fis amans contrarian," he compliments his opponent as a "debating theoretician of lyric poetry"; at the same time, he draws attention to Raimbaut's disavowal of *amor,* the first premise of their genre. Giraut insists: given a choice between making his songs *amatz* and having them appreciated as *denhtatz,* he prefers in-dignity—as long as everyone may sing them:

> Mos sos levatz
> c'us enraumatz
> lo·m deissazec e·l diga mal
> que no·l deing ad home sesal.
> (R d'Aur 31, 39–42)

Lift up my song: let a singer with a cold garble it and sing it badly, for I do not deem it worthy of the tax collector.[10]

Hearing the distorted rendition of the ordinary man, even one who sounds as if he had a bad cold, is preferable, for Giraut, to reserving the song for "the taxable man" (*home sesal*). Worth, Giraut implies, is not synonymous with wealth.

Trobar Natural

The last exchange of the *tenso* (strs. 7–8) appears to evade the issue of *trobar clus,* each poet reluctant to upset the cordial relation of guest and host by carrying his argument to the point of offending the other. Yet in these last stanzas, each poet again aligns himself with a particular kind of poetry. It is not immediately obvious whether in these stanzas the poets are extending the ideas they have expressed up to this point or are now reversing their original positions. What is clear is that they are attempting to define the relation between *trobar clus* and the "closure" implied by other stylistic terms—*trobar natural* and *trobar ric.*

That Raimbaut appeals to the authority of Guilhem IX, in lines 43–49, is easy to see; what he means by connecting the *vers de dreyt nien* with *trobar natural* (and both with *trobar clus*), is not. Perhaps the key is in the term *natural* itself, in the associations it calls up here and in other contexts of the time. Both Raimbaut and Guilhem claim ignorance of their "birth":

> Raimbaut: Non sai de que·ns anam parlan,
> ni don fui natz
> si soi torbatz
> tan pes d'un fin joi natural.
> (R d'Aur 31, 45–48)

I don't know what we were talking about, nor from whence I was born, I am so confused, since I think so much about a perfect, natural *joi*.

> Guilhem: Non sai en qual hora·m fui natz . . .
> (Gm IX 4, 7)

I don't know in what hour I was born . . .

Raimbaut's and Guilhem's "forgetfulness of their birth" indicates extreme disorientation. Raimbaut has forgotten who his parents were, and Guilhem does not know how old he is. To "forget one's birth" is to renounce one's orientation in time, place, and the social order, as well as all one's possessions. *Natura,* in the charters, meant family and referred to birthright; when title to a castle was transferred, so were the "men and women who were natural to it"—that is, the bondsmen born there. A formula for donations to the Templars was to give "tot quant eu devia aver per paire ni per maire ni per natura" (all that I should have had through [my] father or through mother or through nature), and one young man, whose father had disinherited him by such a donation, and who had attempted to recapture a castle by force, had to swear that neither he "ne nuls om de sa natura" (nor anyone of his family) would force the castle again.[11] Even when *natura* refers simply to species (e.g., Mcb 2, 28: "seguon la natura del ca," according to the nature of a dog) it insists on origin and lineage, on the privileges and obligations one has been born to rather than deserved or learned. *Natura,* then, is the essence of "history, narration, genealogy."[12] Yet *fin joi natural,* as Raimbaut d'Aurenga uses the term in the *tenso,* disrupts the sense of the past that *natura* stands for:

> Non sai de que·ns anam parlan
> ni don fui natz
> si soi torbatz
> tan pes d'un fin joi natural
> can d'als cossir, no m'es coral.
> (R d'Aur 31, 45–49)

> I don't know what we were talking about, nor from whence I was born, I am so confused, I think so much about a perfect natural *joi* that when I think about something else, my heart isn't in it.

Thus *fin joi natural,* obliterating memory, is the antithetical substitute for *natura,* rather than nature's counterpart in poetry.

One might question Raimbaut's seriousness in alleging *fin joi natural* as an excuse for discontinuity, either in genealogy or in discourse. This is not the voice of the *fis amans contrarian*—the good debater of lyric theory—who has just criticized "equality" and expressed the wish that his song "no torn' en trepeil" (not be stampeded). Raimbaut may be mimicking some poets who, in the name of "natural" inspiration or "song that moves from the heart" ("can d'als cossir, no m'es *coral*"), compose songs in which there is no necessary continuity in the *razo,* no "memory" of what was said in preceding stanzas, and thus no sequence. Raimbaut, as a practitioner of what Ghil (1979) calls "tropeic development," could be pretending to yield (or default in) the debate by adopting the more common "topic development," where it makes no difference which of the conventions one has already activated and there is no need to remember (see discussion in Chapter 4 above).

L. T. Topsfield came to the conclusion that two types of poets, the "reflective poets such as Marcabru and Peire d'Alvernhe and courtly poets such as Bernart de Ventadorn," interpret the word *naturals* in nearly opposite ways (1974, 1157). His synopsis of the many meanings of *natura* and the adjective derived from it does not attempt to explore denotations the troubadours might have borrowed from Latin rhetorics: "The two primary meanings of *naturals* in medieval Provençal are 'conforming to the order which exists in nature' or 'conforming to the particular character of each species, including the human race and its subdivisions, e.g. the feudal ruler, the loyal lover, the good and the wicked.' Since *naturals* refers to the innate individual quality of a person, it has many nuances of meaning" (p. 1154*n*.11). But after Roncaglia's study of the term, especially in "'Trobar clus'—discussione aperta" (1969b), it is no longer satisfactory to associate Marcabru's *trobar natural* primarily with "the moral symbolism of colours and natural objects, trees, plants, animals, insects and birds" (Topsfield 1974, 1155). Of special interest for understanding the term *naturals* are Roncaglia's citations from medieval Latin rhetorical theory, where the "natural" and the "artificial" are two types of word order or narrative sequence:

> Naturalis ordo est, si quis narret rem ordine quo gesta est; artificialis ordo est, si quis non incipit a principio rei geste, sed a medio, ut Vergilius in Aeneide.
> (Roncaglia 1969b, 46, quoting *Scolia Vindobonensia ad Horatii artem poeticam,* ed. J. Zechmeister [Vienna, 1877])

> The natural order is when someone narrates a thing in the order in which it was done; the artificial order is when someone does not begin at the beginning of the thing done, but in the middle, as Vergil did in the Aeneid.

The "natural order," then, is historical—structured by the idea that an event to be told has a beginning, an order, and an end. Neither the "topic" nor the "tropeic" development, described by Ghil, qualifies as this type of *ordo naturalis*. Further, most troubadours' *joi natural* persistently shows itself to be the opposite of the "natural" in this sense, for it is antihistorical.

The "man with no memory," whose *sen* is *natural,* is the hero of the *no-say-que-s'es.* Peire Rogier introduces himself as such a man and then holds a debate with his own conscience. The result is a contest between the "timeless" or "lyrical" impulse of *natural sen* (which makes events inconsequential and thus neutralizes emotional response to them) and the *sen* that is aware of time and place, of beginnings and ends:

> No sai don chant, e chantars plagra·m fort
> si saubes don, mas de re no·m sent be
> et es greus chans, quant hom non sap de que.
> Mas adoncx par qu'om a natural sen
> quan sap son dan ab gen passar suffrir
> quar no·s deu hom per ben trop s'esjauzir
> ni ia per mal hom trop no·s desesper.
>
> (P Rog 4, 1–7)

I do not know what I am singing about, and singing would please me very much if I knew what [I sing] of, but I do not feel good about anything, and song is difficult when one does not know what it is about. But now it becomes apparent that one has "natural sense" when he knows how to suffer his loss by nobly enduring it, for one should not be too delighted about good fortune, nor ever too much despair about bad fortune.

The exordium may in fact be satirical: the "stalling" in the first three lines, the unconvincing and wordy platitude in the last three. The whole song explains *natural sen* as self-deception (vv. 40–41: "Am mai lo sieu mentir / qu'autra vertat," I prefer her lies to another woman's truth), when it confronts the voice of "true" conscience, much like the kindly moralistic voice of Peire d'Alvernhe's religious lyrics (vv. 13–14: "Aisso dic ieu que no·s deu hom giquir / aissi del tot qui·l segle vol tener," I say that a man should not thus abandon everything if he wishes to hold on to the world).

Peire Rogier lets his "conscience" remind him that composing in this "natural" style is a way of renouncing the world, insofar as *fin joi natural* works only from within, drawing on an inherent motivation to compose poetry, and allows the speaker to remain indifferent to actual joy and pain. Creating an inner landscape that bears no relation to sensed experience, Peire Rogier's *natural sen* cultivates a world-upside-down within the speaker. It is no wonder, then, that *natural* is so often associated with madness. Here, Peire speaks as if he were rebelling against a rule that speech should correspond to experience; the dictates of weather (vv. 1 and 3) are overruled by the impulse to sing (vv. 2 and 4):

> Tan no plou ni venta
> qu'ieu de chan non cossire
> frei'aura dolenta
> no·m tolh chantar ni rire
> qu'amors me capdelh' e·m te
> mon cor en fin joy natural
> e·m pais e·m guid' e·m soste
> qu'ieu non sui alegres per al
> ni alres no·m fai vivre.
>
> (P Rog 2, 1–9)

> Neither the rain falls nor the wind blows so hard that I do not think about song; the chill, mournful wind does not take from me my singing and laughter, for love controls me and holds my heart in perfect natural *joi,* and feeds me and guides me and sustains me, so that I am not cheerful for any other reason, nor does any other thing make me live.

The treatment of *amors* as the lord from whom one holds one's fief, and on whom one depends for sustenance, makes of *fin joi natural* a self-sufficient realm, independent of *lo segles* (the secular world). Peire's choice of verbs suggests the Psalms, with *fin joi natural* as the "green pastures" and "still waters" where *Amors* leads him, maintains him, and "restores his soul." The "second nature" created by *Amors* is a verbal one: statement reforms perception. Again, love acts as a metaphor for song. Just as the lover is advised to believe what the lady says rather than what she does, so the poet proposes to give greater value to statements (powered by *joi,* the impulse to compose) than to experience.

Bernart de Ventadorn calls *desnaturar* (denaturing) the same effect that Peire Rogier ascribed to *joi natural:*

> Tant ai mo cor ple de joya,
> tot me desnatura.
> Flor blancha, vermelh' e groya
> me par la frejura,
> c'ab lo ven et ab la ploya
> me creis l'aventura,

per que mos pretz mont' e poya
e mos chans melhura.

(B Vent 44, 1−8)

My heart is so full of joy that it completely denatures me.
Flowers white, red, and yellow to me look like frost, for with
the wind and with the rain my fortune increases, so that my
worth rises and climbs, and my song improves.

Peire d'Alvernhe recognizes that some poets have distorted the meaning of the word *natural*. Those who criticize Marcabru for madness have
in fact identified their own error; it is easy to see his criticism aimed at
Peire Rogier's views of *fin joi natural* and at the "man with no memory":

Marcabrus per gran dreitura
trobet d'altretal semblansa,
e tengon lo tug per fol
qui no conoissa natura
e no·ill membre per que·s nais.

(P d'Alv 13, 38−42)

Marcabru, with great justice, composed in similar fashion—
and they all take him for a fool who does not know [his] nature and does not remember why he is born.

Marcabru had upheld a form of *trobar natural* but never played the
"natural fool." Peire d'Alvernhe, in his own work, emphasizes the genealogical aspect of *natura;* he denounces as "illegitimate" those whose *joi,*
supposedly *fin* and *natural,* induces them to compose poems bearing no
relation to reality. Once "history, narration, genealogy" are removed, action is "inconsequential" and *noncura* prevails, as Peire warns in this passage from "Bel m'es quan la roza floris":

Sel que·l ioi del setgle delis
vei que son pretz dezenansa;
fils es d'avol criatura
que fai avol demonstransa:
e per tan non baisa·l col!
Quar gitatz es a noncura
estai mais entre·ls savais.

(P d'Alv 13, 22−28)

He who destroys the *joi* of the secular world, I see that his
worth diminishes; he is the son of a base creature, for he makes
a base showing, and yet does not bow his head. Because he is
cast into indifference, let him remain longer among the lowly.

What Peire Rogier had called *natural sen* ("when one knows how to suffer his loss by nobly enduring it"), Peire d'Alvernhe calls *noncura:* it is
disengagement from the world, both from *dan* and from the *joi del setgle;*
it divides words from their referents, lets them fall from their original
meanings—even the word *natural*. "Bel m'es quan la roza" insists that
poetry should correspond to politics: when Peire urges Sancho III of Castile to follow the example of his father, Alfonso, in going to battle against
the Moors, he makes a point of showing that he, too, is following the
example of his poetic forebear, Marcabru, who had stirred Alfonso against
the Muslims (Riquer 1975, 321). Peire's song descends from Marcabru's
just as Sancho descends from Alfonso. Peire d'Alvernhe supports a notion
of *trobar natural* best suited to the sirventes. The poet as *castiador,* who
advises men of the world to fight for the traditions and rights of their *natura,* must use a language that "remembers" its source.

Thus—to return to the *tenso* between Raimbaut d'Aurenga and Giraut de Bornelh—it is doubly in opposition to Raimbaut's amnesiac *fin
joi natural* that, for his last parry, Giraut "remembers" his promotion in
rank: "Don't I remember how she appointed me *comtal?*" As a poet and
as a debater, at least, Giraut is the equal of the Count of Orange—and in
affirming it he accuses himself (with an ironical wink) of "forgetting"
gratitude toward his superiors, of stepping out of rank:

> Lingnaura, si·m gira·l vermeil
> de l'escut cella cui reblan
> qu'eu voill dir "a Deu mi coman."
> Cals fols pensatz
> outracuidatz!
> M'a mes doptansa deslial!
> No·m soven com me fes comtal?
>
> (R d'Aur 31, 50–56)

Linhaure, if she whom I praise should turn the red side of her
shield toward me, then I will say, "I place myself in God's
hands." What a mad, outrageous thought—it has given me
disloyal doubt. Do I not remember how she made me a *comtal?*

Giraut has earned this title by merit and not by birth, yet he is more mindful of this feudal bond than Raimbaut is of his "birthright."

Giraut's Shield and the Heraldry of Style

Earlier Giraut had called Raimbaut a "fis amans contrarian," clearly using the word *amans* to designate a "theoretician of lyric poetry"; having once substituted *amor* for *trobar* in the debate, he lets his last contribution to it carry forward the idea that to win the argument is to succeed in love. If "virar lo vermeil de l'escut" is a sign of rejection, then Giraut concedes failure. Yet in calling to mind the heraldic "shield" of his patroness, Giraut replies to Raimbaut's evocation of *trobar natural* and the "man with no memory." He remembers "com me fes comtal"; he is "accountable," and he "recounts." [13] A *comtal*, according to Marc Bloch, was a local chief who organized others under his lord's "banner."

When Marcabru declares himself a follower of *trobar natural*, he describes himself as if carrying its blazon:

> E segon trobar naturau
> port la peire e l'esc'e·l fozill
> mas menut trobador bergau
> entrebesquill,
> mi tornon mon chant en badau
> e·n fant gratill.
>
> (Mcb 33, 5–10)

And in accordance with "natural composition" I carry the flint and tinder and steel, but insignificant rhyme-weaving hornet troubadours turn my song into gaping and scraping.

The three emblems on Marcabru's "shield" are offered as a trademark— of the arsonist's trade, apparently, unless Prometheus used "flint and tinder and steel" (trans. Paterson 1975, 29). The "original" poet, equipped with the tools to make something from nothing wherever he goes, can strike up a blaze from cold stone; the "small-time" troubadours merely "do a lot of scratching" (*fant gratill*). R. Howard Bloch has pointed out the interdependence of "semantic discontinuity and genealogical discontinuity" in similar passages of Marcabru's poetry (1981, 958–960) and, against a broader backdrop of medieval thought, in a trend to "the nominalizing lyric" in Old Provençal (1983, 126; see 108–127, "The Poetics of Disruption"); here morality illustrates poetics. The "trobador bergau" only flirt with his style ("tornon . . . en badau"), while Marcabru makes it conceive: songs as "natural" offspring. The legitimizing coat of arms, then, stands for the creative intelligence of a poet who, at least according to his *vida,* may not qualify for other kinds of "legitimacy."

There are at least two ways to make a fire: one can blow on the old coals in hope that they will flare up again (as the *bufa-tizo* of Marcabru's *vers del lavador* might do), or one can start "from scratch." To "remember"—and this includes history, narration, and genealogy, as well as the transmission and adaptation of other men's songs—is to "blow on the old coals." Marcabru is attempting to reverse our habits of legitimation: his shield proclaims the rise of a "natural" lineage of poetry conceived "from scratch."

Viewed as a statement about *mouvance,* Marcabru's lines on *trobar natural* tend to validate only the "original" version. The "menut trobador bergau" would, then, represent unskilled players who perform the song without authorization in diluted and insipid versions.

Peire d'Alvernhe also uses the metaphor of the heraldic shield, fancying his own style blazoned in gold and azure against a background of other styles in "rusty iron":

> Que cum l'aurs resplan e l'azurs
> contra·l fer ros
> desobre los escutz
> mi det do, tro lai ont es Surs,
> qu'ieu sobriers fos
> als grans et als menutz
> dels esciens
> de trobar ses fenhs fatz,
> don sui grazens
> ad aquilh don m'es datz.
>
>   (P d'Alv 5, 61–70)

For just as gold and azure gleam against red iron, on shields, I was given the gift that I would be, as far as Syria, superior among wise men both great and small in composing without foolish imaginings, for which I am grateful to the one by whom it was given to me.

These lines close a poem that has made no secret of its style, that in fact has overdescribed itself: *senatz, segurs, francs e ferms*, Peire gives his approval to "obscure verses" (*ditz escurs*) recited "without broken words" (*ses motz romputz*, vv. 31–33).

Not all poets aspire to *trobar ses fenhs* (compose without imaginings), however, nor would describe *fenhs* as *fatz* (foolish). Raimbaut d'Aurenga, who in probably his earliest important poem praised the song of the wren as *cars, dous, e fenhz* (rare, sweet, and imagined; R d'Aur 1, 1–2), may have taken offense at Peire d'Alvernhe's condemnation of the imaginative (*fenhs*) in poetry; at least, he composes an emphatic *recusatio* of the image of the "shining shield" Peire had upheld:

> E qar no·i trop pro, en orda,
> lais—car sent paraulas rancas.
> No·m eslag l'amar e·l mel
> d'amor, e non dig parlan
> l'escut, e so que·i resplan.
>
> (R d'Aur 34, 36–40)

And because I find no advantage in invention, I give up—for I smell rancid words. I do not distinguish the bitter part from the honey of love, and I do not describe in speech the shield, and that which glitters upon it.[14]

According to Pattison (1952), this song addresses itself mainly to the *vilania* involved in Alfonso II of Aragon's change in marriage plans. The description of the shield announces a style allied with the lineage it serves to praise. Raimbaut's refusal to use the metaphor of the shield, then, is a protest against what he perceives both as a disruption of lineage (through the irregularity in Alfonso's broken engagement) and as a disruption of discourse (since praise, which Alfonso usually earns, is not now possible): he breaks off, offended by words not yet spoken.

The shield that has been turned against Giraut de Bornelh in the *tenso* belongs to a patroness, "cella cui reblan." Peire d'Alvernhe would have us think Giraut's flattery was directed mainly toward "old water carriers" and other *vilanas*. But Pattison directs our attention to the *tornada* of Giraut's song 27, where the poet thanks the Glove Lady for appointing him *comtal* (although here he seems to regret the appointment). As in the *tenso*, the motif of the poet's recollection accompanies the acknowledgment of his duty as spokesman:

> Amia, d'aisso·m sove
> C'anc, depos que'm fis comtals,
> No m'avenc pois tan grans mals.
> (Gr Bor 27, 73–75)

My friend, this much I remember: that never, since the time
when you made me *comtal,* has anything so bad happened to
me again.

This is the same poem in which Giraut earlier sought

> . . . bos motz en fre
> que son tuch chargat e ple
> d'us estranhs sens naturals,
> e non sabon tuch de cals.
> (Gr Bor 27, 51–54)

. . . good rhymes reined in, which are all charged and filled
with an unfamiliar "natural" meaning, and not everybody
knows what kind.

In evoking this poem (which was an important stylistic manifesto) as an
answer to the feigned "forgetfulness" induced by Raimbaut's *fin joi natural,* Giraut contests the other poet's interpretation of the term *natural* on
a fundamental level.

Not remembering, in the *vers de dreyt nien,* tended to empty the meaning from *bos motz* (good rhymes), for "I don't remember" signals a song
of madness and apathy: of *noncura, foudatz.* Giraut remembers, and fills
his words with *sen,* though of a paradoxical kind. *Estranh* and *natural*
are opposites: the first connotes all that is foreign, alien, outside the range
of local experience—exogenous and "unfamiliar" in every sense. Guilhem IX, in the poem that Raimbaut d'Aurenga linked with *joi natural,*
would not "locate himself" either in the distance or in close range:

> no say en qual hora·m fuy natz:
> no soi alegres ni iratz
> no suy estranhs ni soi privatz
> ni no·n puesc au.
> (Gm IX 4, 7–10)

I do not know in what hour I was born, I am neither cheerful
nor morose, I am neither a stranger nor an intimate, nor can I
be otherwise.

Giraut's *estranhs sens naturals* directly opposes the *foudatz*. It includes both the foreign and the native; his *bos motz* are "harnessed" (*en fre*) and loaded (*chargat e ple*) like a wagon bearing exotic merchandise (*estranhs sens*). "Not everyone knows what kind" of *sens naturals* Giraut means, since for some poets, like Peire Rogier, *sen natural* meant the *foudatz* that allows mere assertion to prevail over what the eyes see.

It is worthwhile to entertain the possibility that Giraut's *estranhs sens naturals* might combine quoted or adapted (exogenous, another's) material with original compositions. The term *natural* has already appeared in other contexts where it meant "original" poetry, as opposed to adaptations. Giraut has accepted and even welcomed the idea that others would adapt his songs to their own use. The opposition *estranh/natural* has also been developed by Marcabru, who from all evidence disapproves of adaptation; the context in which Marcabru places this opposition—the closed garden that requires constant vigilance against poachers—sheds further light on the debate over *trobar clus*.

Trobar Natural and the Enclosed Garden

Marcabru speaks of an *amors* whose "native place" is enclosed and therefore safe from the *estranhs*. Substituting *trobars* for *amors* in this passage yields an interesting view of the relationship between *trobar clus* and the opposition *natural/estranh*:

> L'amor don ieu sui mostraire
> nasquet en un gentil aire,
> e·il luocs on ill es creguda
> es claus de rama branchuda
> e de chaut e de gelada,
> qu'estrains no l'en puesca traire.
> (Mcb 5, 49–54)

> The love to which I point the way was born in a noble lineage [pun: "air, climate"], and the place where it grew up is enclosed by branching boughs, [closed off] both from heat and from cold, so that a stranger may not take it away from there.

Roncaglia discounts the contention of Scheludko and Robertson that this passage may allude to the *hortus conclusus,* "Symbol of the Blessed Mary, her eternal virginity," by identifying the *Desirat* of the *tornada* with a

historical figure, Sancho III, called *desiderabilis Sancius* (1969b, 25).
Marcabru is quite capable, however, of reconciling *doas cuidas* in one
statement. The above passage is the last stanza before the *tornada*, and
this is the normal position for dedications explaining why the song and
the addressee are worthy of each other.

Much has been said about Marcabru's distinctions between *fin'amors*
and *fals'amors*, so that discussions of his poetics usually turn to his eth-
ics. Yet Marcabru himself appears to be conscious of the structural congruity between *amors* and *trobars:* he attempts to match his subject
(*fals'amistatz*) with an appropriate song—a *vers desviatz* sung to a *son
desviatz*. His familiar reproval of husbands who cuckold one another:

> Tals cuid' esser ben gardaire
> de la so' e de l'altrui laire
> (Mcb 5, 25–26)

> So-and-so thinks he is a good guard of his own belongings, and
> the robber of another's

is punctuated with a comment on the progress of the *vers desviat* itself

> Si l'us musa, l'autre bada
> E ieu sui del dich pechaire.
> (Mcb 5, 29–30)

> If one gawks, the other gapes, and I am a sinner against the
> poem.

In all the manuscripts (*AIK*), as Dejeanne (1909) notes, line 26 is hyper-
metric; that is, the poet has "sinned against" his *dich,* and it is probably
wrong to correct the line as Dejeanne suggests ("De la so'e d'altrui laire").
Further, the verse is deliberately unspecific about what these men believe
they are guarding. Dejeanne's translation begins, "Tel pense être bien le
gardien de sa femme . . . ," and already he has supplied a detail that was
not in the Provençal original: the *femme*. Perhaps Marcabru intended a
broader meaning. One is reminded of Giraut de Bornelh's application of
the same terms to a problem specific to poetry: "c'us s'en fezes cla-
maire / dels dichs don altre era laire / com fes de la gralha·l paus" (one
makes himself the claimant [screamer] of poems whose thief [barker] was
another man, just as the cricket does [complains] against the peacock;
Gr Bor 62, 33–35).

The major part of Marcabru's *vers desviatz,* then, develops a parallel between *fals'amistatz* (improper love) and improper verse: it is continually being stolen by someone who hypocritically "guards his own"; it is "easy to pick up or drop," and it is "marketable," like Giraut de Bornelh's *vers levet e venarsal:*

> C'aissi leu pren e refuda
> puois sai ven e lai mercada.
> (Mcb 5, 4–5)

For it is so easily picked up and then set aside, since it is sold here and purchased there.

In the last strophe, however, Marcabru changes his subject from the *amors* (and the *trobars*) he must censure to the *amors* he would recommend ("don eu sui mostraire"). Line 54 echoes the more explicit stylistic statement of "Aujatz de chan":

> *vers desviatz*, v. 54:   Qu'estrains no l'en puesca traire.

So that a stranger cannot take it away from there.

> "Aujatz," v. 4:   Si que autr'om no l'en pot un mot traire.
> (Roncaglia 1957, 23)

So that another man cannot take away one word from it.

The last stanza of Marcabru's *vers desviatz* does propound an ideal for *trobar* as well as for *amor;* it thus helps to explain the connection the troubadours perceive between closure and *vers naturals.* "Original" poetry, worthy of its attribution to an "author" and fully "pedigreed" ("nasquet en un gentil aire"), requires for its growth and maintenance an impossibly sheltered place, where there is neither heat nor cold, where no "stranger" can reach it ("the place where it grew up is enclosed by branching boughs, closed off both from heat and from cold"). Marcabru only claims to point the way to this ideal, to be its *mostraire.* For him it is the verbal counterpart of love in the *terrenal paredis,* where things went by the names Adam gave them, and there were no "strangers."

The connection between "closed rhymes" and "closed gardens" becomes still more apparent in a song of Peire d'Alvernhe that explicitly favors *motz clus.* The motif of the *hortus conclusus* recurs; rather than deny the biblical allusion altogether, we might learn from it how *clus* po-

etry situated itself within a complex of images that had come to stand for
a theory of interpretation.

> Be m'es plazen
> e cossezen
> que om s'ayzina de chantar
> ab motz alqus
> serratz e clus
> qu'om no·ls tem ja de vergognar.
> (P d'Alv 8, 1–6)

It pleases me well and suits me fine that one should undertake
to sing with few words, locked and closed so that one may never
be afraid of spoiling them.

> Mais am un ort
> serrat e fort
> qu'hom ren no m'en puesca emblar
> que cent parras
> sus en puegz plas:
> qu'autre las tenh ez ieu las guar.
> (P d'Alv 8, 25–30)

I like better one garden, locked and strong so that no one can
steal anything from me, than a hundred gardens up on a plateau
such that another man owns them and I watch them.

The parallelism of the two strophes sets up the garden as the analogue of
the poem: *motz serratz*, like the *ort serrat*, are safe from those who might
invade and dishonor it. *Trobar plan*, through its geographical counterpart
puegz plans (flat peak, plateau) is also being set in contrast to the more
desirable "closed" and "tight" writing of the closed garden.

Ulrich Mölk interprets the first of these two strophes in the context of
mouvance, working with the assumption that Peire intends to influence the
transmission of his song by installing formal safeguards. According to his
translation, Peire expects his "closed and dark" style to intimidate the
performer: "words which one does not hesitate to respect" inspire reverence for the original, precluding unauthorized revision, especially at the
rhyme word (Mölk 1979, 5). Mölk compares the passage to the opening of
Marcabru's "Aujatz de chan," where the poet claims that he "knows how

to bind up the *razo* and the *vers* so that another man cannot remove one *mot* from it": "Peire d'Alvernhe argues in similar fashion that it is precisely the bizarre and obscure words—*motz* meaning primarily rhyme word here as well—which will function as protectors of the integrity of the song" (p. 5).

Paterson also links Peire's closed garden of verses with this "stylistic ideal" of Marcabru: "Peire . . . himself prefers such poetry, which is strong and tightly locked so that each word is strong and necessary to the whole, to 'a hundred parcels of land up on the open plain' which another might own" (1975, 81). This raises the question of "textual integrity," discussed in the next chapter: can Peire have expected a poem in which "each word is necessary to the whole" to survive the relay of transmission? More important, is it accurate to attribute to the troubadours such a modern ideal of "the text"? *Serrat* may have been meant more as a guarantee of the position of a rhyme word within a "closed" stanza than as a guarantee that the entire stanza will not drop out of the poem. If Peire had written "Be m'es plazen" as a song "in which each word is necessary to the whole," then available texts fall too far short of "necessity" for the modern reader to recapture "the whole" and to comment on it.

A related issue, that of the "ownership" of poetry, also arises in Peire's and Marcabru's metaphor of the closed garden. *Emblar* (to steal) has no meaning except in the context of property, whether fief or allodium, movable or immovable goods, and insofar as the garden stands for the song, this means literary property. Marcabru calls his garden an *alos,* a freehold. This is consonant with my interpretation of his remarks on *trobar natural:* the original maker of the poem owns it free and clear, without obligation to any higher *senher* on earth. Peire d'Alvernhe's dislike of the hundred plateau gardens, "c'altre las tenh e ieu las guar," also implies a preference for the role of proprietor over that of spectator (perhaps "watchman") in poetry. Translated into the terms of poet and audience, Peire's lines favor the unique "original creation" and seem rather hostile to its dozens of circulating versions—more so even than Raimbaut d'Aurenga's "mi non cal sitot non s'espan" (I don't care if it does not circulate).

The "closed garden" as a metaphor for "closed poetry" is an interesting one: it not only implies an effort on the poets' part to control *mouvance* (since "no one can remove a single word" and "no one can steal anything" from such a closed poem), but it also situates this kind of "closure" within a well-known area of medieval theory of interpretation:

Dolce, tu ies jardins enclos
ou ge sovent gis en repos,
tu ies fontaine soz gelee
ki deseur totes bien m'agree.
Li soiels guarde les secretz
qe nuls n'en soit avant mostrez
s'a celui no cui om velt faire
consachable de son afaire.
Tels est tis cuers, quar ben conois
A cui tu descovrir le dois.
(Song of Songs, 12th-cent. O.F. version,
2302–2312; Pickford 1974)

Sweet one, you are a closed garden where I often lie at rest;
you are a fountain frozen on top which is pleasant to me above
all else. The seal protects the secrets of which not one may be
revealed, except to someone whom one wishes to make the
confidant of his doings. Such is your heart, for you know well
to whom you should uncover it.

The author of this popular interpretive "translation" has thus made the
maiden of the *Canticus* a symbol of the hermetic text, "sealed" to those
who should not be *consachable*.[15] The "sealing of the heart" becomes the
"sealing of a message." Raimbaut d'Aurenga has borrowed this image:
the injunction of the *Canticus*—"pone me ut sigunaculum cor tuum" (8,
6)—is answered by Raimbaut:

Car s'eu dic so que·s cove
de leis que mon cor sagel,
totz lo mons sap, per ma fe,
cals es; car tota gen cria
e sap, et es pron devis
cals es la meiller que sia!
Per qu'eu la laus et enquis.
(R d'Aur 29, 29–35)

For if I say what is fitting about her whom my heart seals, all
the world knows, by my faith, what she is like; for everyone
shouts it, and knows, and is fully informed who is the best
woman in existence. Therefore I praise and petition her.

The "seal" on this particular lady is not very hermetic, since the "message" she embodies ("cals es") is common knowledge, and is transmitted by everyone ("car tota gen cria"). The lady of this poem is in the same situation as Raimbaut's *trobars plans,* a style (again contrasted with the "closed" style) in which Raimbaut believes he can excel because a poet capable of truly original work surely can surpass the common singers in their "bleating," everyday style of rhyming:

> Qi tals motz fai
> c'anc mais non foron dig cantan,
> qe cels c'om totz jorns ditz e brai
> sapcha, si·s vol, autra vez dir.
>   (R d'Aur 16, 5–8)

> Anyone who composes such rhymes as have never before been
> recited in song, can also at other times, if he wishes, recite
> those [rhymes] that are sung and bleated every day.

Raimbaut lets us know that he cannot specify "her whom my heart seals" because she consists of pure convention: ironically, "the best woman in the world" (*la meiller que sia*) was also, in Raimbaut's time, the most talked about woman in the world, and had as many lovers among the troubadours as "Anonymous" has titles to his credit.

The analogy, then, works three ways: the song is a garden, the lady is a song, and the garden is a lady. Any of the three can be either "serratz e clus / qu'hom no·ls tem ja de vergonhar" (locked and closed so that one never fears that they may cause disgrace) or shared (*envazit, parsonat, comunal*—"invaded, divided, communal"). Erich Köhler (1970) has argued that the *gilos* in troubadour poetry represents a growing ideal of private property that had begun to extend its claim to the *domna* herself and that therefore found *fin'amors* inimical; the proponents of *fin'amors* themselves eventually absorbed some of this attitude toward property, and the *amador* too became *gilos.* This theory can be applied metaphorically to the concept of literary property: the "jealous poet" would see in his verse a potential source of dishonor—"temer de vergognar," in Peire d'Alvernhe's phrase. Thus, rival poets might "corrupt" a song, produce in it a "change of heart" (represented by such phrases as "virar lo cor") that alters the intended form or meaning and leads to the creation of "illegitimate" versions.

Vernacular literary convention of the twelfth century is more familiar with ladies who are locked inside gardens than with ladies who *are* locked gardens: we might cite Chrétien de Troyes's Fenice and the lady of Marie de France's "Guigemar," among others. Yet the *locus amoenus* is often identified with the lady herself. The troubadours often designate an "implied lady" as a place, a *loc* "over there" (*lai*); Rigaut de Berbezilh addresses a song to his "Bels Paradis." Guilhem IX's "bosc en un deveis" (3, 14) stands for a lady, and her situation is apparently the same as that of the *domna esserrada* of song 2, who complains to Guilhem about her *gardadors*.

If we follow the isomorphism *ort serrat/motz serratz/domna esserrada* (locked-up garden, words, lady), then Guilhem's resentment of *gardadors* amounts to skepticism about the value of keeping poetry as a "private preserve." The manuscript tradition attests that in many cases, for every line that is "pruned out" from a poem, "two or three more crop up": "E quam lo bocx es taillatz nais plus espes" (And when the wood is trimmed, it comes forth thicker). Moreover, even the best-guarded poem sooner or later yields to its natural inclination for "infidelity" and escapes its owner, like the resourceful woman of whom Guilhem predicts, "If she can't have a horse, she'll buy a pony." The poet soon finds attributed to him numerous songs not of his own making, though they bear a family resemblance to his own wayward poem. Guilhem's comical "remedy," that one may as well agree peaceably to the unexpected "increase," take credit for the "abundance," and call it "profit," proposes a cheerful response to the hazards of transmission not only in families but in songs. If anyone should accept Guilhem's argument, the joke would be on him.

That "pruning stimulates new growth" applies equally well to polysemic texts: to remove one specifying detail may cause the range of possible meanings to multiply. Guilhem may actually have been alluding parodically to the exegetical tradition, specifically to that of the ending of the Song of Solomon: the "closed garden" is the Virgin Mary, but it is also the divine Word of the Scripture, whose meanings multiply according to the interpretive ingenuity of its commentators (see Minnis 1984, 42–58). When Guilhem adds that there is no loss of profit to the *senher*, he may have had in mind the *mille argenteos* of Solomon's final parable (Song of Solomon 8:11):

> e·l senher no·n pert son comte ni sos ses;
> a revers planh hom la tala . . .
>
> (Gm IX 3, 17–18)

And the lord does not lose his account from it, nor his taxes. A
man is wrong to complain about the harvesting . . .

For the Scriptures, a single text in the hands of its temporary caretakers
produces a great abundance of *sermones*—the equivalent, according to
Rupert of Duize, of the thousand coins paid for fruit cut from Solomon's
orchard after it was entrusted to *gardadors:*

> "Tradidit eam custodibus," commisit eam rectoribus; "vir affert pro
> fructu ejus mille argenteos," id est quivis operarius fidelis ac virtuosus,
> Scripturarum peritus et ore facundus, cunctas fidelis sermonis copias im-
> pendit praedicando, ut percipiat tempore suo quidpiam de fructu ejus.
> Omnes argentei eius mille, id est omnes sermones ejus consonant in una
> fide, quia sicut jam supradictus est, qued arithmeticis non incognitum est.
>
> (Rupert of Duize, *Patrologia Latina*, sec. 426, vol. 168, col. 959)

> "He gave it over to guardians," he entrusted it to leaders; "a man brings
> for its fruit a thousand pieces of silver," that is to say, anyone who is in-
> dustrious, faithful and virtuous, experienced in the Scriptures and fertile
> of tongue, is inevitably going to produce publicly a great abundance of
> faithful discourses, so that in his time something of its fruit may be
> picked [understood]. All his thousand pieces of silver, that is to say, all
> its discourses, resound together in a single faith, for the same reason
> mentioned above, which is something not unknown to those who make
> accountings.

The parallel among the lady, the poem, and the garden (or hunting
ground, borrowing the Ovidian motif of "love as a chase") may be presented from the point of view of the poacher as well as of the jealous
proprietor. Guilhem IX took the poacher's stance. Marcabru's *gap* plays
up the interchangeability of *drutz* and *gilos* in their relation to various
dompnas; by analogy, the jealous holder of the "rights" to one poem
might seek to "poach" from another man's repertory to increase his
own, "adulterating" the song and recreating it in his own image:

> En l'altrui broill
> chatz cora·m voill
> e fatz mos dos canetz glatir
> e·l tertz sahus
> eis de rahus
> bautz e ficatz senes mentir.
>
> (Mcb 16, 37–42; in Roncaglia 1951a)

> In another man's woods I go hunting whenever I wish, and
> make my two dogs bark, and the third hound leaps forward,
> bold and tense, toward the prey—it is no lie.

Marcabru hints that his repertory is not limited to songs that "anc mais non foron dig cantan" (were never before recited in song), even though his own songs are "claus . . . que nuills no lo·m pot envazir" (closed . . . such that no man can invade it against me): he plays the *gilos* with his own works, but makes the private preserves of others resound with the barking of raiding hounds. Peire d'Alvernhe's "ort / serrat e fort" (garden locked and strong), which he equates with "motz alqus / serratz e clus" (few words locked and closed), certainly derives from Marcabru's *deves claus*. Both set up the poem as a "closed garden" and, to the extent that they refer to *amors* at all, speak from the point of view of the *gilos drutz* keeping close guard over a *domna esserrada*—a lady quite opposite to the biblical *sponsa*. She represents a thoroughly secular kind of discourse; the "private place"—*ort, cambra, aizi, deves*[16]—is in troubadour poetry the site of just the kind of love, earthly, not divine, that one might find if one failed to read the Song of Solomon allegorically.

It is not surprising that the troubadours should give some thought to the greater-than-usual need of this part of the Bible, so popular in the twelfth century, for exegesis to bring it into conformity with divine charity.[17] Surely they were aware of its resemblance to many of their own lyric conventions:

> Iam enim hiems transiit:
> imber abiit, et recessit.
> flores apparuerunt in terra nostra.
> (Cant. Cant. Salomonis 2 : 11 – 12;
> Colunga and Turrado 1959, 642)

> Now the winter has passed; the rain has gone away, and has
> retreated; flowers have appeared in our land.

No doubt their works reflect an effort to set themselves in some clear relation to this text. They do so, apparently, with playful contrariety. First, their songs are not *Scrichura* but contemporary airs designed to entertain audiences rather than enlighten souls. Second, the love-languishing they sing of concerns not the love of the Church for Christ but "amor jauzida / de don'e de cavalier" (love enjoyed by a lady and a knight; B Mar 7, 59 – 60). Only a very few troubadour poems, such as those framed as the poet's interpretation of his patron's symbolic dream, are allegorical in the sense of using imagery to refer to abstractions (although another type of allegory, in which personified abstractions like *Jovens*, *Largueza*, and *Proeza* refer to specific political events and persons, is more common). At least, insofar as they employ this type of allegory, they remain strictly on secular ground. Marcabru, as much as his invasion of *l'autrui broill* with his "two dogs" evokes the role of the "little foxes that spoil the vine," flaunts a sexual implication that would discourage the exegete and that may not have been intended for mixed company.

Drawing the Honey from the Wax

The literal level of meaning vanishes, or is transformed, when scriptural commentary applies its principles of interpretation to passages whose literal meaning seems unacceptable for moral instruction, and this phenomenon is exaggerated with the Song of Solomon. Its Old French translator explains patiently to his reader how the actual "letter of the text," sacred though it may be, serves as a mere container—disposable and, in itself, not spiritually "nourishing"—for the "honey of meaning" that it is the commentator's duty to extract:

> Molt a de miel en ceste ree
> que nos avoms ici trovee.
> Or covenroit fors le miel traire.
> Deus le nos doinst dignement faire.
> (Song of Songs, 12th-cent. O.F. version,
> 2535–2548; Pickford 1974)

> There is much honey in this honeycomb which we have found here. Now it would be fitting to draw out the honey: may God grant that we do it worthily.

When the Occitan poets adapt this image to their poetry, they observe that with *amors* the wax at times becomes as important as the honey, just as *trobar* values form as highly as meaning. In Marcabru's "Dirai vos senes duptansa," *amors* reverses the normal interpretive procedure: she extracts the wax from the honey. After this action, it will be difficult for her to be "true" in the future:

> Greu sera mais Amors vera
> pos del mel triet la cera

anz sap si pelar la pera;
—Escoutatz!—
Doussa·us er com chans de lera
Si sol la coa·l troncatz.
(Mcb 18, 31–36)

With difficulty will Love be true hereafter, since she drew out
the wax from the honey; but she does know how to peel the
pear—Listen! She will be as sweet to you as the song of a lyre,
if only you cut off her tail.

Raimbaut d'Aurenga, much less resistant to the appeal of *amors* than
Marcabru was, is intrigued by the geometric form of the honeycomb; he
uses the image in conjunction with that of the chain, since the *bresca*
(honeycomb) consists of interlocking compartments and expands the linear structure of the *cadena* (chain) to three dimensions. His thought
(*pessars*)—which will become the *sens* and *ric'entendensa* for his song—
takes like form, proceeding from one "link" inevitably to another:

Qu'Amors m'a mes tal cadena
plus doussa que mel de bresca;
quan mos pessars en comensa
pus pes que·l dezirs m'en vensa.
(R d'Aur 5, 29–32)

Because love has contrived for me such a chain, sweeter than
honey from the honeycomb, that once my thinking begins,
then thought more than desire overcomes me.

Raimbaut's "meaning," then, is the counterpart not merely of the *mel*,
but also of the "interlocking" structure that holds it:

Ben ai ma voluntat plena
de tal sen que s'entrebesca.
(R d'Aur 5, 36–37)

My will is full of a meaning of such kind that it intertwines
itself.

In a song that "conceals its meaning" yet can be "easily understood"—

li mot seran descubert
Al quec de razon deviza
(R d'Aur 3, 7–8)

The words will be revealed to one who divides [interprets] them properly

—Raimbaut uses both *triar* and *devezir* to describe aesthetic discrimination:

> Ben saup lo mel de la cera
> triar, e·l miels devezir
> lo iorn que·m fes lieys ayzir;
> pus, cazen clardat d'estela,
> sa par no·s fay ad contendre (*CR:* ad entendre)
> beutatz d'autra, si be·s lima,
> ni aya cor tan asert
> de be s'aribar en Piza.
>
> (R d'Aur 3, 25–32)

He knew well how to separate the honey from the wax, and to discern the best, that day when he introduced me to her; since, when light is falling from the stars, she has no peer to compete with [*CR:* understand] her, no matter how well polished is the beauty of another woman, nor may anyone's heart be so certain of having actually arrived in Pisa.

The lady surpasses others in beauty as honey is sweeter than wax. She is the "pure meaning," extractable by wise men, from the general form of womankind. Raimbaut, however, uses the terms of carefully shaped poetry to describe her *beutatz:* the phrase "si be·s lima" (if it is well polished) belongs to *trobar plan* and applies the metaphor of sculpture to song. The "starlight" by which she looks best, along with Raimbaut's "cor asert," recall the combination of *clar* and *ferm* that distinguish the songs of Arnaut Daniel. In embodying an ideal she is "essential," as honey is the essence of honeycomb, but it is her *forma* that interests Raimbaut and not some more specifically interpretable message underlying *beutatz.*

A striking feature of the passage is its comparison, by the choice of terms of praise, between the Creator and the poet. Raimbaut does not praise God so much for having *made* so many beautiful ladies, but rather for being able to *discern* what is finest among all his creations: "He knew well how to separate the honey from the wax, and to discern the best" (R d'Aur 3, 25–26). This metaphor of "trying out the honey from the wax" (in the terms *triar* and *devezir*) appears to function like *entendre:* it serves to designate both interpretation and composition, that task of "making distinctions" that all parties to the message must undertake—the "original" poet, the performer (who recomposes), and the auditor, who reconstructs the message in his mind.

We have thus distinguished two concepts of the "text" in the lyrics of the troubadours: one is a distinctly "open" text that is made for the pleasure of the retransmitter—permutable, conventional, additive, and with movable parts in the style of Bernart de Ventadorn and Jaufre Rudel. The second, the "closed" text, admits the possibility of literary property that traces the "lineage" of a song to its creator, of a text intricately shaped like a honeycomb, such that its honey can be extracted only by the worthy. Poets who speak of the closed text are not incapable of comparing divine Creation with poetic creation: the poet is elevated to Author. The task of interpretation inherent in reception is also viewed as an act of poetic creation, since it is an act of aesthetic discernment. For those advocating "closed" poetry (here represented by Marcabru and Raimbaut d'Aurenga), only a select audience deserves a share in this privilege of recreating discernment. In the *tenso* with Raimbaut, Giraut de Bornelh plays on both sides of the net: he understands Raimbaut's concern with "legitimacy" and "lineage" for song, but he favors a classless aesthetics that makes song openly available to even the poorest of singers and listeners.

It will become more and more apparent, as we trace the metaphorical vocabulary of "open" and "closed" poetry in the works of the troubadours, that with the twelfth-century troubadours we are in the presence of massive ambivalence surrounding their medium. On the one hand a successful song is innately beautiful; on the other hand a successful song circulates widely and in the process adds some shady characters to its lineage. Exclusive, limited circulation could prevent tarnish or shame to a song's "legitimacy," yet it could also doom the song to oblivion. It is the rare poet who takes a fixed, immobile stance; the others uphold now exclusivity, now commonality. But a great many of them, even those who change their minds, are aware that their songs are to be judged. They therefore ask themselves who holds the aesthetic standard by which songs are to be judged: small, select court audiences, or large indiscriminate "marketplace" audiences.

SEVEN

The Metaphorical Vocabulary of *Mouvance* and Textual Integrity

Texts that confer editorial license on their performers do not, as a rule, confer it unconditionally. In such cases, the recipient is invited to "melhurar lo vers" (improve the poem) as befits its flaws and virtues. The pun *vers/ver(s)* (poem/truth) discourages departures from the poem's metrical, logical, and thematic decorum as well as from publicly held belief, for any *mot fals* would disqualify its context as "true" poetry by excepting it from an equivalency built into the language itself. "Melhurar lo vers" is to enhance the poem's approximation to *lo ver,* the truth.[1]

In "Bel m'es lo dous chans per la faia" (323,6), *fals motz* would provide the one condition under which the poet asks of the addressee "q·el melhur . . . / los vers." The uncertainty of the poem's authorship may be the result of how little proprietary control its original poet claimed:

> Lo vescoms que gran ben aja
> vuelh que lo·m melhur, si·l plai
> lo vers, si fals motz lo sec.
> (Zenker 1901, 798, vv. 56–58)[2]

I would like the viscount—may he have great good—to improve the poem, if he likes, if false words follow it.

The liberty offered at first only to one trusted nobleman, the addressee, might easily have been taken by jongleurs who, in adding the poem to their repertories, "improved" a few lines and, in time, took credit for its creation. This may explain its attribution to Bernart de Venzac, a poet named only in manuscript C, whose entire corpus (as reconstructed by Rudolf Zenker) consists of songs more defensibly attributed to Peire d'Alvernhe and Marcabru. Whether or not he foresaw the effacement of his individual claim to authorship, however, the poet repeats his invitation, using the same deferential qualifying phrase *si·l plai;* he shows more interest in the appropriateness that his words maintain, and in their future as a song to be sung over and over, than in attaching his name to a fixed text:

> Lo vers vas la fin s'atraja
> e·lh mot sion entendut
> per N'Isart, cui Dieus aiut,
> quez el ama en autum;
> se i a mot que non s'eschaia,
> volh que l'en mova, si·l plai
> e que no·i l'en teigna nec.
> (Zenker 1901, 798, vv. 50–56)

The poem draws to an end, and may the words be understood by Lord Isart—may God help him—for he loves in eminence, and if there is a word which is not appropriate, I would like him to alter it, if he likes, and may he not keep it silent.

Clear evidence that *mover* can mean "to alter a poem" as well as "to begin singing" appears in Jaufre Rudel's "No sap chantar qui so no di," where in one version he uses the verb *mover* as an amplifying synonym for *camjar,* with *lo vers* as its object: "E cel que de mi l'apenra / gard si non mueva ni camgi" (And he who learns it from me, let him take care neither to alter nor to change it; J Rud 6/1A, 21–22). Jaufre's prohibition of change asserts that the poem, as composed, contains no *mot fals* (c.f. *falhir*): "Bos es lo vers s'ieu no·y falhi / Ni tot so que·y es, ben esta" (The poem is good if I am not mistaken, and everything in it well suffices; J Rud 6/1, 37–40). The only version to forbid change without exception ("Gard si non mueva ni camgi," 6/1A) is also the only version to omit the *tornada* foretelling that its hearers in Toulouse and Limoges or Quercy will make new words for the song: "Bons er lo vers e faran y / Calsque motz que hom chantara" (The poem will be good and they will make there whatever words someone will sing; 6/1B).

Ulrich Mölk demonstrates that in many instances, the word *motz* seems to refer specifically to the rhyme words and thus to entire metrical schemes (1979, 3–5). If this meaning is intended in "Bel m'es lo dous chans per la faia," then the phrase "mot que non s'eschaia" refers not to a breach of decorum in diction but rather to a possible defect in the rhyme scheme. We should perceive here a distinction between transmitters' changes that alter a poem's form and changes that preserve it. Mölk follows Rupert T. Pickens in identifying certain words as belonging to the lexical field of poets' reference to transmission and performance: "*Franher, pessar, mudar, peiurar, desfaissonar*: the troubadours use these and other terms to express their concern for the integrity of the metrical structure. This concern can rightfully be seen less as a topos than as an obviously significant moment in literature" (Mölk 1979, 5). Yet "Bel m'es lo dous chans per la faia" teaches us that a poet could believe in the stability of the rhyme scheme even if he left further revisions to the hearer's discretion; it also shows that even the "integrity of the metrical structure," the *motz* or rhyme scheme, could be fair game for emendation if it were defective, *fals*. "Integrity" was something that could be restored, or even conferred for the first time, by a new performer.

References to future singers are often linked to the polarity "deterioration/improvement" and to a boast about the poem's structure. Guilhem IX affirms the enrichment of a poem well understood; the construction *mais . . . qui* suggests repeated performance ("the more . . . the more"), and the song's "equal rhymes" are supposed to guarantee appreciation rather than depreciation:

> Del vers vos dic que mais ne vau
> qui be l'enten, e n'a plus lau:
> que·ls motz son faitz tug per egau.
> (Gm IX 7, 37–39)

Of the poem I tell you that it is worth more, the better one understands it, and gets more praise for it: for the rhymes are all created equal.

Jaufre Rudel's "Quon plus l'auziretz, mais valra" (The more you will hear it, the more it will be worth; 6, 6) is colored by the ambiguity of Jaufre's previous line, "*pero mos chans comens' aissi*" (but [therefore] my song begins thus); is this "only the beginning of the song" because Jaufre has sung only the first stanza or because the song has yet to undergo all the transformations that will realize its full potential value? A less ambiguous version of this topos occurs near the end of a song by Bernart de

Ventadorn: "Lo vers, aissi com om plus l'au / vai melhuran tota via" (The more the poem is heard, the more it continually improves; B Vent 21, 57–58). Literally, his song improves "all along the road" (*tota via*). Not just one hearer, whose understanding deepens, but many hearers and many performers enhance the song.

"Rust" and "Splinters"

In Peire d'Alvernhe's "Belh m'es qu'ieu fass' huey mays un vers," the boast about the durable structure takes the form of a metaphorical description:

> On plus hom mos vers favelha
> fe que·us deg, on mais valon elh
> e no·y a motz fals que y rovelh
> ni sobredolat d'astelha.
> (P d'Alv 15, 65–68)

> The more my song is repeated, I swear to you, the more it is
> worth; and there are no false words that might rust in it, nor
> [words] too smoothly filed free of splinters.

"Rust" suggests a song made of metal; "splinters," of wood. Both metaphors express Peire's confidence in the future of his song: its rhymes are neither prone to rust nor *sobredolat d'astelha*, "polished too smooth of splinters." Whether *sobredolat* connotes excessive or merely superficial smoothness, Peire is content that the "barbs" remain. *Astelha* can refer to sharp sticks as large as war spears, and Peire's invective against those who abuse language is intended to prick the conscience. "Splinters" might be viewed as flaws in fine woodworking, but Peire has already disavowed artistic roughness (*mot fals*); he ends with a paradox, transferring a metaphor from the poet's technical craft (*dolar*, "polish") to his moralistic intention.

Marcabru first linked *mot fals* with "rust" and transferred the moral term into the lexical field of poetry. In the last strophe of "Lo vers comens quan vei del fau," a song composed "segon trobar naturau" (v. 7), Marcabru defies future singers in a passage that compares his song to a miner's lode, an archaeologist's dig, or a vandal's buried treasure:

> Marcabrus ditz que no·ill en cau
> qui quer ben lo vers'al foïll

> que no·i pot hom trobar a frau
> mot de roïll
> intrar pot hom de lonc jornau
> en breu doïll.
> (Mcb 33; Roncaglia 1951b, 31, vv. 49–64)

> Marcabru says he does not care if someone searches the poem
> well with a ransacker's tool, for one cannot find there hidden a
> word of rust; one can enter after a long day's work through a
> small hole.

The medieval Latin equivalency *rubigo:malitia* (Roncaglia 1951b, 45*n*.52) is expanded here to accommodate Marcabru's artistic "morality"; "a word of rust" would make way for the chipping and chiseling of the vandal's *foïll* ("*fodiculum*, to designate the instrument used to *fodiculare*"; Roncaglia 1951b, 45*n*.50). As it is, they merely "scratch the surface" (*fant gratill*):

> Mas menut trobador bergau
> entrebesquill
> mi tornon mon chant en badau
> e·n fant gratill.
> (Mcb 33; Roncaglia 1951b, 31, vv. 9–12)

> But petty troubadours, drones, fabricators, turn my song into
> gaping and scratching.

This portrait of a "droning" performance (*bergau*, "hornet, fool"; Roncaglia 1951b, 37*n*.9), where the singer "scrapes" at his lyre and "stands with his mouth open" instead of singing meaningful sounds ("tornar chant en badau"), catches the *cantador* overacting his rôle of *amador* at the expense of poetry, gaping with feigned desire (*badar*) and "tickling" (*gratillar*) the imagination of other men's wives.

But these enemies of Marcabru, who profane *his* song, are not merely performers but *trobador* who compose, or recompose it: the designation *entrebesquill* (interweavers) alludes to the creation of rhymed lines. Thus, Marcabru's reference to his song's "freedom from rust" as a safeguard against "ransacker's tools" suggests, like Peire d'Alvernhe's "there are no false words that might rust in it," that its structure is "impenetrable." Indeed, Marcabru has found twenty-seven different words in each of his two rhymes, so that it might be difficult to replace a line without telltale repetition.

Because it does not rust or tarnish, and because it is "rare" and valuable, gold becomes a favorite metal for poets who use the metaphor of sculpture to describe poetic composition. Although Peire Vidal once compares the "tempering" of a love song to the goldsmith's method of purifying a lump of gold by "breaking" it in the fire, Peire more often alludes to a nonstructural, decorative exterior of gold:

> Qu'era que sui malmenatz
> fas meravelhatz
> motz ab us sonetz *dauratz*.
> (P Vid 4, 12–16)

For now that I am ill treated, I make marvelous rhymes with a gilded little tune.

> Senher N'Agout, no·us sai lauzar
> mas de vos *dauri* mon chantar.
> (P Vid 7, 81–82)

Sir Agout, I know not how to praise you, but with you I gild my song.

In both of these instances, the context indicates that Peire has reason *not* to produce a "solid gold" song: in the first passage, he has been mistreated, and in the second, a man unworthy of Peire's praise provides the "gilt" with which he adorns his song. Peire gives a comic twist to the familiar idea that a poem should be worth the price paid for it and worthy of its addressee.

The combination of noble and base metals or of metal and wood as materials for "sculpture in words" reappears in Peire Vidal's "En una terra estranha," where Peire points to the futility of "gilding and filing" with words. He observes that whoever applies the gold leaf first and then shapes his words with a file destroys his own work, revealing his "ill-schooled" heart. Such a man's work, the *amors* he fabricates in words, can last no longer than a spider's web:

> Quar pus qu'obra d'aranha
> no pot aver durada
> amors, pus es proada,
> qu'ab ditz daur'ez aplana
> tals qu'al cor de vilan escuelh.
> (P Vid 25, 49–53)

For no more than a spider's web can love have duration, since
it has come to the test [been proven] that such a man as gilds
with words, and [then] files, gets his intention [heart] from an
ignoble school.

Taken together, Peire's uses of the verb *daurar* to describe poetic orna-
mentation disapprove the thin film of glitter, applied to conceal an un-
sound structure.

The troubadour who best reconciles the constructive metaphors for
poetry—sculpture, building, and metallurgy—is Raimbaut d'Aurenga. In
his *rimeta prima* that he "built without rule or line" (2,3) as well as in
"Cars, dous e fenhz" (1), Raimbaut associates the process of filing (*limar*)
with the removal of rust. More descriptively than in Marcabru's *trobar
naturau,* the search for "rust" takes the form of a probing inspection;
Marcabru's ransacker ("qui quer ben lo vers'al foïll") has his counterpart
in Raimbaut's *falsa genz:*

> De la falsa genz qe lima
> e dech'e ditz (don quec lim)
> ez estreinh e mostr'e guinha
> (so don Joi frainh e esfila),
> per q'ieu sec e pols e guinh;
> Mas ieu no·m part del dreg fil,
> quar mos talenz no·s roïlha
> q'en Joi nos ferm ses roïlh.
> (R d'Aur 2, 9–16)

[I complain] about the false people who file and dictate and
speak (wherefore I file each of them) and squeeze and point
and stare at that which causes *Joi* to break and unravel; because of them I follow [or "dry out"] and pound and squint,
but I do not leave the straight wire, for my intention does not
rust, because it encloses us in *Joi* without rust.

Like Marcabru, Raimbaut regards the critical scrutiny of his enemies
("estreinh e mostr'e guinha") as something closely related to vandalism.
The two poets' enemies use comparable tools in their destruction: the
lima and the *foïll* have in common the fact that both wear away their
object and risk breaking it ("frainh e esfila"). One is reminded of Bernart
Amoros's caution against overediting, to illustrate which he quotes "a
wise man":

> Blasmat venon per frachura
> d'entendimen obra pura
> maintas vetz de razon prima
> per maintz fols qe·s tenon lima.
> (Stengel 1898, 350)

Pure works come to be blamed through breakage of understanding, very often [works] with outstanding arguments, because of many fools with files ["erasers"] in their hands.

Bernart too speaks of "breakage" (*frachura*) as the result of emendation
by "fools with files in their hands."[3]

Raimbaut criticizes the *falsa genz* for actions that he and other poets
associate with the making of legitimate *vers*. The least of it is the parallelism between Raimbaut's attentiveness ("ieu sec e pols e guinh," v. 13)
and that of his enemies, who "estreinh e mostr'e guinha" (v. 11). Their
"filing," which Raimbaut deprecates, is part of the work that goes on in a
poet's *obrador;* Raimbaut himself admits to doing it:

> Cars, bruns e tenhz   motz entrebesc
> pensius-pensanz   enquier e serc
> (com si liman   pogues roire
> l'estraing roill   ni'l fer tiure)
> don mon escur   cor esclaire.
> (R d'Aur 1, 19–23)

Rare, dark, and colored words I intertwine; pensively ponder-
ing I search and seek (as if by filing I could rub off the incon-
gruous rust or the hard calcifications) how I might clarify my
obscure intention.[4]

The skepticism expressed by "com si" admits that "filing" will not really
remove "rust" from "dark words": it is only a simile. *Cor* can mean intention or will, and Raimbaut seeks to clarify his intention despite the
"darkness" of his rhymes. The impurities that obscure his words—rust
and calcium deposits—create a context in which Raimbaut's intention resembles a vein of gold surrounded by a mineral crust foreign to it, or a
statue that has been left out in the rain for years and needs cleaning and
restoration. The former image, "intention as a vein of gold," is consistent
with the lines in Raimbaut's *rimeta prima,* where his "intention does not
rust" because he "does not depart from the straight wire": "mas ieu no·m

part del dreg fil, / quar mos talenz no·s roïlha" (R d'Aur 2, 14–15). The excellent poet does not need to "file" because he works in rustproof materials. Raimbaut's implication of this "straight wire of gold" may be a sort of signature, a play on his nickname, Linhaure, "Golden Line."[5] Raimbaut identifies with this noble metal in several poems. In his view, anyone who "mistakes copper for gold" is courting danger: "Que vau doptan / aur per coire / cor al perill / on ie·m liure" (Because I go mistaking gold for copper, I run toward the peril to which I surrender myself; R d'Aur 1, 48–49). In the *tenso* with Giraut de Bornelh, he compares the rarest and best of songs to the rare metal: "Per so prez'om mais aur que sal / e de tot chant es atretal" (That is why one values gold more than salt, and it is the same way with every song; R d'Aur 31, 34–35).

Arnaut Daniel recalls Raimbaut's criticism of "la falsa genz que lima" (the false people who file) when he describes the art of his "Chansson do·ill mot son plan e prim," defending himself against anticipated objections like Raimbaut's:

> Pel bruoill aug lo chan e·l refrim
> e per c'om no men fassa crim
> obre e lim
> motz de valor
> ab art d'Amor.
>   (Arn D 2, 10–14)

> Through the grove I hear the song and I echo it, and in order
> that this not be made an accusation against me, I work and file
> words of value by the art of love.

To what *crim* might Arnaut be referring? Through the woods he hears the song *e·l refrim,* and to avoid being accused of error for this, he applies his poetic craft. My solution to the question is that *refrim* is a verb: *refrimar,* "retentir, résonner" (Levy 1961). Arnaut *echoes* the song he hears in the woods and "polishes it up." As he did in the famous *razo,* he adapts the song of another to his own art—but this time it is the song of a bird, and he jokingly suggests that he might be accused of plagiarism. Arnaut justifies using the *lima* by asserting the value of his results ("motz de valor") and the worthiness of the guiding aesthetics ("ab art d'Amor"). Like Raimbaut d'Aurenga, Arnaut combines the workshop metaphors with the idea of "following a (straight) line" and alludes to the possibility of "digression," inadvertent separation from the "right way": "ans si be·m faill, / la sec a traill" (vv. 16–17). It is worth noting that although there is a tradition associating "filing" with "rust," the obvious rhyme *ruoilla* does not appear in extant copies of Arnaut's poem, although it meets the requirements of the leonine rhyme *fuoilla/bruoilla/tuoilla*.[6]

Arnaut also flouts Peire Vidal's criticism of "Amors, pus es proada / qu'ab ditz daur'ez aplana" (Love, since it has been proven that with speeches she gilds and [then] polishes; P Vid 25, 51–52), except that he does his "filing and gilding" in the more sensible order:

> En cest sonet coind'e leri
> fauc motz e capuig e doli
> que serant verai e cert
> qan n'aurai passat la lima
> q'Amors marves plan'e daura
> mon chantar, que de liei mou
> qui pretz manten e governa.
>
> (Arn D 10, 1–6)

In this graceful and gay little melody, I construct rhymes and hone them and file them so that they will be true and sure when I have passed the file over them, for Love without hesitation planes and gilds my song, which originates in her who supports and controls worth.

He defends love and his craft in one breath, declaring that love is not the creation of poetic artifice, but its creator. He counters Peire's taunt that the gilded works of *Amor* "can last no longer than a spider's web" by weighting his "graceful and frivolous little tune" with the sense of substantial, reliable carpentry that, he claims, will make his words "true and sure."

Level, Plumb, and True: Songs as Buildings

Architectural metaphors, for us, suggest the creation of a permanent edifice, perfected on a blueprint before the first board is cut. Some troubadours do speak of "building" their poems, likening the work of composition to a great stronghold made of wood and stone. It is the motif of the artisan working in his *obrador,* but on the largest scale. Raimbaut d'Aurenga draws on the idea that the master craftsman no longer needs the crude tools on which his apprentices must rely; his great skill and experience allow him to measure and level his work by sight. Raimbaut's equivalent of the carpenter's skill is the sureness of his poetic intention (*volers*):

> En aital rimeta prima
> M'agradon lieu mot e prim
> Bastit ses regl'e ses linha,
> Pos mos volers s'i apila.
> (R d'Aur 2, 1−4)

In such a first-quality little rhyme, I am pleased by light and fresh words, built without rule or [plumb] line, since my will inclines toward it.

Like Arnaut, Raimbaut contrasts the delicacy of his project ("lieu mot e prim") with the heavy tools of construction, as if the lightest of these tools (*regla, linha*) could damage the finely finished work.

Guilhem de Berguedà makes the same claim, but his mastery exempts him from using even grosser tools. In lines reminiscent of Arnaut Daniel's *sonet coind'e leri*, Guilhem satirizes the metaphor of the love poet as builder and of poets whose "hearts have wings" yet who carve their words with blunt instruments. Being the "master of the school," Guilhem has no need of the adz and hatchet; in implying that other poets do use these, he compares them not to architects but to clumsy woodcutters who bring rough lumber to the building site:

> Cel so qui capol'e dola:
> tant soi cuynde e avinen
> si que destral ni exola
> no·y deman ni ferramen
> qu'esters n'a bastidas cen
> que maestre de l'escola
> so, e am tan finamen
> que per pauc lo cor no·m vola.
> (Gm Berg 15, 1−8)

I am the one who planes and trims: I am so gracious and pleasing that I do not require an adz or a hatchet, nor other tools, for I have built a hundred [songs] without them, because I am the master of the school, and I love in such a refined way that my heart nearly flies away.

Elsewhere Guilhem de Berguedà develops the expression "sirventes bastir" into a full conceit; the poem as "building" becomes a stronghold, a battle station, that not only protects itself but also shelters the poet during his fight for revenge on its attackers:

> Ara voill un sirventes far
> tal que, quan l'aurai bastit
> non hai negun tant ardit
> enemic no·s posca pensar
> que si m'offen qe ja mais fi ni patz
> aia de me tro qe·n sia venjatz.
> (Gm Berg 24, 1–6)

> Now I wish to compose a sirventes such that, when I have built it, there will be no enemy so bold as to be able to think that he will ever have an end [to war] or peace from me, if he offends me, until I am avenged.

By 1190, "bastir sirventes" was a cliché for Guilhem de Berguedà: in song 21, Guilhem scarcely pauses to comment on this "building," so intent is he on obtaining patronage "hastily" (*astivamen*, v. 9):

> Un sirventes ai en cor a bastir
> que trametrai a·N Sanchon en Espaigna.
> (Gm Berg 21, 1–2)

> I have it in my heart [mind] to build a sirventes, which I will transmit to Sir Sancho in Spain.

Already *bastir* means nothing more than "compose": one cannot "send" a fortress. Raimbaut de Vaqueiras uses the same verb to signal the completion of his "Kalenda maia":

> Bastida, finida, N'Engles,
> ai l'estampida.
> (P.-C. 392, vv. 71–72; cited from Riquer 1975, 839)

> Mr. Englishman, I have built, I have finished the *estampida*.

Although Raimbaut probably chose the verb *bastir* to draw attention to the artful "construction" of his poem, he is content to leave the term in the realm of the dead metaphor. *Estampida* is a dance and cannot be "built."

The lasting monuments of the Middle Ages—cathedrals, castles, and towers—were the work of many, sometimes of generations, and there would be no Frank Lloyd Wright to credit with designing the whole and seeing it completed according to his original plans. The metaphor of the poet as builder, too, must be in harmony with medieval ideas on building. Giraut de Bornelh develops the metaphor at length. He first compares the poem to a friendship, then likens both poem and friendship to a tower, built stone by stone until it finally reaches a defensible height. Then battlements can be built, and it can be armed, and the tower—or poem, or friendship—is safe from attack:

> E pois auziretz chantador
> E chansos anar e venir!
> Q'era, can re no sai m'assor,
> Me volh un pauc plus enardir
> D'enviar no messatge
> Que·ns porte nostras amistatz
> Que sai n'es facha la meitatz,
> Mas de leis no n'ai gatge
> E ja no cut si'achabatz
> Nuls afars, tro qu'es comensatz.
>
> Qu'eu ai vist acomensar tor
> D'una sola peir'al bastir
> E cada pauc levar alsor
> Tan josca c'om la poc garnir.
> Per qu'eu tenh vassalatge
> D'aitan, si m'o aconselhatz.
> E·l vers, pos er ben assonatz,
> Trametrai el viatge,
> Si trop qui lai lo·m guit viatz
> Ab que·s deport e·s do solatz.
>
> (Gr Bor 40, 41–60)

And then you will hear singers and songs come and go! For now, when nothing uplifts me here, I wish to become a little more courageous to send my messenger, that he might carry for us our friendship, for here only half of it is made—though I have no token [down payment] from her, and never, I think, can any business be completed until it is begun.

> For I have seen a tower begun from one single building block and little by little rise higher until it can be armed. Therefore I keep this much of chivalry, if you advise it; and the verse, when it will be well set to music, I will send on the journey, if I find someone who will guide it there for me quickly, whom it will amuse and provide with conversation.

If Giraut de Bornelh sends a messenger to "carry for us our friendship," he will surely have it conveyed in the form of a song. But now Giraut is so distressed (nothing "raises" him, v. 43) that he cannot dignify the work in progress with the name of *chanso*. In better times, he promises, "you will hear the singers and songs come and go." Now it will take more courage to send off his work, for it, like the friendship, is only half-made "here" (i.e., by Giraut): "Que sai n'es facha la meitatz" (v. 47).

The implication is that the other half (*meitatz*) will be made *lai*, there where the addressee is.[7] Since the lady has sent no *gatge* (surety), no first word as "earnest money" on the song, Giraut can feel justified in sending a mere beginning: someone must lay the first stone. A song, like a friendship, is the work of more than one person. Contrasting the stationary, upward growth of the tower with the song's travel by long relay over time and space, Giraut sends his provisional song as the foundation of a great tower of *amistatz*, hoping that it will grow higher *cada pauc* (gradually) until the verse and the friendship together have become as unassailable as the best-armed fortress. *Ben assonatz*, well fitted with its music, the future poem will be provided with a solid foundation, but its ultimate height has not been limited by its architect.

Poetic "Wholeness": *Vers Entiers*

The controversy over *vers entiers* ("entire" or "whole poetry") among Peire d'Alvernhe, Bernart Marti, and other poets of the period bears a close relation to Jaufre Rudel's admonition, "Take care not to break it." The poets discuss "integrity" as a property of poetry itself, of its content, of the jongleur, and even of the poet; they invoke it, disclaim it, accuse others of destroying it, or deny that it can exist. The poems that tell us most about *vers entiers* and *vers frach* emphasize the dangers of performance to a song's "wholeness," and they hint at methods by which the poets could, or believed they could, protect it.

When Peire d'Alvernhe claims to be the first to make *vers entiers*, he also boasts that his song will be understood by posterity:

> qu'entendon be   aquels c'a venir son
> c'anc tro per me   no fo faitz vers entiers.
> (P d'Alv 11, 3–4; in Paterson 1975, 60)[8]

> . . . so that those who are yet to come may fully realize that a
> truly whole song was never composed until by me.
>
> (trans. Paterson)

We cannot be sure that he is referring to the "obviously significant moment in literature" announced by Mölk, but we can expect the poem to try to exemplify (and thus help us to define) "whole poetry"—despite an irony of transmission that breaks the poem with a one-line lacuna. Peire "steals from" (Levy 1961, *apanar* 2) those who practice the trade of poet or jongleur "without an accord that does not get broken along the roadside"; because he has "the bread of poetry" which they lack, other performers must content themselves to be his mere hirelings (*apanar* 1; cf. *apanat*):

> Q'ieu tenc l'us e·l pan e·l coutel
> de que·m platz apanar las gens
> que d'est mestier   s'an levat un pairon
> ses acordier   que no·s rompa·l semdiers.
> (P d'Alv 11, 7–10; in Paterson 1975, 60)

> For I have the experience and the bread and the knife with
> which it pleases me to feed [get the better of] the people who
> have raised up a model for themselves in this profession, without recognizing that a task should not be left half-finished.
>
> (trans. Paterson)[9]

The kind of "accord" that befits "this profession" is not a contractual "agreement" or political "harmony" but rather that fitting of *motz* to *son* which derivatives of *acordar* so often signify in troubadour poetry.[10] Travel—that is, transmission—was hard on poems, and Peire evokes the bumpy roads of the time and their hazard to fragile things. The song should be composed for durability in recitation, so that the jongleur can sing it without fits and starts, without changing his mind midword about what word comes next:

C'a un tenen ses mot borrel
deu de dir esser avinens;
quar qui trassaill   de Maurin en miron
entre·l mieg faill   si no·s pren als ladriers,
com del trebaill   quecs motz fatz trezagiers,
qu'en devinaill   met l'auzir de maison.
(P d'Alv 11, 13–18; in Paterson 1975, 60)

For at one stretch, without broken words, he should be pleasing in recitation; for he who leaps across from *Maurin* to *miron* falls down in between, if he does not cling to the sides, as he makes every [rhyme] word the occasion for turmoil, so that he sets in riddledom the hearing of the house [*maison*].[11]

In lines 15–18, the words *maurin, miron,* and *maion* (MS *E*) function in two ways: in addition to their semantic value, they represent the near homonyms among which a jongleur must choose correctly in order to make sense. "He who takes a leap between *mauri* and *miro,*" if he "falls down midway," will produce a hybrid of vowels and consonants from each word: *maio.* His poor memory for sound produces an aural riddle.

Peire thinks it best not to hesitate, but to sing without stopping to ponder and blunder (v. 13). Yet this is not an argument for rote memorization; the hesitation among *mauri, miro,* and *maio* is the sort of error that would be made by someone who tried to memorize only the sound and could not remember or reproduce the sense. It may also be an argument for reinforcing rhymes: the jongleur should know whether the word ends in *-i* or in *-o* and should not try to compromise by singing *-io.*

The poem is in *coblas unissonans,* with four internal rhymes. Thus, no rhyme sound is so rarely used that one can forget it; even the internal rhymes, each of which is confined to a single stanza, recur four times in four lines. Perhaps, like Marcabru, Peire believed that the form of *coblas unissonans* would protect his song from others' detractions, and thought of the repeated rhyme as a way to "bind up the *razon* in the verse." Peire does derive the proof that his *vers* is *entier* from his strict adherence to his argument: "Auia dese con estau a razon" (Hear right now how I stick to the argument; v. 6).

There is no sign, however, that Peire concerns himself with the *order* of stanzas. Although the modern reader might suppose that a coherent argument must develop its ideas in a necessary order, it is possible that the troubadours' conception of the *razo* differs from modern expectations. Perhaps the "argument" consisted of movable parts: one might *estar a razo* without depending on a particular sequence.

Rather than derive "security in his song" from an exclusionist principle that restricts access to his song, Peire explains his "certainty" with farmers' metaphors:

> Q'ie·m sen sertans   del mieils qui aqui fon
> ensegurans   de mon chant e sobriers
> ves los baisans   e sai que dic, qu'estiers
> no vengua·l grans   don a trop en sazon.
> (P d'Alv 11, 27–30; in Paterson 1975, 60)

> For I feel confident about the best that ever was, self-assured
> about my song and superior to those on the decline, and I know
> what I am saying, for in no other way is the grain forthcoming,
> of which there is much in due season.
>   (trans. Paterson)[12]

Peire attributes the "security" of his song to its abundance, to the fact that the original version (the "seed") is more than sufficient. The biblical parable of the Sower enters the picture, and its application appears to be that the song will "grow" when it is seeded in the "good soil" of audiences and performers who "heed the word." Peire declares himself the "root," "the first" in "finished recitations" ("qu'ieu soi raitz e dic que soi premiers / de digz complitz," vv. 22–23); by emphasizing growth from "root" and "seed" (*raitz, grans*), Peire describes the lyric as an organism whose quality depends on its origin and that illustrates the genealogical aphorism of *trobar natural* that only good trees bring forth good fruit.[13] Peire d'Alvernhe thus, with his talk of "root" and "seed" of "complete poetry," achieves an effect similar to what Pickens observes in Jaufre Rudel's work, where "the erotic movement in the composition, transmission, destination and retransmission of the song associates . . . the spring topos with the topos of the 'seminal word'" (1977, 327).

The "abundance" of Peire's original work, what makes it *ric*, comes from the creative force of *joi:* "D'aisi·m sent ric per bona sospeison / qu'en ioi m'afic" (In this respect I feel rich, through a pleasant apprehension that I am fixed in *joi*; vv. 38–39). The manuscripts give *asic* in line 38, from *asezer* (sit, seat); this makes good enough sense to render emendation unnecessary. "I am seated in *joi*" would give the same sense of stability and well-being as *m'afic,* except that instead of the overtones of being "fixed" or "attached," *m'asic* has the additional sense of "being set to music."

Sung performance, then, was clearly one of the major considerations in "securing a song" ("ensegurans de mon chant," v. 28), in keeping it "whole." Peire trusts in the reinforcing rhymes of *coblas unissonans,* as well as in the more than sufficient creative virtue of the original "seed" or "root" song, which should guarantee that the quality of its "offspring" will be as high as its own. Peire d'Alvernhe, today remembered most for his Marcabrunian satire, was known in the thirteenth century for his outstanding melodies. The superiority that he claims in "Sobre·l vieill trobar" was explained by his Provençal biographer as justifiable by the excellence of his musical compositions:

> E trobet ben e cantet ben, e fo lo premiers bons trobaire que fon outra mon et aquel que fez los meillors sons de vers que anc fosson faichs.
>
> (Boutière and Schutz 1964, s.v. "Peire d'Alvernhe")

> And he composed poems well and he sang well, and he was the first good troubadour who went beyond the mountains and the one who made the best lyric melodies ever made.

In general, Peire seems to rely on large, encompassing structures such as the melody (*son, acordier*), the argument (*razo*), and the rhyme scheme to keep the song *entiers.* "Breakage" (*frachura*) in details, like the blurring of *mauri* and *miro* into *maio,* he blames on jongleurs' failure to sing consistently ("a un tenen") and thus to ensure meaningful sequences of sounds, rather than on their inability to remember the exact wording of the original composition.

In this way, Peire d'Alvernhe's view of what constitutes the "integrity" of the song—its *son,* its *razo,* and its *rima* (melody, argument, and rhyming)—strongly affirms the view of Jaufre Rudel:

> No sap chantar qui so non di
> ni vers trobar qui motz no fa
> ni connoys de rima quo·s va
> si razos non enten en si.
> (J Rud 6/1, 1–4)

> One cannot [know how to] sing without uttering the melody, nor compose a poem without making rhymes [words], nor

know how the rhyme goes if he does not comprehend the argument within himself.

Understanding the *razo* ensures that one will know "how the rhyme goes," and not vice versa. The need to match rhyme and melody while making sense is the singer's, as well as the poet's, task; the rhyme does not precede the sense but follows it. Otherwise one sings well-rhymed nonsense, the *devinaill* referred to in Peire's song.

In "D'entier vers far ieu non pes" ("I care not for making 'entire' poems"), Bernart Marti discusses "textual integrity" as the counterpart of personal integrity, challenging Peire d'Alvernhe's boastful song on both levels, at times blending these levels. Even his own songs, Bernart admits, are not "whole," although he himself has not made "breaks" in them: "D'entier vers far ieu non pes / ni ges de frag non faria" (I am not thinking of making a "whole" song, nor would I make a broken one; B Mar 5, 1–2). Bernart denies that he, as the "original composer" of a song, could presume to claim the high perfection that *entier* implies; nonetheless, his songs' distance from that perfection does not brand them *vers frag*. He also does not blame others for whatever flaws might be found in his songs: transmission neither corrects their imperfections nor creates new "breakage." He composes two or three songs each year, he says, "et on plus sion asses / entier ni frag no son mia" (5, 5–6). In this context, *asses* may again mean "set to music" (from *asezer*): "the more they are set to music, the more they are neither whole nor broken."[14]

Bernart interweaves personal criticisms of Peire d'Alvernhe—his "sin of pride," his disloyalty to monastic vows—with criticism of presumptuous aesthetic claims; the language of secular poetry, he insists, is a fallen language that can no more aspire to perfect "wholeness" than men can aspire to the "wholeness" that preceded original sin:

> E so quez entier non es,
> ni anc no fo, cum poiria?
> Fols hom leu so cujaria
> que chans melhs entrebesques,
> qu'om de vanetat fezes
> entiers ni frags non seria.
> (B Mar 5, 13–18)

And that which is not "whole," nor ever was, how could it become ["whole"]? A foolish man might easily believe that he

> could weave the song better, but whatever a man might make
> out of vanity would not be either "whole" or "broken."

Here, Bernart criticizes the vanity of the reviser: if a song never was "whole," and is not "whole," how can its "wholeness" be restored? "The fool might think he could weave the song better" (v. 16), perhaps better than the original poet made it. However, the works of vanity are flawed by their own motive; they cannot even be "broken" because the word implies a preexisting "wholeness."

Bernart also appears to recommend a division of labor between poets and musical composers; this supports my reading of the first stanza, where the phrase "on plus sion asses" (the more they are set to music) represents the time when the song leaves the poet's jurisdiction and becomes the work of others.

> De far sos novelhs e fres,
> so es bella maistria
> e qui belhs motz lass'e lia,
> de belh'art s'es entremes;
> mas non cove q'us disses
> que de tot n'a senhoria.
>   (B Mar 5, 73–78)

> To make new and fresh melodies—that is a beautiful craft to
> master, and he who laces up and binds beautiful words has in-
> volved himself in a beautiful art; but it is not suitable that one
> man should say that he holds dominion over all.

The making of a song requires the blending of *two* arts, the *maistria* of melodic composition and the *belh'art* of "tying and binding fine rhymes," but no one can claim absolute supremacy in both. Again, Bernart's comment indicates that a "whole" song would, ideally, create a perfect bond between the *motz* and the *son*. This responds to Peire's claim of superiority over others in his trade whose "acordier . . . se romp'al semdier."

Bernart also reminds Peire that he cannot keep constant vigil over transmission: he cannot spread his own praises over the countryside by himself, and it would be a disgrace if he tried to do so:

> Pro sap e ben es apres
> qui so fay que ben estia
> et es mager cortezia

> que sos laus es pels paës
> per autruy que per el mes,
> qu'ab pobol par vilania.
>
> (B Mar 5, 67–73)

> He knows enough and is well educated, he who makes a mel-
> ody that may suit; and it is a greater courtly refinement that his
> praise is spread through the countries by others than himself,
> for among the population, baseness appears.

This stanza includes a backhanded compliment to Peire's musical compositions: it is enough that he "makes a melody that is perfectly ade-
quate" (*ben estia*). Peire should allow others to "spread his praises"—
that is to say, he should leave the making of *vers* to others and stick to
what he does best, the *son*. Among country audiences, the courtly song
may acquire some new *vilania* that would wound its author's sensibility;
he had better stay home. Bernart mentions the peasant audience to deflate
Peire's lofty claim to have achieved the aesthetic ideal of "wholeness."

Time and performance leave songs neither "untouched" nor "broken";
they are mended as often as they are rearranged by other hands, other
voices. Bernart laughs at the claim of absolute and personal control (*sei-
gnoria*): once a song is known, it no longer belongs to its creator, and re-
creators share the credit (*laus*) for making it, or the discredit (*vilania*) for
unmaking it.

Giraut de Bornelh uses Bernart's own argument to refute him: Bernart
denies the poet's right to boast of his songs, since once they enter the public domain they may only distantly resemble his original productions.
Giraut argues that, on the contrary, these conditions leave the poet at liberty to praise his own songs as loudly as if they had been made by another. A song's virtues are intrinsic in it and not conditional on the
hearer's acquaintance (or identity) with the author:

> S'es chantars ben entendutz
> e s'ofris pretz e valor,
> per qu'es lach de trobador,
> desque sos chans er saubutz
> qu'el eis en sia lauzaire?
> Que be pareis al retraire
> si·lh n'eschai blasmes o laus.
>
> (Gr Bor 62, 1–7)

> If a song is well planned, and offers in itself value and worth, then why is it unbecoming in a troubadour, after his song is known, that he himself be its praiser? For it is quite apparent at the performance whether blame or praise redounds to him because of it.

Giraut further clarifies the process of disjunction between the poem and its original author. A song may have an excellent author and yet come to a bad end (as Bernart Amoros later pointed out) because the jongleurs squabble over distorted versions of what was once a good poem by a good troubadour—just as the shrill grackle and the screaming peacock squabble over which of them produces the superior cacophony:

> Lo vers auzitz e mogutz
> coma de bo trobador
> pois reverti en error,
> lo chans can er' asaubutz,
> c'us s'en fazia clamaire
> dels dichs don altr'era laire,
> com fetz de la gralha·l paus.
> (Gr Bor 62, 29–35)

The verse is heard and "moved"[15] as the work of a good troubadour; later, the song turns back into error when it becomes known, for one man makes himself the claimant of verses another man stole, just as the peacock does [complains] against the grackle.

In "un vers que volh far leuger" (a poem that I want to make light), Giraut turns Peire d'Alvernhe's notion of "textual integrity" upside down: poetry too pure to be shared by all never achieves its full potential value:

> Be·l saupra plus cobert far;
> mas non a chans pretz enter
> can tuch no·n son parsoner.
> (Gr Bor 4, 8–10)

I could easily have made it more obscure; but a song does not have its full worth when all are not sharers in it.

That Giraut intends this to be paradoxical is clear from his description of
the aristocratic *pretz enter* as something to be found even in the voice of a
hoarse servant who has gone to fetch well water:

> Qui que·s n'azir, me sap bo,
> can auch dire per contens
> mo sonet rauquet e clar
> e l'auch a la fon portar.
> (Gr Bor 4, 11–14)

No matter who is angered by it, I savor it when I hear my song
sung in rivalry, both hoarse and clear, and hear it carried to the
wellspring.

The kind of "sharing" to which Giraut refers is access not only to the
understanding of poetry but to its performance as well. He draws on the
idea of the *fon* as a source of inspiration; even the lowliest performer who
"takes the song to the wellspring" will contribute new lines to it, will recast and recreate its imperfect passages, will "refresh" it.

Peire d'Alvernhe, in 1170, calls Giraut's music "thin and sad," "the
song of an old woman with a bucket." Answering Giraut's idea of integrity through communality, and at the same time replying to Bernart
Marti's attacks, Peire defends the poet's personal responsibility for his
song and (with a touch of comedy) returns *pretz* to a matter of beauty
and not politics. The poet's "vanity," so disparaged by Bernart Marti, is
quite suitable by comparison with the vanity of the "viella porta-seill"
who dares try her voice at the *canso*. As Peire pictures for us the old
bucket woman donning the persona of the *canso*'s poet/lover and gazing
into the mirror, the reflection we glimpse is of a burlesque Giraut in drag;
the typical modesty of the lover is transformed into the old woman's comment on her beauty ("not worth an eglantine"):

> Q'es chans de viella porta-seill
> que si·s mirava en espeill
> no·s prezari'un aiguilen.
> (P d'Alv 12, 16–18)

For it is the song of an old woman, a bucket carrier, who, if she
saw herself reflected in a mirror, would not value herself worth
an eglantine.[16]

Can such a performer confer *pretz enter* on a song, when her own *pretz* is "hardly worth a stick"? Peire makes uproarious fun of Giraut's faith in literary partnership with humble folk ("can tuch en son parsoner"). The beauty of "carrying the song to the wellspring" is lost on a singer who would use even the *fons Bandusiae* for dishwater. She is the antithesis of the powerful lady whom the *canso* honors, and who in turn does honor to the *canso* by learning to sing it. Peire lets the bucket woman stand as the disheveled Muse of Giraut's aesthetic democracy, capable of frank self-judgment but unlikely to beautify a song.

In this exchange, then, it would appear that Giraut's views on textual integrity—comparable to those he expressed in the *tenso* with Raimbaut d'Aurenga over *trobar clus* versus *trobar leu*—concern accessibility or exclusivity to the performer, not just to the listener. This is consistent with other ideas Giraut defends: the initial composition of a song as the first stone in a tower "only half-built here" and completed through a long process of interchange, and the idea that a poet can no longer take full credit for his works once they enter the public domain. Peire d'Alvernhe, if he heard the *tenso,* would probably have sided with Raimbaut d'Aurenga: *rauquet* or *enraumatz,* a *vilain* is more likely to damage a song than to improve it.

"Dry Verse"

In "Cantarai d'aquestz trobadors," Peire d'Alvernhe criticizes Giraut above all for his dryness: "e sembla oire sec al soleil" (and he resembles a dry wineskin in the sun). The troubadours appear to associate dryness with a sort of insincerity or inconstancy: Peire Vidal brings alive the double meaning of *pics* (woodpecker; or, as adj., piebald, black and white; changing, inconstant), suggesting that the dryness, or untrustworthiness, of the woodpecker comes from the fact that he has "his mouth full of garbage":

> Et es assatz plus secs que pics
> e non pretz tot quant elh retrai
> sa boca plena d'orrethai.
> (P Vid 25, 82–83)

And he is somewhat more dry than a woodpecker, and I do not deem valuable all that he reports [with] his mouth full of garbage.

Raimbaut d'Aurenga associates the dry with the deaf: "Car sabran li sec e·il sort . . ." (For dry men and deaf men will know . . .). *Sec* describes an interference with *entendre* in both senses, deflecting intention as well as understanding.

Alegret's *vers sec* turns on a *rime équivoque* that reappears in the first line of each stanza; the refrain word *sec*, one of the "dos motz ab divers sens" (two words with varying meanings), sets equivocation itself as the theme for some stanzas—equivocation, hypocrisy, insincerity.[17] The *mal sec* that afflicts Larguetatz in lines 22–25 seems harmless, creeping up, imperceptible to the hearing, sight, and touch until it suddenly "skins and plucks" its victim. Dry people promise more than they accomplish:

> Aqill son dinz e defor sec
> escas de fag e larc de ven
> e pagan home de nien.
> (Alegret, "Ara pareisson ll'aubre sec"
> [P.-C. 17,2], 29–31; in Riquer 1975, 239)

These people are dry inside and out, stingy with deeds and generous with wind, and they pay a man with nothing.

They are "windbags" (*larc de ven*). The association of *sec* with contract breaking or "paying with nothing" leads into a suggestion of stinginess: "Joven vei fals e flac e sec / c'a pauc de cobeitat no fen" (I see Youth so false and weak and dry that it nearly bursts with coveting; vv. 15–16). The natural "dry trees" of the opening lines, in their setting of wintry fog and lightless or "unclear weather" (vv. 1–4), become the biblical dry trees that can bear no fruit, just as "malvatz hom no poc esser valen" (a bad man cannot become worthy; vv. 13–14). This theme appears in numerous sirventes, including Marcabru's challenge to Alegret:

> Alegretz, fols, en qual guiza
> cujas far d'avol valen
> ni de gonella camiza?
> (Mcb 11, 65–67)

Alegret, you madman, by what trick do you expect to make the base into the worthy, or trousers into a shirt?

For Alegret, "dryness" or equivocation is despicable in every situation but one: it is *avol* for youth, liberality, patronage, and love, yet *valen* as a device of versification, of rhyme and wordplay. His entire poem turns on the shifting meanings of the word *sec;* while denouncing shifty people, it celebrates the shifty style.

Alegret anticipates objection to his *vers sec,* and his challenge to its detractors focuses on defending the style rather than the moral content of the song. *Non-saben* (know-nothings) who equate *sec* with *avol* might also equate *vers sec* with *vers avol.* But the listener must "double his understanding": Alegret is willing to prove, by fistfight if necessary, that he is too good a poet to blunder. He "foams up" the words on purpose:

> Hueymais fenirai mon vers sec,
> e parra pecx al non saben
> si no·i dobla l'entendemen,
> q'ieu sui cell que·ls mots escuma
> e sai triar los auls dels avinentz;
> e si fols ditz qu'aissi esser non dec,
> traga s'enan, qu'Alegretz n'es guirens.
>
> Si negus es del vers contradizens,
> fassa·s'enan, q'eu dirai per que·m lec
> metr' en est vers dos motz ab divers sens.
> (Alegret [P.-C. 17,2], 50–59; in Riquer 1975, 240)

Now I will finish my dry poem, and it will appear stupid to a know-nothing if he does not double the interpretation, for I am he who foams up the rhymes, and I know how to separate the bad ones from the suitable ones; and if a fool says that it should not be this way, let him come forward, for Alegret is its protector.

If anyone is a contradictor of the poem, let him come forward, for I will tell why I allow myself to set in this poem two words with various meanings.

Alegret's repeated request that his critic "come forward" suggests a challenge to combat, but it may be that instead Alegret wishes him to "contradire lo ver" in some form of public debate. One possibility is that the "fool" who "says that it should not be this way" would be charged to recite the poem as he believes it should be, the "counterversion" qualifying him as *contradizens.*

The poet, too, is a "dry tree" that puts forth no rhetorical flowers when he lacks the "sap" of inspiration: a troubadour may be *sec* when he cannot "express" his complaint in poetic flowers and leaves. It is this blocking of expression that Peire d'Alvernhe struggles to overcome in the sirventes "Belh m'es qu'ieu fass' oimais un vers":

> si que flurisc e bruelh defors
> so que dedins mi gragelha.
>
> (P d'Alv 15, 7–8)

So that what grumbles within me may bloom and leaf out, outwardly.

In this poem, *sec* is the final blow in a long accumulation of adjectives denouncing those who "fan que quascus aprent un quec" (bring it about that each of them should learn something or other). What the dry people have tried to learn, the "un quec" in question, is a song; Peire lets us know this by describing the results of this education as a parody of genuine creativity. The real troubadour, when he makes a new song, "nais e cresc e bruoill" (is born and grows and bushes out), his words blossoming like spring branches. But for these low-born "degenerates," "volpillos, blau d'enveja, sec" (negligent, white with envy, dry; v. 38), the excitement of "learning *un quec*" causes them to break out in boils:

> fan que quascus aprent un quec
> don nays e bruelha·l pustelh.
>
> (P d'Alv 15, 39–40)

They arrange that each one may learn a [little] something, from which cause a boil is born and leafs out.

Peire's comment on Giraut's "dryness," then, may include both reproof of his populism (suggesting that the uninspired and vulgar can mimic but never invent good poetry) and a response to Giraut's claims for the refreshment of the public fountain. The "dry-wineskin" poet may hear his songs "carried to the wellspring," but the Muses' wineskin is empty, and likely to be refilled with the commonest water.

Giraut's answer to the criticism of resembling "a dry wineskin in the sun" (or perhaps part of what provoked that criticism) comes in his "Leu chansonet'e vil" ("Light little song and lowly"), a poem composed especially to be sent to Alvernhe (*al Dalfi* [to the Dauphin], though, and not to Peire):

> Car ges aiga de vi
> no fetz Deus al manjar

ans se volc esalzar
e fetz esdevenir
d'aiga qu'er ans
pois vi per melhs grazir.
(Gr Bor 48, 15–20)

> For not at all did God make water from wine at the feast, but
> rather he wished to exalt himself, and he caused what was for-
> merly water to become wine, the better to confer grace.

Sharing with the public the "wine of poetry," by the same token, does not
instantly convert it to water. The poet who wishes to "s'esalzar" and
"melhs grazir" should follow the example of Christ, and having transformed something common (ordinary language, water) into something
precious (a song, wine), he should distribute it freely in proportion as the
original substance was plentiful. Rarity and expensiveness, says Giraut,
do not guarantee excellence in a song; the troubadour's work is a craft,
not a parade of furs and jewels. This is his objection to *trobar car* and *ric*
("rare" and "rich poetry"): a craftsman cannot sharpen his tools on a
sable cape (a symbol of lavish payment for poetry, as well as of "soft"
poetry) even if he has received such "rich" compensation for "rich" work:

E qui de fort fozil
no vol coltel tochar
ja no·l cut afilar
en un mol sembeli.
(Gr Bor 48, 11–14)

> And anyone who is unwilling to strike his knife on a strong
> whetstone certainly can never expect to sharpen it on a soft
> sable.

For Giraut, the general public is the strongest "whetstone" (*fort fozil*) for
a poem, and their "sharpening" a better recompense for the poet than
furs and other wealth.

Writing and Monumentalism:
Some Modern and Medieval Views

Concern for the preservation of one's works has no doubt changed in character since the Middle Ages. For the modern author, "preserving" one's

works means supervising one's publisher. The poet studies the typesetter's proof sheets, requests fine paper and sewn binding to improve the durability of the book, campaigns for wide distribution, and finally buys up all the unsold copies to save them from being "pulped." One must, if possible, issue a *Collected Poems* late in life, to make sure one's best work, at least, does not go out of print before it has time to become a classic.

Air and stone (or the voice and the inscription) as two opposing media for poetry have long fascinated poets who could look back on the durable literature of antiquity, or of the nearer past. Aware of composing in sound rather than in printer's lead, the modern poet often seems to envy by turns the immortality of stones and the immortality of the nightingale. Basil Bunting, a poet who destroys his "imperfect" works, appears to distrust the printed word as sufficiently permanent to preserve the poems he has chosen to publish: "Pens are too light / Take a chisel to write" (1978, 41).

In "Briggflatts," Bunting's metaphor of the poet as stonecutter makes the analogue of the poem the ultimate monument: the tombstone. Yet other works are ambivalent: Bunting describes the words of his "Ode 33: To Anne Porter" as "a peal after / the bells have rested" (1978, 106). Robinson Jeffers with optimism compared poets to "stonecutters fighting time with marble": the "foredefeated" and "cynical" builders, like the poet who "builds his monuments mockingly," underestimate the power of stones and poems to weather the fall of civilizations (1925, 249). These poets come late in a long tradition of monumentalism. Shakespeare calls it a "miracle" "that in black ink my love may still shine bright" (*Sonnets* 65, 14), yet expects no less than that miracle: "Not marble, nor the gilded monuments / of princes, shall outlive this powerful rhyme" (*Sonnets* 55, 1–2). Horace, who could perhaps count on readers who read aloud, insisted that verse could be both permanent and alive. The dance measures he had transformed into a metal harder than bronze, making of them a "monument," could still escape oblivion through oral performance: *dicar* (I will be recited; *Odes* 3.30). The Occitan troubadours appear to be much more interested in "gathering from the air a live tradition"[18] and, having shaped it into song, returning it "alive" to the air it came from. Peire d'Alvernhe asks a viscount to do what he will with his song, "but please do not keep it silent" (*e que no·i l'en teigna nec;* Zenker 1901, 798). Pons de la Guardia hopes his song will find favor so that "it will be sung in many a good place" thereafter.[19] All the troubadours' references to memorization and relay point to the idea that circulation in performance meant more to these poets than did scrupulous control over the precise words to be sung. Poetry was the "air they breathed," not their graveyard.

Instead of fussing over manuscripts, the troubadours fuss over performance, believing perhaps that one's songs were sufficiently preserved if they remained alive, regenerating themselves with each new recitation. The poet-as-phoenix has no need of a "well wrought urn" for his ashes:

> Plus que ja fenis fenics
> non er q'ieu non si'amics.
> (R d'Aur 4, 64–65)

> No more than the phoenix was ever finished will I ever stop being your friend.

The persona of the lover, as well as something of the poet behind it, revives with each new voice taking up the song:

> Amiga, tant vos sui amics
> q'az autras paresc enemics
> e vuelh esser en vos Fenics
> qu'autra jamais non amarai
> et en vos m'amor fenirai.
> (P Vid 35, 90–94)

> My friend, I am so much your friend that I seem an enemy to other women, and I wish to be a phoenix in you, for I will never love another and in you I will complete my love.

Both of these passages, the first from Raimbaut d'Aurenga and the second from Peire Vidal, are *tornadas*—the usual location for poets' comments on the song itself and its destiny. The simplest interpretation, in each case, is that the poet's *amiga*, like Peire Rogier's patronesses, will learn the song and thus "resuscitate" the voice of the poet. Peire Vidal's use of the phoenix occurs at the end of his last datable song (1204–1207; Avalle 1960, 286), but even a young poet might enjoy the prospect of "being a phoenix in" the memorizing patron's voice.

Rigaut de Berbezilh, in "Atressi com l'orifans" ("Just like the elephant"), wishes he were artful enough to transform his song into something perfectly artless. If he could "contrafar fenis" (36–37), this self-immolation would destroy the "voice" of the "controlling poet" and would thus free the song of all its artifice, indeed of its very words. The song would live again as pure emotive utterance (sighs and tears) in the addressee's safekeeping:

> e mos fals ditz messongiers e truans
> resorsera en sospirs e en plors
> la on beutatz e iovenz e valors
> es . . .

(R Berb 2, 40–43)

> And my false speech, lying and truant, will rise again in sighs
> and in tears, there where beauty and youth and worth are . . .

The troubadours seem to have been conscious of a phenomenon we can observe retrospectively in the *chansonniers*. To transmit a song is to transform it: a single poem, both by rearrangement of stanzas and by abundance of variants in detail, comes down to us in a great many avatars. The lyric "phoenix" could take many different shapes, emerging into each new life with its structure significantly altered.

In summary, we have no reason to suppose—and good reason not to suppose—that literary self-consciousness, or a need to make salable commodities of their works, or even concern for reputation and posterity, should have compelled troubadour poets to commit their works to parchment. All of these motives can be satisfied independently of writing. The troubadours developed a different kind of monumentalism from that which depends on printed publication and copyright—a monumentalism no less flattering to the self-conscious poet, no less profitable, and no less concerned with posterity. Each new learner of a song speaks partly with the voice of the original poet and partly with his own voice: he can use the poem for fame or for profit, he can teach it to singers of another generation, and he can tell or withhold the name of the original poet:

> E diga·l can l'aura apres
> qui que s'en vuelha azautar.
>> E si hom li demanda qui l'a fag, pot dir que sel que sap be far
>> totas fazendas can se vol.

(R d'Aur 24, 40–43)

> And let him recite it, when he has learned it, anyone who
> wishes to embellish it. And if someone asks him who com-

posed it, he can say it was that man who knows how to create all kinds of things when he wants to.

A system of transmission that depended primarily on sung performance could not satisfy a desire for letter-perfect transmission comparable to that of Scripture, or of modern printed poetry. But as I have shown, that type of literalism runs counter to the predominant spirit of troubadour song.

CONCLUSION

Because troubadour poetry was so central to the beginnings of European lyric poetry in the vernacular, it has been reinterpreted by each generation of poets and readers who discovered it for themselves. Thirteenth-century biographers found true stories hidden in the songs and used them as springboards to fictional creation; the grammarians found in them examples of correct and incorrect usage. Dante saw in this poetry not only models of versification but also models of love and of political action. Italian scholars of the Renaissance, such as Barbieri, traced their national lyric tradition back to the troubadours, and never tired of comparing the old and the new.

On the horizon, no end to this need for reinterpretation has appeared. The twentieth-century reader can bring to troubadour poetry some kinds of insight that were never before possible. Meanwhile, some of the materials for interpretation have fallen by the wayside. For example, to recapture the political allusions in a *sirventes* may require years of detective work; fine, if the poet was well-documented in his time, but otherwise half his meaning can elude us. I have identified and explored an equally fundamental category of knowledge needed by the modern reader—needed but forgotten, since the advent of book culture, because of literary assumptions made by generations of readers who received troubadour songs as written poetry.

"Adjusting the Ash Heaps": Paper Poetry

Our own century has seen the complete identification of the poem with the page it is written on. After Mallarmé's ventures into the mysteries of "the white page" and *poésie pure,* the invention of the typewriter allowed poets to compose in the standardized visual shapes of the alphabet, where before that was possible only for poets who doubled as typesetters.

Guillaume Apollinaire and Marianne Moore used the physical bound-aries of the page to set a visual frame around their compositions, and the shapes of the letters themselves nearly replace the voice. Yet "the sanctity of the poetic text" remains an essential issue, even in this kind of mostly "immobile" poetry. Let me illustrate with an example of textual mobility from the print history of Marianne Moore.

Of Moore's "The Fish" Hugh Kenner observes, "It is a poem con-ceived in a typewriter upon an 8½" × 11" sheet of paper" (1975, 99). The reader will recall its counted syllabic rhythm, its visual shape mimetic of the "injured fan" and "ash heaps" under constant "adjustment" by wa-tery bivalves (Moore 1951/1961, 37). After the poem's third appearance in print, Moore changed its typographical layout, merging a one-syllable line with the previous line. Kenner writes: "It is not a trivial change, since it affects the system by which pattern intersects utterance, alters the points at which the intersections occur, provides a new grid of impedi-ments to the over-anxious voice. . . . We can nearly say that we have a *new* poem, arrived at in public and without changing a word, by applying a system of transformations to an existing poem" (1975, 100).

This much is certain: memory and re-creation shaped troubadour song, just as the typewriter shaped the poetry of Marianne Moore. Or, just as visual shape was essential to the *Calligrammes* of Guillaume Apol-linaire, just so essentially the troubadours' object of desire, and hence of expression, was an auditory shape. What the page itself can mean for a twentieth-century poet, the voice itself meant for twelfth-century Occitan poets. Their poetry needed, above all, to survive in the minds and memo-ries of those who heard and sang it: parchment survival, at best, could offer a memento of a living performance. At the most fundamental level, this new knowledge of the troubadours' medium inevitably changes our reading of every song.

"Her" and "Him": *Amor* Consists of Language

Once we recognize the subtext of songs apparently about love but also about poetics, we rediscover a stratum of meaning that has scarcely been touched by studies on the troubadours' philosophy of love. The poet questions his voice, the voices of his immediate audience and of strangers who eventually will sing his song. "She," the feminine Other in many songs, is not just the autobiographical object of affections but represents all potentially benevolent alterity, particularly the alterity of the audience that will challenge the song and transform it. To win *merce*—the audience's acclaim or the lady's kiss—the poet must triumph in speech. Love, in the context of troubadour lyric, consists of speech, and stands for the much more generalized desire, not limited to poetry but epitomized in it, to reach others perfectly with words. The congruity of *eros* and *logos* in this tradition, then, should not prompt us to fabricate amatory biographies, but rather should alert us to the poets' preoccupations with matters much more abstract.

One might cite a comparable case in modern poetry, where the questioning of a single presupposition has allowed a new approach to interpretation. In the poetry of Emily Dickinson, the masculine pronoun *he*, and other evocations of the masculine, exert inexorable and often violent power over the speaker: "He put the Belt around my life— / I heard the Buckle snap." In an essay on Dickinson, Adrienne Rich rejects threadbare assumptions about the way poets convert experience into art; she thereby escapes the literalism of some biographical criticism:

> Much energy has been invested in trying to identify a concrete, flesh-and-blood male lover whom Dickinson is supposed to have renounced, and to the loss of whom can be traced the secret of her seclusion and the vein of much of her poetry. But the real question, given that the art of poetry is an art of transformation, is how this woman's mind and imagination may have used the masculine element in the world at large. (1979, 164–165)

By reading Dickinson's poems without assuming that "he" stood for an *amor de lonh,* Rich concludes that the poet's obsessive subject is neither a real man nor an ideal man but her "relationship with the daemon—her own active, creative power" (p. 170). "The pronoun is masculine; the antecedent is what Keats called 'The Genius of Poetry'" (p. 174). The legend of Emily Dickinson's secret life, like the Old Provençal *vidas* depicting the troubadours actually pining away for love, can stand in the way of our view of the poet as a conscious artist. Conflict or harmony between the sexes can, among other things, represent a problem of poetic creation.

This insight comes alive in many contexts, as we shift our attention from dualities of pleasure and pain to the spectrum of creative action. Understanding that a poet can identify himself or the lady with the poem, that it was common practice to fully exploit the analogous roles of *amador* and *trobador,* and that much of the courtly vocabulary does double service as a vocabulary of poetics has armed us with a lexicon of poetic terminology and a repertory of topoi formerly unrecognized as belonging to the register of poetics. In Part One, this approach to reading yielded direct statements from the poets themselves about the creation and transmission of their works. The words of the song bridge any time between composition and performance; in becoming aware of the separateness of the poet and the potential "other" singer, we are able to see how the poet both shares his mask and separates himself, drawing back from the jongleur to instruct him, and how the performer repeats, adopts, or reinterprets those admonitions. In Part Two, it allowed us to balance the poets' own comments on the rhyme schemes versus the mutability of their poetry against the external, objective evidence provided by manuscript copies and by modern schematizations of rhyme schemes. Stability *could* result from metrical complexity, and many poets expected as much. In Part Three, the structural isomorphy of *amar* and *trobar* enabled us to clarify some of the literary terminology and imagery associated with textual integrity.

At the level of meaning where poetry speaks of itself, the troubadours have demonstrated their awareness of *mouvance*. Some have expressed their ideals regarding the circulation of their work. Many demand of their audience something more than to pay attention: they ask auditors to re-create the song *well*. A public of *entendadors* could have been expected to do this. Like modern poets, who are aware that their books will be purchased and read primarily by other poets, the Occitan troubadours could expect a high level of literary discrimination in these audiences accustomed to learning and circulating songs. When the audience participates in creation, a troubadour song cannot stand as a purely personal statement; instead it offers a persona to be worn by many, a form, subject, and stance to be represented at other times and in other places.

A Diversity of Viewpoints on Textual Integrity Versus *Mouvance*

Jaufre Rudel recognized early that transmitters would take part in circulating and re-creating his songs. His conception of the *razo* as prior to "the way the rhyme goes" may reflect an existing tradition, reinforced by practical realities, of nonsequential composition. Performers had to learn or create a sense of the argument's progression, because only the beginning and the end of a song were clearly marked to indicate their position and function, but stanzas in the middle were not. In the absence of sestinalike stanzaic linkage, only *razo*, or a workable conception to guide the movement and progression of the song's sense, could array the central stanzas appropriately. And Jaufre allowed that conception to be a function of the singer's understanding, not exclusively a product of his own original creation. Despite his place in the mainstream of the development of *fin'amors*, Jaufre was an extremist as regards transmission. He is more explicit than most others in his invitation to improve his songs, and, on nearly every graph of my statistical study, he is an excessively mutable "outlier."

Certainly, it is clear that many troubadours parted ways with Jaufre: Marcabru and poets like him valued authentic, "natural" transmission and sought "legitimacy." But the transmitting culture, from the time the troubadours composed until the *chansonniers* were compiled, refused to support the notion of a fixed text. The singer's importance as a character in the courtly lyric reflects his role in shaping what poets could or could not expect to achieve through their medium; of necessity, poets either accommodated the transmitters or complained about them. A few appear to have idealized the fixed text—fixed, that is, in ways that were important to *them;* the troubadours' ideal of fixity often leaves out the notion of sequential stability. Fewer still took effective action toward the ideal of sequential fixity. Yet those who *did* take such action could do so spectacularly when they chose to.

The notion of the fixed text is related to social concepts that some poets valued and others tended to reject. Closure, exclusive distribution, and strict observance of legitimacy—these poetic and social "goods" were valued to protect the transmission of property and power in a feudal hierarchy that was changing in the twelfth century. That words could pass like currency from one to another, at a time when money was on the rise as a form of exchange, discouraged the idea of poetry as an authentic, original, pedigreed object and thus inhibited the success of the budding concept of the vernacular lyric as a fixed text.

Ambivalence toward the idea of fixing the text is the rule rather than the exception. Marcabru, the possessive poacher, the cuckoo in the nest, who seeks closure only for his *own* garden, takes a consciously mixed and even hypocritical stance on the issue of stability versus accessibility. Overall, he jealously (and ineffectively) champions the authentic text.

Nevertheless, several poets consistently friendly to the transmitter acknowledge the possibility of loss in performance but conclude that if a song is never heard, its perfection matters little. Giraut de Bornelh severely castigates the irresponsible jongleur Cardalhac and compares the competition of unoriginal jongleurs to that of grackles and peacocks, yet overall he opposes exclusivity in performance. Bernart Marti, who scoffs at *vers entiers,* as well as poets who call on the addressee to aid in circulating their songs—Rigaut de Berbezilh, Peire Rogier, Pons de la Guardia, Peire Vidal—all speak somewhat protectively of their songs, expressing optimism that the addressee can be trusted to reproduce their songs well and in good faith. Berenger de Palazol adapts his songs to the capabilities of his primary audience, thus protecting them from immediate and severe rearrangement but at the same time releasing them to the care of his hearers. Bertran de Born answers a jongleur's request for songs with an anti-jongleur song: like Gioglaret of the muddy cape, Mailolis could scarcely be trusted with a delicate work of art. In any case, we see that trust or distrust of transmitters was a central issue in the second half of the twelfth century. How far could they go as perfectionist poets and still retain singers and audiences?

Among those who did envision an ideal of textual stability, even poets who consistently criticize their transmitters still occasionally commend them. Raimbaut d'Aurenga, who argues in favor of restricted transmission, also praises the singing voice of the jongleur Levet and dedicates songs to his Joglar; in the *no-say-que-s'es,* he invites recital by anyone capable of memorizing the song. In the *tenso,* Raimbaut identifies what was in fact most significant in increasing stanzaic permutation: popularity. He understands that the less frequently a song is repeated, the less change it will undergo. But even Raimbaut recognizes the absurdity in ensuring perfection at the price of oblivion.

Peire d'Alvernhe, who usually follows Marcabru in validating only the original version, may be the author of the song "Bel m'es lo dous chans per la faia," where a viscount is invited to correct false words; but even Peire's views on literary property and textual integrity are mixed, and in "Cantarai d'aquestz trobadors" he makes light of the theft of literary property in his vignette of Peire de Monzo.

The hypothesis that the troubadours invented their complex verse forms in order to protect their songs' stanzaic sequence has not proven entirely groundless. The efficacy of these forms in reducing *mouvance* may have been evident to the poets as they listened to early performances. What is surprising for the modern reader is that the poets used forms like *coblas capfinidas* so rarely. Surely a poem is destroyed, its intention fundamentally subverted, if the sequence of its stanzas is altered by a performer. However obvious this principle may seem today, I find evidence that only a few troubadours before 1200 believed it. In experimenting with rhyme schemes, certain poets found schemes that would help to fix the sequence; yet even these poets discard the idea. Arnaut Daniel's sestina simultaneously creates and destroys the possibility of fixing the order of stanzas: the poem is, as Jernigan (1974) shows, a satire; I believe its target, *lo ferm volers,* is "the firm intention" as well as "the firm desire." The obsessive repetition of rhymes, required by the form that "confirms" the sequence of stanzas, accumulates; but instead of conferring seriousness, dignity, and gravity on the rhyme structure, it invites us to laugh, just as audiences laugh when for the fourth and the fifth time Punch utters the one word that will make Judy strike him with a broomstick. Arnaut's sestina is an experiment, a demonstration: only one other of his eighteen extant poems makes use of stanzaic linkage for the possible purpose of fixing the sequence. As I have shown, fewer than ten percent of troubadour poems use stanzaic linkage other than simple *coblas doblas.*

This body of poetry, then, evidently developed without—and even perhaps rejected—an assumption today considered vital to poetry and to its interpretation: the imperative to preserve an intended sequence of words, lines, and stanzas. This means that some kinds of interpretation are entirely inappropriate. In reading fixed written poetry, we can assume an implicitly reasoned progression of argument or of imagery. For most troubadour song, to infer reasoning from one sequence (especially from the sequence of an editor's composite version) would be presumptuous. At the very least, the reader of troubadour poetry needs to know whether the sequence he judges necessary and meaningful can hold primacy over rival versions: is it merely one of eight possible arrangements, evenly represented by sixteen manuscripts, or is it the one sequence preferred by nine copies out of ten? Has the poet provided signposts to mark an intended order? These are questions that the informed reader can no longer neglect to ask.

Nonsequential Reading, Multiple Reading, and the "Open" Text: Adapting to Medieval Reception of Troubadour Lyric

This is not to say that sequence was a matter of indifference to the troubadours, performers, and audiences. Rather, the "literary" experience of troubadour audiences probably included hearing each song more than once and in more than one form. This multiple "literary" experience also, for at least some contemporary audience members, allowed them to participate in the creation of new forms. We can thus use sequences (taking sequence as a unity of meaning in itself) to reconstruct the reception of a particular song—the way in which it, as an ontological whole, was perceived by its audience—only by studying the poem in all its sequential forms. For a poem that comes down to us in three orders, for example

$$1\ 2\ 3\ 4\ 5\ 6$$
$$1\ 3\ 2\ 5\ 4\ 6$$
$$1\ 6\ 2\ 3\ 4\ 5,$$

we must understand three different *aspects* of the same song—at least three performances (or writings) in which the emphasis, progression, and argument developed the strengths and interrelations of the given stanzas in three unique ways. If it is possible to prove one of the versions "authentic" and the others not, fine, let us privilege the "authentic" sequence.[1] Otherwise we must acknowledge the medieval audience's plural experience of the song. Who is to say that medieval audiences did not *prefer* new permutations of old songs—that they did not enjoy hearing "Can vei la lauzeta mover" nine different ways? If medieval audiences did take pleasure in such subtle variations on texts they knew by ear, then surely the pleasure of renewal derives partly from intense awareness of the sequence (and thus of the line-of-argument or *razo*) rather than from aesthetic indifference to sequence. The idea that variation was valued as a good, rather than hated as a violation, is supported by the fact that the most popular songs are the most variously permuted songs.

The often authorized textual mutability of troubadour poetry brings strongly to mind the "open work" described by Umberto Eco (1965). Especially in view of Zumthor's idea of the sort of lyric "keyboard" of conventional motifs from various registers that can be "actualized" at will, in endless combinations, the movable text finds its counterpart in a musical composition Eco uses to illustrate *opera aperta:* "the work constitutes less a piece than a field of possibilities, an invitation to choose. *Scambi* is composed of sixteen sections, of which each can be connected to two others—without, however, compromising the logical continuity of the sound movement" (1965, 15). An "open work" would be one that invites recombination and permutation, and its meaning, its ability to carry specific information, would be accordingly problematic. This is not merely the openness of all art, open in the sense that it becomes particularized to its audience at the moment of its consumption or interpretation (cf. Eco 1965, 17), but the openness of a work that lacks some element of authorial control in its very constitution and, as such, awaits the receiver/performer as its co-author.

The "open" musical works described by Eco, when performed, become sequential. The "open" works of Bernart de Ventadorn and Jaufre Rudel also become sequential when performed or written out. Yet these sequences, constituted by performance, carry with them the potentiality of other sequences. No one performance is the "complete" work.

In place of the inappropriate assumption that each work of art can admit of only one sequence, we will have to develop an understanding of simultaneous structures in poetry, or rather of structure that assumes the sequence of performance but not the single *necessary* sequence of fixed poetry. Bernart de Ventadorn's "Can vei la lauzeta mover" was successful in its multiple sequences; can Bernart have foreseen them and have designed his *coblas unissonans* to cohere in any order? My findings suggest that he probably did. The "topic development" described by Ghil (1979) may have belonged to the fine art of creating flexible poetry, capable of withstanding popular transmission.

Pickens's edition of Jaufre Rudel (1978), then, offers a very desirable model for future editions of troubadour poetry—especially for poets who seem willingly to consent to *mouvance*—given what we now know about the importance that many poets assigned to transmitters in the continuing creation of their poetry. But only six songs of Jaufre survive. Such an edition is not practicable in every case; for example, to make such an edition of Giraut de Bornelh's work, with nearly eighty songs, would be a Herculean task. Fortunately, the serious reader can extract much of the needed information from the critical apparatus of existing editions. With Carl Appel's *Bernart von Ventadorn* (1915), for example, the readers are equipped to construct for themselves a mental "edition," on Pickens's model, of a given poem; they would lack only the certainty provided by comparison of actual manuscripts. Although few readers will have occasion to reconstruct a dozen versions of "Can vei la lauzeta," even beginning readers of Provençal poetry deserve to know to what extent they can base their interpretation of a poem on its details of language, its progression of ideas, and the resolution of its ending.

"Informed Readers" in Literary Theory

Most experts today still read troubadour lyric as if it followed the principles of style and stability we expect in poetry written after the invention of the printing press. Indeed, some find it hampering to scholarship to be deprived of any of the techniques available to modern literary criticism. William Calin would like to eradicate the "otherness" of medieval poetry altogether, viewing the denial that sequence bears meaning as "denigrating the beauty of the past." He makes a strong case for the meaningfulness of stanzaic sequence in sung lyric (1983, 76; see discussion at the end of Part Three). I would like to emphasize, however, that we need not disassociate meaning from stanzaic sequence, but only disassociate it from an expectation of finding there the "original poet's single intended meaning." Calling on modern reception theory to legitimize the twentieth-century audience and its unprecedented possibilities for the interpretation of Old French poetry, Calin asserts, "Any approach is valid provided that it respect the text and not denigrate the beauty of the past":

> Whatever our views on the Otherness of the Middle Ages as history, culture, mind-set, and so on, it is our duty to apply the same critical approaches that we apply to modern ones. . . . Our triumphs now lie in the remarkable number of books and articles devoted to practical criticism: scrutinizing, examining, and rehabilitating all the major and minor masterpieces of the French Middle Ages. (p. 90)

Whether or not Calin's praise of "practical criticism" intentionally alludes to the I. A. Richards variety (just the kind of approach that could lead to presumptuous readings of troubadour songs as "fixed texts"), one can clearly see in his exhortation a unique effort to blend New Criticism with Reception Theory. We should not misunderstand Calin's advice: he is not, I am sure, calling for a scholarly free-for-all that "rehabilitates" medieval texts by misreading them. One of the best contributions of New Criticism has been to prescribe carefulness and precision in reading. After New Criticism, we can never again be satisfied, as Romantic critics sometimes were, with commenting on "general impressions" and "waves of feeling" created by unspecified elements of a given poem. Thus, there is no need to unlearn all of the disciplined reading habits instilled by New Criticism or to avoid other forms of literary theory that sprang from the study of modern literature. These methods can be *adapted* to the medieval lyric, in full consciousness that we cannot completely succeed in reproducing the experience of the medieval audience, but knowing that it is worthwhile to try.

Indeed, the types of reading that only our century can bring to medieval poetry—psychoanalytic, structuralist and anthropological, speech-act, deconstructionist, and so forth—do enrich the body of reader responses that each troubadour song has accumulated to its credit. The medieval audience was not the only audience; our understanding does matter. New layers of readings, even misreadings, do enhance the perceived richness of this body of poetry. For example, thanks to that moment in the history of Provençal studies when Arnaut Daniel's "e l'olors de noigandres" seemed to fill the air with the perfume of some rare or extinct nut tree, even the correct word division, "d'enoi gandres" (warding off ennui), will for some readers always evoke "noigandres" and exotic nut trees in flower. For Pound readers, "noigandres" probably also evokes Freiburg in early summertime. But these are private associations, or "intertextual" readings relevant to the later text but not to the early one.

The best of applications of twentieth-century ideas to medieval literature are those that provide tools for drawing nearer to medieval literary experience, to compensate for what we, as "nonnative speakers" of medieval vernaculars, no longer know, to make up for our shortcomings of "competency" in the idiom from which these texts were made. For example, a reading that draws on modern arts and sciences can manipulate abstract symbols designating "variables," using mathematics a century or less old and equipment of much more recent vintage to tabulate and interpret data, apply formulas, and generate graphic representations. Such a reading both elucidates medieval reception and reflects an entirely new reception unique to the computer age.

However seductive is the medieval nut tree or however intriguing the juxtaposition of old and new when IBM meets Raimbaut d'Aurenga, first privilege must be given to medieval reception. Otherwise we study our own minds and not Raimbaut's craft. In order to avoid that "affective fallacy" that "begins by trying to derive the standards of criticism from the psychological effects of the poem and ends in impressionism and relativism" (Wimsatt and Beardsley 1954, 21), we have to educate our "affect" and adopt, for "psychological effects," a psyche appropriate to the work under consideration.

Stanley Fish allows himself an "affective stylistics" (affirming what the poem *does* in the reader over what it *is*) only on condition of positing an "*informed* reader," one fully competent in the idiom "out of which the text is built up." He therefore observes:

> In its operation, my method will obviously be radically historical. The critic has the responsibility of becoming not one but a number of informed readers, each of whom will be identified by a matrix of political, cultural and literary determinants. The informed reader of Milton will not be the informed reader of Whitman. . . . The question is not how good it is, but how does it work; and both question and answer are framed in terms of local conditions, which include local notions of literary value.
>
> (1980, 86–88)

What I have tried to do in this study is recapture a portion of that locality, its "conditions" and its "notions of literary value," by examining local definitions of "informed" audiences and transmitters. The study of "what a poem does, how it works," is essentially rhetorical study (sometimes in its details grammatical study) and must thus aim to describe the interactions among the poet, his audience, and his work. The modern "informed" reader is two audiences: one understands as oneself (heeding or suppressing the private vision of nut blossoms), and one does one's best to understand as medieval hearers would.

This latter task, to "be like" a medieval audience, is one that Jauss views as off-limits to the intuition. "Psychology" misleads and traps; logical "analysis" relies on what is "objectifiable."

> Thesis 2. The analysis of the literary experience of the reader avoids the threatening pitfalls of psychology if it describes the reception and influence of a work *within the objectifiable system of expectations that arises for each work in the historical moment of its appearance*, from a pre-understanding of the genre, from the form and themes of already familiar works, and from the opposition between poetic and practical language.
>
> (Jauss 1982, 22; emphasis added)

Jauss's version of the informed reader "objectifies" one's own literary experience in order to describe and analyze another's: one "expects," "pre-understands," and "is familiar with" elements of the poem and its context, but only as a way to mirror what a member of the medieval audience might "expect," "pre-understand," or "be familiar with." The "pitfall" avoided by Jauss's informed reader is thus that of studying oneself as a receiver of the poem.

I would modify Jauss's warning, not to give free rein to the "modern experience of medieval lyric," but to emphasize that the modern reader must be two readers: in order to objectify a medieval system of expectations, one must account for one's own system of expectations and carefully separate one's own literary experience from that which "arises for each work in the historical moment of its appearance."

We must therefore distinguish between anachronistic interpretations (however "beautiful" they may be) and those that attempt to re-create the experience of contemporary audiences. In a sense, modern editors have joined the chain of retransmitters and re-creators; appreciating that they have their place, we should not confuse their essentially twentieth-century texts with medieval texts. The medieval troubadour song should be understood as it was "in the historical moment of its appearance": as an inevitably moving thing. Only then—and with full consciousness of the role played by medieval transmitters and by the modern transmitters who make readable texts available to us—do we earn the right to extoll the beauty of hybrid texts and of the forms that textual criticism, in the last hundred years, has created.

Nevertheless, it is useful to know that for a large segment of the troubadours' medieval audience, the experience of reception was closely linked to the experience of re-creation. To hear a song, to understand it, to learn and retransmit it: these interlocking activities are recommended by the poets—too many to overlook—as suitable responses both from specific addressees and from general audiences. In a sense, the need to re-create the song is a point of convergence between the medieval audience and the modern reader. We are under a similar obligation to the text. We lack the medieval audience's freedom to import our experience wholesale into readings of troubadour texts; I have argued that we ought to abstain from behaving like medieval transmitters by creating new versions and passing them off as "closer to the original text." But insofar as every reading re-creates a text, we should (as medieval audiences knew *they* should) abide by the poets' instructions to the good listener and the good jongleur: we should re-create it well, see that it is circulated in good places, not scramble the words and music, and do what we can to become *entendadors*.

> Cantarey mentre m'estau
> Cantaret ben e leiau
> Che xanton macips de Pau
> (Gm Berg 5, 1–3)

> I will sing, while standing here, a good and legitimate little
> song that the small boys of Pau may sing.

The song remains *leiau* (legitimate) even when street urchins are singing it—boys even more amateurish than the jongleur from Pau to whom Guilhem seems to be alluding. To treat these songs as fixed texts, therefore, is to risk serious misinterpretation.

The reader who reads only one of many versions of a song is at best in the position of a medieval hearer who hears the song only once. Songs are mutable: the poets who compose them change them, and so do their competitors and audiences. Bob Dylan sounds as angry as Marcabru (against the "small-time hornet troubadours") in the September 1974 outtake version of "Idiot Wind":

> I've been double-crossed too much
> At times I think I've almost lost my mind
> Ladykillers load dice on me
> Behind my back while imitators steal me blind.
> (Bowden 1982, 205)

Although the author chose not to release that version (it exists only in a "bootleg" recording; see Bowden 1982, 200), it is part of the lyric entity that the song comprises, a dramatic monologue whose success and effect depend almost entirely on the performance and whose flexibility in the wording reflects that character: it is a performance more than it is a piece of music or poetry. To "understand the song," we would be wrong to create a *composite* version that was never performed, and equally wrong to ignore the "ladykillers" passage above as "inauthentic." But we would be justified in taking all recorded versions as aspects of the *same* song, and in observing carefully which parts of the song remain constant (like the "skeletal song" Pickens isolates for each one of Jaufre Rudel's many-versioned songs) and which parts are subject to momentary conditions: the constitution and mood of the audience, the performer's response to public or private events of the day.

At worst, one-version readers deny themselves not only the possibility of interpreting a moving text credibly, but also the full sense of its interaction with its audience in a performing tradition.

To learn to read troubadour lyrics as songs in constant flux requires us to develop new skills in constructing a *multiple* reading of "the moving text." This could mean a serial reading of all the versions, followed by a synthesis, mustering all available resources (including interpretation of the stanzaic sequence) to do justice to individual realizations, and then evaluating their aggregate. It certainly means that readers will have to discriminate between songs where the "intended sequence" cannot be determined and songs where it can.

With an ideal set of documentation, a song could be analyzed with all its versions and each version explained according to the preferences of the audiences and performers of its region and time; and some versions could then be soundly classed as "inauthentic." In the absence of such ideal documentation, however, we can still learn much more from the *chansonniers*—much more that can be applied to the understanding of these "manifestations of texts . . . like bubbles accidentally rising to the surface" (Pickens 1978, 20). A multiple, simultaneous, or synthesizing reading of a many-faceted and "slippery" text will not come naturally to readers trained on New Criticism, but perhaps it will to readers who learned to read and write on a Macintosh and who, teethed on the mouse, are unperturbed by textual mutability.

Adjusting our reading selves to the alterity of the Middle Ages, which cannot be wished away, and adopting whatever we can learn of the medieval audience's expectations and experience will reward the effort to develop these techniques. The ability to attune our expectations about poetry to the troubadours' own understanding of their medium, and to hold in our minds a moving text in its entirety, will bring us closer to the experience of the medieval audience. It will enrich our comprehension of the songs that gave rhyme and *razo* to the beginnings of Western vernacular lyric.

APPENDIX A

Quantitative Survey
of *Mouvance*

The material in this Appendix is provided in support of claims made in Chapters 4 and 5. The computerized analysis of statistics primarily serves as the basis for Chapter 4; the analysis of stanzaic linkage is of interest for Chapter 5. Fuller interpretations of the results are given in those chapters.

For each of the poets surveyed, a large mass of data was tabulated. Looking at the way these indices show the quantity and manuscript quality of surviving works attributed to him, we develop a profile of each troubadour. From that point, we can compare the artists in terms of their popularity in the transmitting traditions, their susceptibility to version production, their usage of linked stanzas, and the success of their poems in resisting transposition. The list below explains each index and abbreviation.

Components of Each Poet's Data Profile

The following abbreviations are used for raw data:

P   Poem Count: total number of poems attributed to a given poet.

P+   Poems in Multiple Copies: number of his poems surviving in more than one manuscript copy.

T   Transposition Count: number of his poems with more than one stanzaic sequence in comparison of manuscript copies.

A   Array Count: number of his poems with more than one array of stanzas; this includes abridgments as well as transpositions.

M   Manuscripts: total number of manuscript copies of poems attributed to him.

Ma   Manuscripts (unlinked): Total number of manuscript copies of his poems with unlinked stanzas.

V   "Versions Narrowly Defined": total number of *sequentially distinct* versions of his poems (that is, distinguished from one another by stanzaic transposition). V is the counterpart of T: T asks "Does this poem undergo transposition, yes or no?" while V asks "*How many* distinct sequences are there?"

Va   Versions (unlinked): same as V, but only for poems with unlinked stanzas.

W   "Versions Broadly Defined": total number of stanzaic arrays (versions), including abridgments and fracturings as well as stanzaic transposition. W is the counterpart of A: A asks "Does this poem occur in more than one arrangement of stanzas, yes or no?" while W asks "*How many* arrangements are there?"

L   Linkage: number of his poems using linked stanzas.

L+   Linkage (more than one manuscript): number of his poems using linked stanzas *and* surviving in more than one manuscript.

Y   Year: assumed midpoint of poet's life span, using dates given in Riquer 1975 for each poet.

Z   Stanza Length: average number of lines per stanza (total number of lines per stanza in all poems, divided by total number of poems).

The following abbreviations are used for indices derived from the raw data:

TR   Transposition Rate: percentage of poems (in more than one manuscript) that show stanzaic transposition. $TR = T/P+$

MS   Manuscript Survival: average number of manuscripts per poem. $MS = M/P$

VM   Versions (narrowly defined) per Manuscript: average number of versions (distinguished by stanzaic transposition) per manuscript. $VM = V/M$

VMa Versions (narrowly defined) per Manuscript (unlinked):

average number of versions (with transposition) per manuscript, in poems with unlinked stanzas. VMa = Va/Ma

WM   Versions (broadly defined) per Manuscript: average number
of stanzaic arrays, including abridgments as well as
transpositions, per manuscript copy. WM = W/M

LK   Linkage: percent of poems using linked stanzas. LK = L/P

LK+   Linkage (more than one manuscript): percent of poems
using linked stanzas *and* preserved in more than one
manuscript. LK+ = L+/P+

Compilation of Data

The primary data were compiled manually rather than mechanically. No
available machine can conveniently count poems, determine whether or
not there is more than one stanzaic sequence in a poem, and analyze the
rhyme scheme to decide whether stanzas are "linked" or not. Decisions
had to be made during the tabulation; thus, an account of my criteria
is needed.

First, in making the poem counts (P, P+), I eliminated any poems that
were immune from transposition by virtue of their brevity. Since the first
stanza is always stable, I did not count any poems with fewer than three
stanzas extant. Usually such poems exist in only one manuscript anyway,
or their editors mark them "coblas" and take them as incomplete works.
Manuscript copies with three stanzas or fewer were also discounted when
they appeared in certain *chansonniers* designed to present only "coblas"—
selections from favorite poems. The compilers of these collections had no
intention of offering a whole poem but rather only an *estrat* (extract; see
discussion of Ferrari de Ferrara, Chapter 2).

The Transposition Count (T) literally records as having produced
"versions" only those poems that exhibit more than one stanzaic sequence. This is the "narrow definition" of "version." I stayed with the
criterion of "transposition" so strictly that a separate "version" would
not register if a stanza were omitted in the middle of the poem or, as
much more frequently occurs, at the end. For example, in a hypothetical
poem where the sequences are as follows, there was no transposition
(T = "no" = 0) and the number of "sequentially distinct versions" was
recorded as "1" (V = 1):

```
ABDE    1 2 3 4 5
C       1 2   4 5
FGHIK   1 2 3 4
```

Similarly, poems with "fractured strophes," if the fractured strophe did contain lines from the "standard" strophe for its position, were not counted as having extra "versions, narrowly defined."

By the broader definition of "version," the poem just cited would count as having three different "stanzaic arrays." Thus, it would contribute to its author's data profile the following scores: A = "yes" = 1; W = 3.

A source of uncertainty in the data is that the editions used probably vary in the reliability with which they present the information tabulated here. I used the best editions available to me; they range in date from 1909 to 1986, and editorial styles change. A poet's canon may be redefined; more manuscript copies may be discovered or simply used for the first time. Some early editors were able to use only manuscripts that were geographically convenient for them to consult. Modern editors have access to microfilm copies of all the *chansonniers*. Some of the data for Bertran de Born changed, for example, when I was revising this book and switched from the Stimming edition to the new one by Paden, Sankovitch, and Stäblein: his transposition rate (TR) rose from 56 percent to 66 percent, his popularity (MS) rose, and the percentage of poems with linked stanzas (L) rose. Newer editions are not always "better" for this kind of analysis, however; for my statistical purposes I needed data that some excellent newer editions omitted. For example, despite the high quality of Riquer's 1971 edition of Guilhem de Berguedà, I had to omit that poet from my survey because no information on stanzaic sequence was provided. Some of the recent Italian editions of troubadour poets presented the same problem. The tables and charts that follow this discussion are offered as documentation for generalizations made elsewhere. I provide them to assure the reader that my results can be duplicated.

Statistical Analysis

Once the data were gathered, we used a statistical analysis package (SAS) to determine which variables were correlated with one another, and to what degree. The results fall into three groups of correlations: those tied to manuscript survival, those connected with quantifiable formal properties of the poetry (stanza length and linkage), and those related to chronology. Full interpretations of these correlations are presented in Chapter 4. Here, I wish only to make available to the reader the statistical documentation of conclusions presented in Chapter 4 and to offer visual illustrations, through the graphs, of the relative "weakness" and "strength" of correlations discussed.

The correlation matrices (Tables A-3—A-4 below) show two numbers for each pair of variables. The top number (two decimal places) is the correlation coefficient. It measures the strength of the linear relationship between the two variables, that is, how closely the various points, when plotted, fit the model of a straight line. The bottom number (four decimal places) represents the so-called significance level. This term should have been named the "*in*significance level," since the number actually increases as significance decreases. The smaller the number, the stronger the correlation: the significance level estimates the "probability of the null hypothesis," that is, the likelihood that the data could have come from a larger mass of data with no real trend at all, from "a no-slope population." Thus, the highest numbers among the correlation coefficients and the smallest numbers among the significance levels indicate the strongest and most trustworthy correlations.

For each pair of highly related variables, with a correlation coefficient of at least .4 or a significance level of .05 or better (i.e., or *less*), we made the computer plot a graphic representation of the data. In a few cases I have presented fainter correlations because useful information could be gained either from the absence of a correlation or from a slight one. Conversely, numerous high-correlation graphs have been omitted because they were redundant with the information given in those chosen for presentation.

Each graph also shows, beneath the correlation coefficient and significance level, an equation in the form: $Y = m(X) + b$. This equation tells exactly how to plot the trend line on a graph, showing the line's "slope" and "intercept." In the generalized equation just given, b represents the point at which the trend line intercepts the X-axis; the $m(X)$ part of the equation shows how steeply the line rises, by showing the normative proportions of X to Y. If m is a negative number, the line will drop from left to right and the two variables will be inversely correlated.

Factors in Transmission: Circulation and Stability

CORRELATIONS WITH MANUSCRIPT SURVIVAL

When we look to the interrelations of numerical counts (primary variables M, P, T, A, V, W, L), it emerges that the single most "influential" variable was the number of extant manuscript copies of each poet's work (M).

The number of poems preserved under a given poet's name bears a strikingly constant relation to the number of manuscript copies of poems attributed to him (Fig. A-1). Further, the relationship of manuscript copies to transpositions is even more constant (Fig. A-3), and the proportion of manuscripts to arrays (including abridgments as well as transpositions) more constant still (Fig. A-2).

Version production can thus be said to "depend" almost totally on the circulation of a given poet's work. Otherwise the creation of new versions—whether we take "version" to refer only to stanzaic transposition or count also abridgments—would not be distributed so democratically among poets who vary widely in their beliefs about textual integrity, their stance with respect to literacy, their habits and styles of versification.

The more manuscript copies of a poet's works survive, the more likely is a given poem to survive with more than one arrangement of stanzas. The more times a poet's songs were transmitted, the greater number of his songs "moved." The more instances of transmission, the more instances of version production. A sequentially distinct version was created about once in every five manuscripts;[1] a distinct stanzaic array (by the "broad definition of version") occurs about once in every three manuscripts.[2] The unusually stable poets, "nonconformists" on the stable side of the trend line (Fig. A-3), are Guilhem de St-Didier, Raimbaut d'Aurenga, Folquet de Marselha, and Giraut de Bornelh; "nonconformists" on the unstable side are Bernart de Ventadorn, Bertran de Born, and Raimon de Miraval.

STANZAIC TRANSPOSITION AND ABRIDGMENT

Each poet has about 1.4 times as many poems showing alteration of the stanzaic array as poems showing transposition (Fig. A-4). For the kind of *mouvance* documented here—alteration in the series of stanzas—"versions" broadly defined are distinguished by about 40 percent abridgment and 60 percent sequence.[3] For every poem showing transposition, there are 4.36 sequentially distinct versions.[4] For every poem showing more than one stanzaic array (including abridgments as well as transpositions), there are 4.46 different stanzaic arrays.[5]

From Figure A-5, we can tell which poets had more trouble with transposition and which ones suffered more from abridgment, compared with the norm drawn by the trend line. Giraut de Bornelh, Raimbaut d'Aurenga, Marcabru, and Guilhem de St-Didier undergo relatively little transposition; their songs were more often abridged than their sequence of stanzas transposed. Conversely, Arnaut de Mareuil, Bertran de Born, Berenguer de Palazol, and Bernart de Ventadorn more often had stanzas transposed than abridged.[6]

Thus, the primary indices all point to regular increases in *mouvance* in proportion to manuscript survival. When we look to the relationships among derived indices, we find a similar situation. The more manuscripts per poem, the more versions per poem were produced and the higher the percentage of poems that underwent transposition (Fig. A-5).

Assuming that the number of extant copies reflects frequency of performance and/or of transcription, we can say that a "popular" or oft-repeated poem not only was *more likely* than others to develop stanzaic shifting during transmission (MS vs. TR, Fig. A-5), but also was likely to develop *more shifting*.[7]

In quantity and quality, manuscript survival "should" reflect both a conservative element and an innovative element, if it reflects both written and oral transmission. These data show conclusively that innovation, as a concomitant of popularity, far outweighs the conservatism expected either from familiarity or from literalism, whether from singers or from copyists.

CORRELATIONS WITH POEM SURVIVAL (P)

That the incidence of transposition correlates better with the number of manuscripts of a given poet's work (M) than with the number of his poems (P) supports the idea that popularity and circulation, not productivity, were the governing factors. The only primary indices that correlate better with "Poems" than with "Manuscripts" are the counts of "Poems showing alternate arrays" (A) and of "Poems using linked stanzas" (L).[8]

The trends of correlation with poem survival offer precise information about extremely regular patterns of version production per poem. Poets surveyed conform surprisingly well to the trend for about 42 percent of poems to show transposition (T vs. P),[9] even given that one of our initial "burning questions" was how to explain variations in the ratios of T to P (T/P = TR, "Percent showing transposition").

Visibly much closer statistical conformity appears, however, in the fact that about 75 percent of each poet's songs show alternate stanzaic arrays, whether these consist of abridgments, transpositions, or both (A vs. P).[10] With a correlation coefficient of .98, this pattern of version production seems almost inhuman in its regularity. Other factors do not disrupt it in the least—neither chronological progress of any sort nor stylistic variations among the poets made any impact at all on the trend: three poems out of four will show some alteration in stanzaic array. Only one in four will be left "intact" (bearing in mind, of course, that "intactness" of stanzaic arrays far from guarantees "intactness" at the level of lines and word choice). This last figure, that only 25 percent of songs were transmitted "intact," is remarkable given that over 12 percent (68/552) of songs surveyed exist in only one manuscript and therefore *can* have only one stanzaic array. This means that only 13 percent of the songs surveyed show the same stanzaic array in two or more manuscripts.

V vs. P and W vs. P show the number of actual versions, by each definition, per poem. The number of sequentially distinct versions is approximately twice the number of poems (which means that most poets average two sequences per poem).[11] Stanzaic arrays, including abridgments, are about three times the number of poems (W vs. P: most poets average roughly three "broadly defined versions" per poem).[12] The regularity of these correlations may help to explain why the index VP, "Versions per poem," failed to produce many significant correlations: it was too "flat," with few poets deviating far from the ratio of 2:1, two versions per poem.

The number of poems showing stanzaic linkage (L) is much more loosely related to the total number of poems (P). Here, the stylistic character of individual poets affects the statistics dramatically. We still see a correlation coefficient of .64, indicating that the transmitters did tend to preserve a certain proportion of linked-stanza poems in each poet's canon, but the "scatter" on the graph of L vs. P (Fig. A-11) makes visible the fact that some poets preferred to use stanzaic linkage while others avoided it. Since L is a subset of P, it makes sense that the number of poems using linked stanzas should maintain a relatively constant proportion to the number of poems. Figure A-11 will be discussed in greater depth under the discussion of stanzaic linkage.

CORRELATIONS WITH CHRONOLOGY

The temporal index used (Y for "Year") did not correlate at all with my initial index of *mouvance*, TR, the percentage of each poet's works showing transposition (Fig. A-6). It did, however, correlate with *mouvance* indices tied to manuscript survival rather than to poem survival: with "Sequentially distinct versions per manuscript" (VM) and "Stanzaic arrays per manuscript" (WM) (Fig. A-7). This trend is more pronounced in the production of versions by the broad definition including abridgment (with WM) than by the narrow definition including transpositions only (VM). Possibly the phenomenon of abridgment is more closely related to the growth of the book culture than is the phenomenon of stanzaic transposition; but see Chapter 4 for an in-depth discussion of Figure A-7.

Further, the chronological trend to fewer versions per manuscript is more pronounced in poems with unlinked stanzas than in the general body of poetry, and it scarcely exists as a trend at all for poems with linked stanzas.

In regard to changes in the formal properties of troubadour lyric, I confirmed that stanza length did gradually increase over time (Fig. A-8, Z vs. Y) at the rate of about two additional lines per hundred years. Nevertheless, as the "scatter" of that graph indicates, many early poets composed long stanzas and many later poets composed short ones.

Of particular interest (though the correlation is among the weakest that qualify as significant) is that the use of linked stanzas tended to drop over time. Figure A-9 illustrates this rather "scattered" trend. The actual "course of literary history" can be seen more sharply in Figure A-12, where we can see distinct "clusters" of poets. The earliest groups (1098–1158 and 1151–1179) used stanzaic linkage heavily, perhaps increasingly. Then 1180–1195 marks a "reactionary" period in which stanzaic linkage was seldom used, even though poets in this group created some of the most memorable poetic forms with stanzaic linkage. Later (1205–1248), poets returned to composing 20–25 percent of their poems in forms with stanzaic linkage.

CORRELATIONS WITH STANZA LENGTH

Stanza length proved valuable in the overall stability of a poet's works. It correlated very significantly with versions per manuscript by all definitions—with VM, VMa, and WM (see Fig. A-10). This means that generally, the longer the stanza, the more instances of transmission it requires to create a transposition or an abridgment.

The tendency toward an increase in stanza length over time (Fig. A-8) has been discussed. Now that we can see longer stanzas as a stabilizing feature, we can see how their increased use may have contributed to the historical decrease in version production shown in Figure A-7.

A positive correlation of stanza length and manuscript survival (M vs. Z) means that performers and copyists did not shy away from poets who used long, perhaps involved, stanza patterns. On the contrary, this feature seems to encourage retransmission.

CORRELATIONS WITH STANZAIC LINKAGE

Figure A-11 gives us a better picture than would a mere tally of how frequently poets use stanzaic linkage, because it provides a more accurate description of the norm. Filtering out differences caused by the varying sizes of the poets' bodies of works, we can see which ones are unusually favorable to stanzaic linkage and which ones are unfavorable. Poets decidedly favoring stanzaic linkage are Marcabru, Bernart de Ventadorn, Raimbaut d'Aurenga, Guilhem de St-Didier, Pons de la Guardia, and Raimon de Miraval. Poets decidedly rejecting stanzaic linkage are Berenguer de Palazol, Aimeric de Belenoi, Arnaut de Mareuil, Arnaut Daniel, Peire Vidal, Bertran de Born, and Giraut de Bornelh. Note that some of these last were the inventors of new and foolproof rhyme schemes.

The higher the percentage of linked stanzas, the more transpositions per manuscript (Fig. A-12). If anything, the habitual use of linked stanzas contributes to instability, even in the stanza-linked poems![13] The performer or scribe knows that such-and-such a poet uses linked stanzas frequently, yet even though confronted with a stanza-linked poem he transposes the stanzas anyway.

In looking at Figure A-12 (LK+ vs. VMa), one can see that linkage correlates overall with instability. The circled areas identifying chronologically close clusters of poets, however, show a fascinating phenomenon. The first historical group, roughly 1098–1158, uses stanzaic linkage heavily "to no avail"—it does not help them a bit in discouraging stanzaic transposition. The second group, 1151–1179, uses stanzaic linkage even more heavily *and much more "successfully"*: version production drops dramatically for these poets, including Rigaut de Berbezilh, Bernart de Ventadorn, Raimbaut d'Aurenga, and Guilhem de St-Didier. The third group, 1180–1195, manages to keep version production low while dramatically curtailing the use of stanzaic linkage. Finally, a fourth group (1205 – 1248) returns to moderate stanzaic linkage, without increasing version production in the process.

The Graphs

HOW TO READ THE GRAPHS

Some of the labeling of the graphs has necessarily taken the form of abbreviations. Decoding these abbreviations consists mainly of understanding (1) the abbreviations for variables compared statistically (the captions on the graphs indicate the names of the variables; full explanations of each variable are given in the introduction to this appendix under "Explanation of Data Indices"); (2) the numbers representing "data points" (each number refers to a specific poet, each of whom retains the same "code number" throughout the survey); and (3) the statistical information given with each graph (the letter *r* represents the correlation coefficient; the "significance level" appears below it; and the equation below that describes the "slope and intercept" of the trend line).

KEY TO POETS:
ABBREVIATIONS AND CODE NUMBERS

The numbers assigned to each poet are in approximate chronological order; they are the same as in Tables A-1 and A-2, which give the "Data Profile" of each poet.

No.	Abbrev.	Name
1.	GmIX	Guilhem IX
2.	JRud	Jaufre Rudel
3.	Mcb	Marcabru
4.	BMar	Bernart Marti
5.	RBerb	Rigaut de Berbezilh
6.	Pd'Alv	Peire d'Alvernhe
7.	BVent	Bernart de Ventadorn
8.	Rd'Aur	Raimbaut d'Aurenga
9.	BPal	Berenguer de Palazol
10.	PRog	Peire Rogier
11.	PonsG	Pons de la Guardia
12.	GmSt-D	Guilhèm de St-Didier
13.	GrBor	Giraut de Bornelh

No.	Abbrev.	Name
14.	ArnD	Arnaut Daniel
15.	BBorn	Bertran de Born
16.	PVid	Peire Vidal
17.	ArnMar	Arnaut de Mareuil
18.	FMars	Folquet de Marselha
19.	RmMir	Raimon de Miraval
20.	JsPcb	Jausbert de Puycibot
21.	AimBel	Aimeric de Belenoi
22.	DPrad	Daude de Pradas
23.	GmMont	Guilhem de Montagnagol

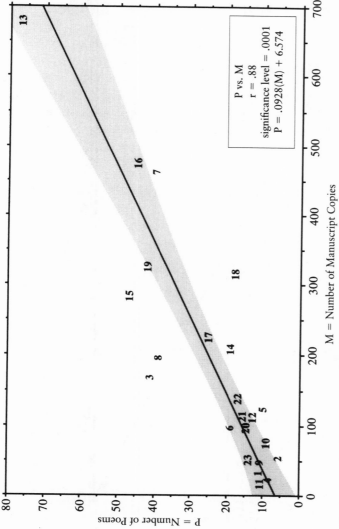

Fig. A-1. Number of Poems versus Number of Manuscript Copies. Consistently, the more manuscript copies of a given poet's work survive, the greater the number of his surviving poems.

NOTE: Numbered points on each graph correspond to individual poets; see "Key to Poets," pp. 223–224. Shaded areas show 95 percent confidence bands.

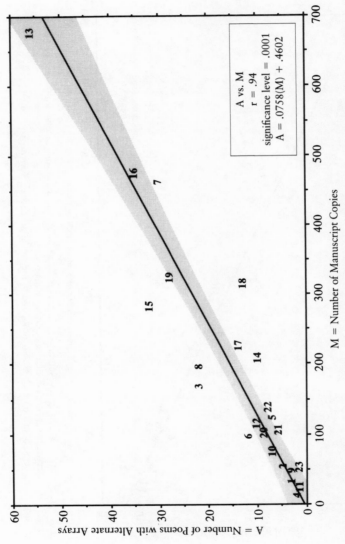

Fig. A-2. Poems with Alternate Stanzaic Arrays versus Number of Manuscript Copies. The number of poems showing more than one stanzaic array is consistently proportional to the number of extant manuscript copies.

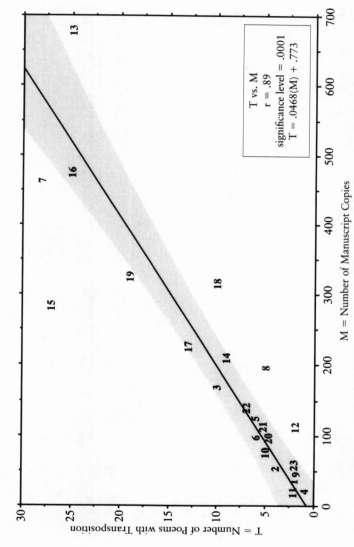

Fig. A-3. Poems with Transposition versus Number of Manuscript Copies. The number of poems showing transposition, within a given poet's works, is consistently proportional to the number of extant manuscript copies of his works.

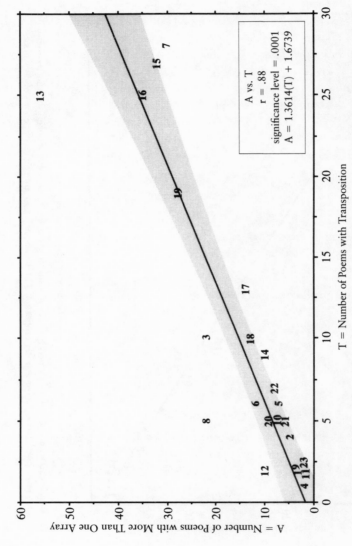

Fig. A-4. Poems with More Than One Array versus Poems with Transposition. The number of poems showing more than one stanzaic array will predictably be about 1.3 times the number of poems showing transposition only (plus 1.7).

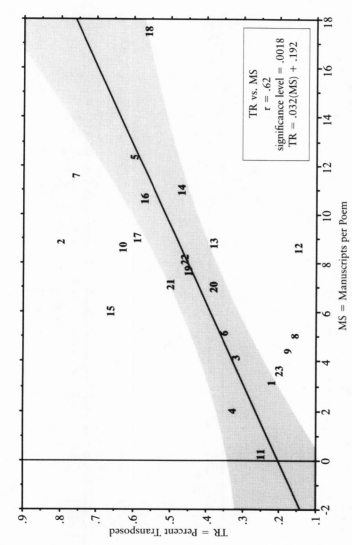

Fig. A-5. Percent Transposed versus Manuscript per Poem. The rate at which transposition affects a poet's work increases with the circulation of his works.

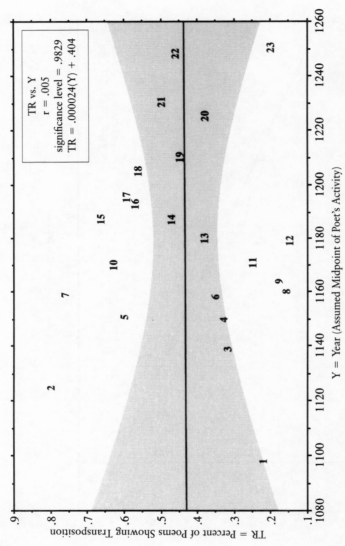

Fig. A-6. Percent Transposed versus Year. Random scatter and no slope: there is no chronological trend whatever toward an increase or decrease in the percentage of poets' works showing transposition.

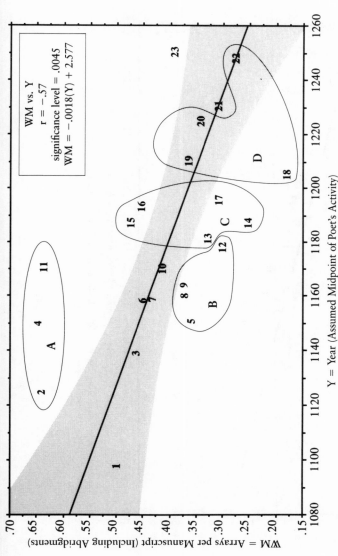

Fig. A-7. Arrays per Manuscript versus Year. There was a chronological trend to produce fewer stanzaic arrays per manuscript. Four clusters show the relationship of array production with the poets' use of linked stanzas (LK+) and stanza length (Z).

NOTES TO CLUSTERS:

A: Early poets with heavy use of stanzaic linkage *and* short stanzas (i.e., high LK+ and low Z) show abnormally high version production.

B: Third-generation poets with heavy use of stanzaic linkage and normal stanza length showing low version production.

C: Middle poets with very low use of stanzaic linkage: those with short stanzas show above-average version production, while those using long stanzas show lower version production.

D: Later poets with good stability showing moderate to high use of stanzaic linkage and medium to long stanza length.

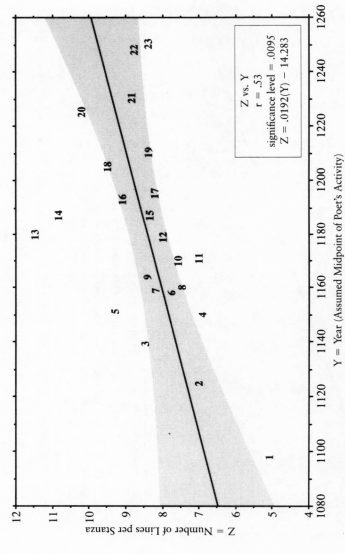

Fig. A-8. Stanza Length versus Year. As time passed, there was a distinct tendency to compose longer stanzas. The increase averages only about two lines per stanza per hundred years.

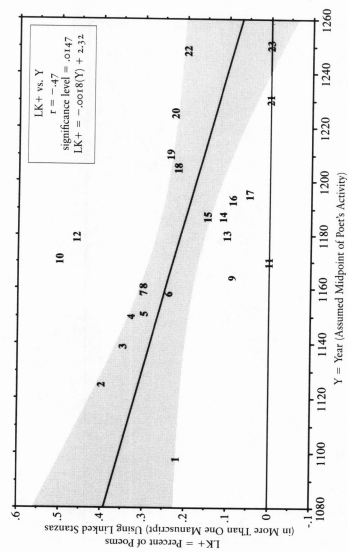

Fig. A-9. Use of Linked Stanzas versus Year. Later poets tend to use linked stanzas in a smaller percentage of surviving songs than do earlier poets. Poets numbered 13–17 show a turning away from stanzaic linkage around 1180–1195, followed by a return to moderate use (poets 18–20, 22).

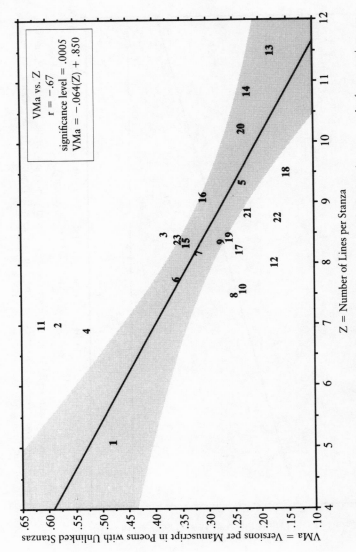

Fig. A-10. Versions per Manuscript (Unlinked) versus Stanza Length. The longer the stanzas, the fewer versions per manuscript—especially in poems with unlinked stanzas.

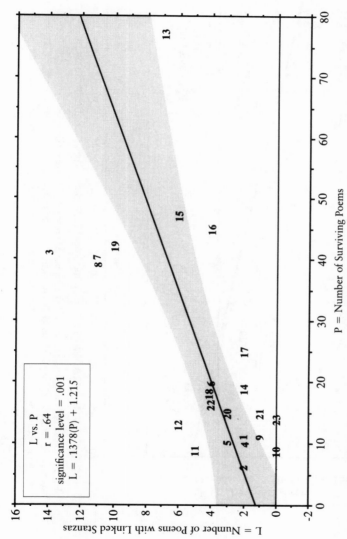

Fig. A-11. Poems with Linked Stanzas versus Total Number of Poems. Generally, we can predict that the number of extant linked-stanza songs by a given poet will be about 14 percent (plus 1.2) of the number of his extant songs. Poets with unusually frequent or infrequent use of linked stanzas fall outside the shaded area.

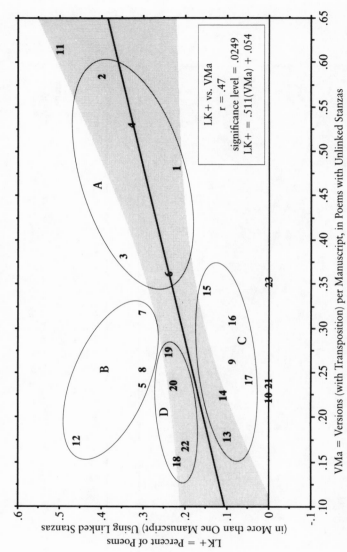

Fig. A-12. Use of Linked Stanzas versus Versions per Manuscript (Unlinked). The more habitually a poet used linked stanzas, the more versions per manuscript his poems (even those with unlinked stanzas) produced. This trend is true mainly of the early poets (1098–1158). Clusters show chronological trends in acceptance or rejection of stanzaic linkage.

NOTES TO CLUSTERS:

A: 1098–1158; B: 1151–1179; C: 1180–1195; D: 1205–1248

TABLE A-1. Primary Data

Poet	Y	P	P+	T	A	M	Ma	V	W	Z
1. GmIX	1098	11	9	2	3	34	25	14	17	5.09
2. JRud	1125	6	5	4	5	53	36	30	34	7.0
3. Mcb	1139	41	31	10	222	168	110	57	78	8.48
4. BMar	1150	10	3	1	2	20	17	11	13	6.9
5. RBerb	1151	10	10	6	7	123	107	28	45	9.33
6. Pd'Alv	1158	19	17	6	12	96	72	30	43	7.74
7. BVent	1159	40	37	28	30	461	347	141	201	8.18
8. Rd'Aur	1160	39	31	5	22	195	139	46	73	7.47
9. BPal	1164	11	11	2	3	48	42	12	18	8.42
10. PRog	1170	9	8	5	7	77	77	18	32	7.56
11. PonsG	1171	9	8	2	2	22	13	13	14	7.0
12. GmSt-D	1179	13	13	2	10	112	52	16	34	8.0
13. GrBor	1180	77	68	25	56	679	612	117	224	11.48
14. ArnD	1187	19	19	9	10	209	165	40	53	10.83
15. BBorn	1187	47	41	27	32	283	251	95	134	8.34
16. PVid	1193	45	44	25	35	475	414	135	215	9.09
17. ArnMar	1195	25	22	13	14	226	207	53	70	8.2
18. FMars	1205	18	18	10	13	315	252	47	57	9.5
19. RmMir	1210	42	41	19	28	325	245	82	119	8.36
20. JsPcb	1225	15	13	5	9	105	85	23	36	10.2
21. AimBel	1230	15	10	5	6	107	106	25	33	8.83
22. DPrad	1248	17	15	7	8	137	107	26	38	8.76
23. GmMont	1250	14	10	2	2	51	51	18	20	8.36
Totals		552	484	220	338	4321	3532	1077	1061	
Averages	1180	24	21	9.6	14.7	188	154	47	70	8.4

NOTE: For the primary indices L and L+, see Table A-5.

TABLE A-2. Derived Indices

Poet	TR	MS	LK+	VM	VMa	WM
1. GmIX	.22	3.1	.22	.412	.480	.500
2. JRud	.80	8.8	.40	.566	.583	.641
3. Mcb	.32	4.1	.35	.339	.382	.465
4. BMar	.33	2.0	.33	.550	.529	.649
5. RBerb	.60	12.3	.30	.228	.234	.360
6. Pd'Alv	.35	5.1	.24	.313	.361	.448
7. BVent	.76	11.5	.30	.306	.317	.437
8. Rd'Aur	.16	5.0	.30	.236	.252	.375
9. BPal	.18	4.4	.09	.250	.261	.375
10. PRog	.63	8.6	.00	.234	.234	.415
11. PonsG	.25	2.4	.50	.591	.615	.637
12. GmSt-D	.15	8.6	.46	.143	.173	.304
13. GrBor	.38	8.8	.10	.172	.178	.330
14. ArnD	.47	11.0	.11	.191	.224	.254
15. BBorn	.66	6.0	.15	.336	.342	.474
16. PVid	.57	10.6	.09	.284	.309	.452
17. ArnMar	.59	9.0	.05	.235	.242	.310
18. FMars	.56	17.5	.22	.149	.151	.181
19. RmMir	.45	7.7	.24	.252	.273	.366
20. JsPcb	.38	7.0	.23	.219	.235	.344
21. AimBel	.50	7.1	.00	.234	.226	.309
22. DPrad	.46	8.1	.20	.190	.168	.277
23. GmMont	.20	3.6	.00	.353	.353	.392

TABLE A-3. Correlation Matrix for Primary Indices

	Y	M	P	T	A	V	W	L	Z
Y	1.0 .00	.15 .5048	.06 .7717	.11 .6106	.04 .8614	.04 .8473	.04 .8476	−.18 .3995	.53 .0095
M		1.0 .00	.88 .0001	.89 .0001	.94 .0001	.92 .0001	.95 .0001	.46 .0263	.58 .0040
P			1.0 .00	.83 .0001	.98 .0001	.85 .0001	.89 .0001	.64 .0010	.44 .0339
T				1.0 .00	.88 .0001	.97 .0001	.94 .0001	.47 .0241	.40 .0578
A					1.0 .00	.90 .0001	.94 .0001	.60 .0027	.47 .0235
V						1.0 .00	.98 .0001	.54 .0082	.37 .0844
W							1.0 .00	.51 .0121	.42 .0434
L								1.0 .00	.06 .7847
Z									1.00 .00

TABLE A-4. Correlation Matrix for Derived Indices

	Y	MS	VM	VMa	WM	LK+	TR	Z
Y	1.0 .00	.20 .3530	−.46 .0265	−.54 .0084	−.57 .0045	−.47 .0253	.005 .9829	.53 .0095
MS		1.0 .00	−.57 .0043	−.58 .0034	−.60 .0024	−.13 .5511	.62 .0018	.53 .0088
VM			1.0 .00	.99 .0001	.94 .0001	.43 .3820	.007 .9738	−.64 .0009
VMa				1.0 .00	.94 .0001	.47 .0249	.04 .8630	−.67 .0005
WM					1.0 .00	.45 .0314	.02 .9258	−.64 .0010
LK+						1.0 .00	−.16 .4737	−.35 .1023
TR							1.0 .00	.17 .4312
Z								1.0 .00

TABLE A-5. Synopsis of Transposition and Stanzaic Linkage

	All Poems		Poems in More than One Manuscript					
	Total (P)	Linked (L)	Total (P+)	With Trans-position (T)	Linked (L+)	Linked with Transpo-sition	Un-linked	Unlinked with Transpo-sition
1. GmIX	11	2	9	2	2	0	7	2
2. JRud	6	2	5	4	2	1	3	3
3. Mcb	41	14	31	10	11	1	20	9
4. BMar	10	2	3	1	1	0	2	1
5. RBerb	10	3	10	6	3	0	7	6
6. Pd'Alv	19	4	17	6	4	0	13	6
7. BVent	40	11	37	28	11	8	26	20
8. Rd'Aur	39	11	31	5	9	1	22	4
9. BPal	11	1	11	2	1	0	10	2
10. PRog	9	0	8	5	0	0	8	5
11. PonsG	9	5	8	2	4	0	4	2
12. GmSt-D	13	6	13	2	6	2	7	0
13. GrBor	77	7	68	25	6	1	62	24
14. ArnD	19	2	19	9	2	1	17	8
15. BBorn	47	6	41	27	6	2	35	25
16. PVid	45	4	44	25	4	1	40	24
17. ArnMar	25	2	22	13	2	1	20	12
18. FMars	18	4	18	10	4	2	14	8
19. RmMir	42	10	41	19	10	2	31	17
20. JsPcb	15	3	13	5	3	0	10	5
21. AimBel	15	1	10	5	0	0	10	5
22. DPrad	17	4	15	7	3	3	12	4
23. GmMont	14	0	10	2	0	0	10	2
Total	552	104	484	220	94	26	390	194
		(18.8%)		(45.45%)	(27.66%)		(49.74%)	

A Quick Guide
to Rhyme Schemes

In the following illustrations, capital letters indicate matching of rhyme sounds in an entire stanza; lowercase letters indicate matching of rhyme sounds in a line.

coblas unissonans: AAAAAA etc.
coblas singulars: ABCDE etc.
coblas doblas: AABBCCDD etc.
coblas ternas: AAABBBCCC etc.
coblas quaternas: AAAABBBB etc.
coblas alternadas: ABABAB etc.
coblas redondas: abcde edcba etc.
coblas capcaudadas: abcde ebcdi ibcda a . . . etc. (Many variations are possible; the important thing is that the first line of each strophe rhymes with the last line of the previous strophe).
coblas capfinidas: Again, many variations are possible; the identifying feature is that the first line of each strophe contains, repeated, the rhyme word of the previous stanza's last line. Illustration, where each of the sentences represents a stanza:

> The black cat / on the mat / in June / looks at the *moon.*
> *Moon* light / is so bright / that he / climbs up a *tree.*
> In *tree* tops / the cat hops / above / people in *love.*
> *Lovely* cat! / Thou art that / which fights / in the *nights* (etc.)

For a more detailed introduction to the Old Provençal repertoire of rhyme schemes, see Frank 1953; and Chambers 1985.

APPENDIX C

List of Manuscripts

For more information about the manuscripts, see Pillet and Carstens 1933: x–xxxv; and Zufferey 1987. The very specific regional provenances are from Zufferey (p. 314). When discussing manuscript versions of a particular poem, I am using the same sigla adopted by the poem's editor.

A   Rome, Bibl. Apost. Vat., lat. 5232. 13th cent., Italy (copyist came from southern France but worked in Venetia).

B   Paris, Bibl. Nat., fr. 1592. End of 13th cent., France (Haute-Auvergne). Closely related to A.

C   Paris, Bibl. Nat., fr. 856. 14th cent., Southwest France (Narbonne region).

D   Modena, Bibl. Naz. Est., α, R.4.4. Second part of ms. End of 13th or beginning of 14th cent., Italy (Venetia).

Dᵃ   First part of D. 13th cent., Italy (Venetia).

E   Paris, Bibl. Nat., fr. 1749. 14th cent., France (region of Béziers-Montpellier).

F   Rome, Bibl. Apost. Vat., Chigi. L. IV. 106. 14th cent., Italy (Venetia).

G   Milan, Bibl. Ambr., R 71 sup. 14th cent., Italy (Lombardy).

H   Rome, Bibl. Apost. Vat., lat. 3207. End of 13th or beginning of 14th cent., Italy (Venetia).

I   Paris, Bibl. Nat., fr. 854. Second half of 13th cent., Italy (Venetia).

J   Florence, Bibl. Naz. Centr., Conv. Sopp. F. IV. 776. End of 13th to 14th cent., France (Eastern Languedoc—Nîmes area).

K   Paris, Bibl. Nat., fr. 12473. Second half of 13th cent., Italy (Venetia). Closely related to I.

L   Rome, Bibl. Apost. Vat., lat. 3206. 14th cent., Italy (Lombardy).

M   Paris, Bibl. Nat., fr. 12474. 14th cent., Italy (Lombardy).

N   New York, Pierpont Morgan Libr., 819. 14th cent., Italy (Lombardy).

N^2 Berlin, Staatsbibl., Phillips 1910 (= d in Zufferey's reassignation of sigla). 16th cent., Italy (Venetia).

O   Rome, Bibl. Apost. Vat., lat. 3208. 14th cent., Italy (Venetia).

P   Florence, Bibl. Med.-laur., XLI. cod. 42. 14th cent., Italy (Venetia or Tuscany).

Q   Florence, Bibl. Ricc., 2909. 13th–14th cent., Italy (Lombardy—region of Pavia or Cremona).

R   Paris, Bibl. Nat., fr. 22543. 14th cent., France (Toulouse region).

S   Oxford, Bodl. Libr., Douce 269. End of 13th cent., Italy (Venetia or Tuscany).

Sg   Barcelona, Bibl. Cat., 146 (= Z in Zufferey). Third quarter of 14th cent., Catalonia.

T   Paris, Bibl. Nat., fr. 15211. 14th–15th cent., Italy (Venetia). The Provençal poems are in cursive script.

U   Florence, Bibl. Med.-laur., XLI. cod. 43. 14th cent., Italy (Venetia or Tuscany).

V   Venice, Bibl. Naz. Marc., fr. App. cod. XI. Completed in 1268; Catalonia.

W   Paris, Bibl. Nat., fr. 844. 13th cent., northern France. (An Old French songbook).

X   Paris, Bibl. Nat., fr. 20050. 13th cent., northern France. (An Old French songbook).

ψ (= K″ in Zufferey) Paris, Bibl. Nat., naf. 23789. Fragment (2 leaves), published in *Romania* 62 (1942–1943): 504–513. End of 13th cent.

a   *chansonnier* of Bernart Amoros [1]

    a = Florence, Bibl. Ricc., 2814 (fols. 1–132). Pp. 1–251 of a copy from Bernart Amoros's *chansonnier* made in 1589 by Jacques Teissier de Tarascon.

    a^1 = Modena, Bibl. Naz. Est., γ, N.8.4; 11, 12, 13. Pp. 252–616 of Jacques Teissier's copy. 1589, paper.

c   Florence, Bibl. Med.-laur., XC inf. 26. 15th cent., paper.

f   Paris, Bibl. Nat., fr. 12472. First half of 14th cent., paper.

NOTES

Introduction

1. The fascination with the troubadours as love theorists appears in studies as diverse as Lazar 1964, Topsfield 1975, and Cropp 1975. The mystique of *fin'amors* has caused the troubadours to be blamed for far-reaching historical and cultural change: their theory of love was supposedly connected with the heresy that brought on the Albigensian crusade (Nelli 1963); they have been blamed for popularizing a destructive concept of romantic love (Rougemont [1956] 1964).

2. Zumthor himself is the first to exclude the troubadours from his analysis of the *grand chant courtois* (1972:190).

3. Throughout this study, I identify poets quoted by abbreviations, citing the songs and lines as numbered in standard editions used, listed in the Bibliography; translations are mine unless otherwise indicated. In some instances, editions of individual poems are preferred to complete editions (for example, I use Roncaglia's texts, when available, for discussions of Marcabru). Such departures from standard editions are clearly marked.

4. Del Monte, in the notes to his edition, draws comparisons between Peire's lines and the songs of the poets satirized (1955, 129−134).

5. See the introduction to Pickens's edition (1978).

6. Despite the doubts later cast on its geographical and historical assumptions (Lejeune 1965), Pattison's thesis preserves the best of its original merits; his dating of the gathering is still considered correct.

7. I.e., banqueters "inflated" with food, wine, and boasting; literally, "swell-bladders." On *als enflabotz* see Roncaglia 1969a, 75−78. Goldin (1973, 175) translates the phrase as reflecting an even more colorful (and loud) setting: "The verse was made to the noise of bagpipes."

8. For the sake of consistency, I have used the dates for each poet as given in the chapter headings of Riquer's anthology (1975). Riquer assesses the historical evidence carefully and discusses the uncertainties in reconstructing a biography for each poet.

9. Pattison (1952) introduces his critical edition of Raimbaut's works with a

thorough study of the historical Raimbaut; he also publishes a "Cartulary of Raimbaut d'Orange" (pp. 215–219) and prints both a photocopy and a transcription of Raimbaut's will (pp. 26a–26b, 218–219).

10. Guilhem's modern editor, Aimo Sakari (1956, 12), cites three historical documents naming Guilhem de St-Didier: two papal bulls dated July 20, 1165, and 1171, respectively; and a sale of property recorded in Provençal witnessed by a W. Disders. The form of his name in the second papal bull is *Guillelmo de Sancto Desiderio*. While reading Raimbaut d'Aurenga's will in Pattison 1952, I discovered near the end of the list of witnesses the name Guill*e*lmus *s*ancti desid*e*ri*j* (p. 219). Pattison makes no remark about this; perhaps it went unnoticed because the poet is sometimes known as Guilhem de Saint-*Leidier*. Another name appears on the roster of witnesses that may contribute to our knowledge of Guilhem: there is also a Bertrand*us s*ancti desid*e*ri*j* (p. 218). Aimo Sakari notes that eight of Guilhem's fifteen surviving songs contain an allusion to one or two "Bertrands" in their *tornadas* (1956, 15). Sakari rejects the idea of the *vida* that one of these "Bertrands" was Guilhem's contemporary, Hugo Marescale. Why should a Hugo be called a Bertrand? Is it implausible, though, that Bertrand*us s*ancti desid*e*ri*j* was one of Guilhem's Bertrands?

11. I follow Riquer's reading of the second line (1975, 340), where Del Monte edits "que canta de sus e de sotz."

12. Because of his literary sophistication, Rigaut de Berbezilh was long believed to have begun his career in about 1175. Rita Lejeune (1957), however, has identified the historical Rigaut, documented between 1141 and 1160, and has argued that nothing in Rigaut's poetry requires us to suppose a later date. Martín de Riquer confirms Lejeune's dating (1975, 281–285).

13. Since Arnaut's earliest datable song is not the work of a beginner ("Doutz brais e critz", 1180), we can safely place him as a younger contemporary of the poets active in 1170, even though he is not mentioned in Peire d'Alvernhe's satire. Arnaut shares a *senhal* with Raimbaut d'Aurenga: "Bons Respieitz" ("Good Expectation"; Arn D 17, 17; and 16, 23); this supports the theory that he was active before 1173, the date of Raimbaut's death.

Chapter 1

1. Pierre Guiraud, writing to confirm Zumthor's view, argues from the etymologies of *trouver*, *chanter*, *aimer*, and *joie* to establish a homology between "la jubilation amoureuse et l'enthousiasme poétique" and to intimate (rather than prove) that "the immediate model" of both trouvère and troubadour song should be sought "dans la littérature latino-chrétienne du haut Moyen Age et, plus particulièrement, dans la technique des tropes liturgiques" (1971, 422, 425). Enthusiasm for the homology has carried Guiraud too far; not only the argument from

etymology but the etymologies themselves are doubtful. Although he mentions Charles Camproux's (1965) distinction between *joy* and *gaug*, Guiraud seems unaware of Camproux's convincing argument that *joy* derives from *joculum* rather than from *gaudium*, and still less aware that generalizations about the language of the trouvères are not universals to be freely extended to the troubadours (p. 421). Guiraud has since taken further his study of Old French *joie* (1979).

2. Gerald A. Bond, in a study of Guilhem IX and his "Ben vueill que sapchon li pluzor," observes that "the count employs ambiguous vocabulary to interweave the double theme" of *amar/trobar,* and lists several words and phrases that, in the *gap,* have application in either semantic field: *aqest mestier, joc d'amor, failli, sobre coissi, joc doussa,* and *bona ma* (1978, 168).

3. Cf. Condren 1972, 184, 193ff.

4. R d'Aur 2, 25–26: "Si que·l cor m'art, mas no·m rima / ren de foras, mas dinz rim." R d'Aur 18, 25–26: "Tant ai prim / mon cor qand rim"; and 18, 37–38: "Amors, rim / Co·s vuoilla prim."

5. Most of these terms have been discussed by Dorothy R. Sutherland 1965.

6. Pickens 1978, 183*n*.39 and Glossary, s.v. "Chausimen." Goldin recognizes *chauzir* as a term belonging to the verbal arts when he translates it as "depict" in a *tornada* of Peire Cardenal: "Clergue, qui vos chauzic / ses fellon cor enic / en son comte faillic" ("Clerics, whoever depicted you without a cruel and vicious heart erred in his account"; 1973, 295).

7. See Sutherland 1965 for the connotations of distraction and transport in *pensius* and *cossiros.* I have collected several occurrences of the word *cabal* (both as an adjective and as a noun) and its derivatives; they lead me to believe that the word refers to the head, and hence to intellectual activity. B Vent 24, 46–47: "Que de fol cove que folei / e de savi que chabalei" (It is fitting for a fool to run mad, and for a wise man to use his head). B Vent 15, 5–7: "Per so es mos chantars cabaus / qu'en joi d'amor ai et enten / la boch'e·ls olhs e·l cor e·l sen" (This is why my song is intelligent—because I direct toward the joy of love my lips and eyes and heart and sense). P Vid 38, 25: "Estiers mon grat am tot sol per cabau / Lieis" (Against my will I love her only with my mind). Pons G 4, 27–28: "Per qu'eu sofer totz mals e deport / que trac per vos soletz en mon cabau" (Therefore I endure all the pains which I suffer for you alone, in my mind).

8. For *merce* as the reward or prize for love's ordeal, see R. Howard Bloch 1977, 182–184.

9. For *entendre,* I rely on the interpretation of A. H. Schutz (1932). Marshall (1972, 107) and Poe (1984, 108) base their opposition primarily on the *Razos de trobar,* where the most "ordinary" level of meaning for *entendre* always at least suffices; nevertheless, I find Schutz's interpretation operative in lyric and other contexts. A full study of *retener* can be found in an article by Glynnis Cropp (1974). Although Cropp concentrates on the transference of the feudal term to

the field of love, many of the passages she cites can be interpreted as the poet's request that the addressee memorize his song.

10. There is a lacuna in the last line.

Chapter 2

1. For example, note these variations between versions 3 and 3A in Jaufre Rudel's "Quan lo rossinhols": *que reversos/que raizos* (backwards/rooted down) and *e pueys sompnhan durmen/e pueys son ja durmen* (and then dreaming asleep/and then I am suddenly asleep), in Pickens 1978, 80, 84. Homophony of two variants sometimes points to a process of deliberate poetic *melhuramen* (improvement) suggested by the sound, as may be illustrated by the way T. S. Eliot revised a line intended for *The Waste Land:* the original reads "In the calm deep water where no stir nor surface"; but Eliot deletes "nor surface," substituting "nor surf is" above it ([1971], 115, v. 30). The sound has changed very little; the sense, drastically. Much more dependent on sound, and also prevalent in the *chansonniers,* is the phenomenon of William Safire's "mondegreens," "inspired by 'Lady Mondegreen,' a phrase of ancient poetry that was originally 'laid him on the green'" (1981, 171).

2. For "fractured strophes," see Pickens's introduction to song 2 (1978, 88–96). For frequency of abridgments, see Appendix A to this volume.

3. Hendrik van der Werf 1972, 26: "If all the usual theories about medieval song are valid, the scribes of the preserved chansonniers wrote more wrong notes than correct ones!"

4. J. H. Marshall takes as the theme for his lecture on the troubadours' medium the "gap between creation and transmission" (1975, 5ff.); it is an excellent introduction to the problems of the manuscript tradition, but I dispute his refusal to recognize "clear signs of memorial transmission" in the variation of texts in the *chansonniers,* although he recognizes troubadour song as "a poetry which was created as song and intended for performance" (p. 6). Marshall does concede the likelihood of authorial redaction, "the poet's second thoughts," but only in the existence of alternate *tornadas;* in these, he says, "we can perceive . . . traces of the life that a particular song had when it was performed before audiences" (p. 14). It is unclear why Marshall considers that only the original author would find reason and feel qualified to make such changes, but one detects an underlying assumption based on modern notions of textual integrity: that the poetic text, especially the lyric text, is sacred and inviolable, down to the placement of commas.

5. For Marshall, a vast rift separates the poets and the transmitters, because "we have extant sources which transmit this poetry to us precisely from the moment when the poetry itself was ceasing to be a living thing in its native land"

(1975, 5). I would argue that this rift does exist between the poets and the "chirographic folk," but not between poets and singing transmitters.

6. The text survives in a copy made in 1589 by Jacques Teissier de Tarascon; the corrections were added later in the sixteenth century by Piero di Simon del Nero, according to Stengel.

7. Avalle (1961, 114) discusses hypotheses on the origin of MS C.

8. For convenience of reference, I have numbered the sections of the text, following the example of Boutière and Schutz 1964.

9. For a critical edition of Bernart's preface, an analysis of his dialect, and a discussion of Bernart's lost anthology, see Zufferey 1987, 80–84 and through 101. Zufferey finds phonological evidence that Bernart's exemplum had "une origine plus méridionale . . . à savoir languedocienne et provençale" than did Bernart himself, or than the Auvergnate tradition of MSS A and B. He gets this information from places where "notre clerc n'a pas imposé son système au point de faire disparaître toute trace de la *scripta* du modèle" (p. 101).

10. Originally published in Léopold Delisle, *Mélanges de paléographie et de bibliographie* (Paris, 1880); cited in Bertoni 1911.

11. Bernart's prologue does not fit into any of the three types of medieval academic prologue described by Minnis (1984, 9–39). The *chansonniers* were not "authoritative texts"; Giraut de Bornelh is *maestre* but not *auctor*, so Bernart is only marginally entitled to use those conventions of the prologue that his discussion of *entencio* hints at. If anything, Bernart's prologue follows the "Type A" structure (Minnis 1984, 16), giving the circumstances under which a work was composed (the journalistic "who, what, when, where, why, and in what manner") but answering these questions in respect to himself (his compilation) rather than to an *auctor* or a troubadour poet (the composition).

12. See Mussafia 1874 for an analysis of the contents of Miquel's book, based on Barbieri's citations. The reference in Peire Cardenal's biography is in Boutière and Schutz 1964, 335–336.

13. Avalle still prefers the idea that a small amount of authorial intervention was combined with heavy deterioration through repeated recopying: "Quanto alla problema della tradizione orale, dirò subito che la tesi sostenuta più de ottanta anni fa del Gröber mi pare ancora la più convincente" (1961, 47).

14. Cf.: "The eleventh-century Eadmer of St. Albans says that, when he composed in writing, he felt he was dictating to himself" (Ong 1982, 95; citing Clanchy 1979, 218).

15. From "Near Perigord," Pound 1926, 154.

16. We now know relatively much about Bertran de Born from historical documents and allusions (Paden, Sankovitch, and Stäblein 1986)—but not the color of his eyes.

17. See Avalle 1961 and Kleinhenz 1976 for collections of such miniatures and for discussions of the question of writing.

18. This is Gröber's conclusion (1877, 342); thus, the starting point for his theory of *Liederblätter* is this absence-of-*Liederblatt*.

19. For a parallel text of the two versions, see Boutière and Schutz 1964, esp. 326–327.

20. Van der Werf (1972, 28) reaches this conclusion on the basis of his study of *mouvance* in the musical texts: "All of this leads to the assumption that initially most or all chansons were transmitted in an exclusively oral tradition and that from about the middle of the 13th century on there was dissemination in writing parallel to the continuing oral tradition."

21. P.-C. 325,5. Most MSS ascribe it to Peire d'Alvernhe, C to Marcabru, and C *Reg.* to Bernart Marti. Zenker believes its author to be Bernart de Venzac; Del Monte, without comment, excludes it from his edition of Peire d'Alvernhe.

22. "E saup mielz trobar qu'entendre ni que dire. Mout fo paoros dizenz entre las genz; et on plus vezia de bons homes, plus s'esperdia e menz sabia" (And he knew better how to versify than to conceive the idea of a poem or to deliver it. He was very fearful among the public, and the more good people he saw, the more he was flustered and the less he knew; Boutière and Schutz 1964, 149; translation of the first sentence from Schutz 1932, 137).

Chapter 3

1. Compare Giraut de Bornelh's jongleur Cardalhac (song 75). Giraut calls him "glotz e lechaders" and warns that if he loses his job as a jongleur he is unlikely to be taken in by a monastery "Car mal etz fachs per escriure legenda" (Because you are ill suited to writing saint's lives; vv. 33–36). Bertran de Born's Mailolis is even more gluttonous, slothful, and violent. Bertran tells him that he sings worse than a peacock, "E gavainatz los motz e·ls sos / per que·s folls qui los vos bailha" (and you muddle up the words and the music, and therefore he who entrusts them to you is crazy!; B Born 27, 46–47; P.-C. 80,24).

2. Pizzorusso, entry 36 (1978, 227–228). *Chansonnier R* gives a slightly shorter version with the same instructions. Entry 47 gives similar instructions, in shorter form, for singing another song that is "encadenat e retrogradat de motz e de son" (p. 230).

3. I read *mos libres* as singular because the plural of the possessive adjective would be *mei;* perhaps the book is in *cas sujet,* " . . . if my book dared to open."

4. Rigaut de Berbezilh defends Ovid's advice, "perfer et obdura" (*Ars amatoria* 2.178), in his poem "Tuit demandon qu'es devengud'Amors" ("Everyone's asking what has become of love"): "C'Ovidis dis el libre que no men / que per soffrir a hom d'amor son grat, / e per soffrir son maint tort perdonat / e sofrirs fai maint amoros iausen" (For Ovid says in the book that does not lie that through suffering a man has his will of love, and through suffering are many wrongs pardoned, and suffering makes many a lover rejoice; R Berb 9, 29–32).

5. In MS *C* we have what Avalle himself calls "exceptional testimony" (1961, 85): "Aissi comensan lo cans d'en Guiraut Riquier de Narbona . . . enaissi adordenadamens cum era adordenat en lo sieu libre, del qual libre escrig per la sua man fon aissi tot translatat" (Here begins the poetry of En Giraut Riquier of Narbonne . . . ordered in the same way as it was ordered in his own book, from which book, written by his own hand, they were straightaway transcribed; Pizzorusso 1978, 221).

6. See Maas 1958, 1ff. The term *the original* is featured in the very first of Maas's "Basic Notions": "1. We have no autograph manuscripts of the Greek and Roman writers and no copies which were collated with *the originals;* the manuscripts we possess *derive from the originals* through an unknown number of intermediate copies. . . . The business of textual criticism is to produce a text *as close as possible to the original (constitutio textus)."* Surely most troubadour texts would be classed by Maas as "irremediable," or "where the original can only be established by choosing (*selectio*) between traditions of equal 'stemmatical' value" (p. 1).

7. That is, the ratio of "versions" (with transposed stanzas) to manuscripts. See Chapter Four.

8. Avalle (1960, xxxviii) considers that songs 1–16 constituted "il libro del Vidal" and that the other songs in the *codice antico* were added later.

9. Avalle 1960, xvi–xvii: "The date of compilation of this manuscript, which I will henceforth call the 'codice antico,' doubtless goes back to before 1260, the year in which Alberic de Romano died, that is, the owner of the manuscript from which the scribe of the Este manuscript (*D*)—or of its exemplum?—transcribed the songs of Vidal that were missing in the first part (*Dª*)."

10. See ibid., xxxviii. The "lost precursors" of *I* and *K* are the following, according to stemma 3: (1) "'l'esemplare del Vidal' (messo assieme fra il 1201 ed il 1202; cfr. xij, 12, e comprendente le prime 16 canzoni di cui alla Tav. VI." Table VI contains songs numbered 1–16 in Avalle's edition. For Avalle, lines 11–13 of poem 12 ("Vol ara liurar francamen / a sels qu'iran ab lo marques / Outra la mar per Dieu servir") date the poem between the election of Bonifacio I de Monferrat as head of the fourth crusade, in August 1201, and his departure in August 1202 (1960, 115). Since this is the latest reference in songs 1–16, Avalle takes it as the date when Peire must have made his book. (2) "Archetipo (si aggiungono da altra fonte le canzoni xvij, xviij, e xxv)." (3) "Codice antico." (4) β, from which come *A, Dª, E, H,* and δ (the "lost precursor" of *Q* and *N*). (5) k (the lost source of *IK*).

11. I experimented with generating random "anthologies," both with a computer and with a deck of cards. I then applied Gröber's procedures (1877) to them to find imaginary "genetic relationships" among "anthologies." The detailed results of this experiment would make very tedious reading; in summary, I found that the probability of finding "matching clusters" varies with: (1) the size of the

"pool" of poems from which their numbers are randomly drawn, (2) the size of the anthologies generated, and (3) the number of anthologies generated. Matching pairs were extremely frequent, and the more liberal the "rules" for determining "matching sequences" (e.g., allowing "inverted series" or "series with gaps"), the more I found that "coincidences" outnumbered sequences that could *not* in any way be understood as "coinciding."

12. Note that I am omitting from Avalle's list of ten poems in chronological order in *A* the three that he calls "non databile," which leaves seven.

13. Sequence of poems in *A* and *N,* and dates for each poem, are put together from information scattered through Avalle 1960. That *N* contains a chronological sequence is my idea, not Avalle's. Yet I am not making any claims for an "author's book" in *N;* I merely wish to show that *A*'s superiority in this regard is doubtful.

14. In his *tenso* with Giraut de Bornelh (song 31; Pattison 1952, 174), Raimbaut seems to argue that the poet should be allowed to restrict transmission. "Mi non cal sitot non s'espan" (I don't mind if it does not broaden its circulation; v. 31) is answered by Giraut's proposal to allow even the worst singer to transmit it: "C'us enraumatz / lo·m deissazec e·l diga mal" (let a man with a cold garble it and recite it poorly; vv. 40–41).

15. Boutière and Schutz 1964, 9: "Cercamons si fo uns joglars de Gascoigna, e trobet vers e pastoretas a la usanza antiga. E cerquet tot lo mon lai on el poc anar, e per so fez se dire Cercamons" (Cercamon was a *joglar* from Gascony, and he composed poems and pastorals in the old manner. And he searched the entire world, wherever he was able to go, and for this reason he had himself called Cercamon ["Search-world"]).

Chapter 4

1. Pons G 7, 5–8: "E pus a lieys ai ma chanso promeza / ben la dei far cuend'e guay'e prezan, / quar ben conosc que, si·l ven en talan, / qu'en mans bos locs n'er chantad'e apreza" (And since to her I have promised my song, I must certainly make it clever and gay and valuable, for I know well that, if it please her, that in many a good place it will be sung and learned). Thus, the song will be sung *and learned* in good society, not merely sung in the *presence* of good society after lowly jongleurs have learned it. Gm Berg 5, 1–3: "Cantarey mentre m'estau / chantaret bon e leiau / que xanton macips de Pau" (I will sing, while I am standing still, a good and loyal little song that the boys of Pau may sing). Riquer notes that "Pau es, sin duda, Pau, en el Ampurdán, de donde seguramente era el juglar de Guillem de Berguedà Ramon de Pau" (1971, 2:65).

2. I use *transposition* with the same meaning as Paden's term *permutation* (1979). Both refer to changes in the sequence of stanzas. The term's role in the

field of music should not confuse the reader, since I make no reference anywhere to melodic "transposition" from one key to another.

3. Stemmas based on word-level variants frequently fail to correspond to the manuscript filiations suggested by "matching" stanzaic sequences. The myriad word-level variants were also too numerous for me to classify and quantify single-handedly, even with a sample of only twenty-three poets. My decision not to study them statistically was based on practicality, *not* on a judgment that word-level variants were unimportant. I do mention them where discussion of variants fits into the questions at hand. But because this study surveys a whole body of poetry, I sometimes choose not to distract the reader from the "panorama" by diverting attention to small-scale textual details.

4. Of course, Guilhem could have dictated a book. But if so, he would still not be using writing as an aid to composition. In this case, the book would have been a "memento," not an embodiment, of the songs.

5. According to Paden 1983, the naming of jongleurs declined from 20 percent (25/127) in 1220–1260 to 10 percent (8/80) in 1260–1300 and 5 percent (1/22) in 1300–1340.

6. Paden draws his conclusions from figures based on names accepted as belonging to jongleurs in Chambers's *Proper Names in the Lyrics of the Troubadours* (1971).

7. Diez 1845, 103: "La rime réunissant les diverses strophes d'une pièce offre le double avantage d'aider à la mémoire par la concordance des sons et de produire une harmonie agréable a l'oreille." Diez also argues that a complex strophic structure may have aided in composition: "Elle ajoute aux difficultés de l'art, mais une forme ardue en tant qu'elle ne soit pas un jeu vide de sens, stimule l'inspiration poétique à s'en rendre maître; l'entraine dans une sorte de lutte corps à corps dont le prix est pour le poète d'atteindre à la noblesse de l'expression."

8. Riquer (1975, 41–44) recognizes the weakness in *coblas unissonans* and *singulars;* he sees in their lack of mnemonic guides to sequence a direct cause for the variety of different shapes each poem takes in the manuscripts.

9. It is all too easy to take the editor's text for "the poet's text" and to assert that the poet has succeeded in his intention because this text represents his intention. Thus Mölk's description of Guilhem IX's songs no. 1, 8, and 10 (Pillet-Carstens numbers) as "pentastanzaic," "octostanzaic," and "decastanzaic," respectively (1979, 7), assumes that the manuscripts preserve these poems intact, without adding or subtracting stanzas. Yet song 10 is "decastanzaic" in only four out of eight manuscripts. For the "pentastanzaic" song 1, Mölk credits Guilhem with inventing a "peculiar rhyme pattern" because the poem shifts from *coblas doblas* to *coblas ternas* (1, 2: *el, i, an;* 3–5: *i, an, el*). How can we assume that this "pentastanzaic poem" did not lose a sixth stanza? How can we be sure that the pattern was not originally *coblas alternadas,* for example 1324—5, with the

missing stanza in -*el*, -*i*, -*an*, or that there was never another set of stanzas with the complementary structure -*an*, -*el*, -*i*?

10. This calculation excludes the 68 poems preserved in one manuscript only. There were 484 poems in more than one manuscript (P+), 4,253 single-song manuscript copies (M+—again, excluding "unique MS." songs), 1,009 "versions" distinguished by stanzaic transposition (V+), and 1,533 "versions" counting all arrays (W+).

11. In the terms of Appendix A, why does T/P (= TR) vary?

12. LK+ vs. Z is a negative correlation, of only 35 percent; there is a 10 percent chance that there is no actual trend (see Appendix A, Table A-5).

13. VM = 46 percent and WM = 57 percent (see Fig. A-7).

14. Note that this trend does not hold true at all for poems with stanzaic linkage. When I distinguished between stanza-linked and unlinked poems in subindices of Versions per Manuscript, the stanza-linked poems tended to follow their unlinked counterparts and usually offered a weak reflection of their pattern of correlations. In this case poems with linked stanzas sharply diverged from the trend (i.e., Y vs. "VM-linked" gave a correlation coefficient of .00038, indicating near-perfect randomness). This type of stability in poems with unlinked stanzas thus may have been influenced by some chronological factor that did not affect poems with linked stanzas.

15. I had for a long time assumed that abridgment was more likely to be produced by lazy scribes (or by the constraints of space on pages) than by singers. I went so far as to think that a song version had to have at least three stanzas in order to show any sequence at all. Very recently, though, I heard sung a beautiful rendition of "Can vei la lauzeta mover"—in only two stanzas: short and sweet. The circumstances of the performance—a mixed audience perhaps unwilling to pay attention to the long version of a song that can seem interminable, and the need to fit the song into the rest of the musical program—made the two-stanza version seem best for reasons of performance. Manuscripts giving only two to three stanzas might, therefore, reflect performed versions. Such manuscripts are the only ones that frequently begin other than with the first stanza.

16. BVent: Y = 1159, WM = .437; VM = .306; LK+ = .30; Z = 8.18 (see Appendix A).

17. Berenguer de Palazol, also in quadrant 2, has an unusually small corpus of poetry, with eleven songs in only forty-eight extant copies: BPal: Y = 1164; WM = .375; LK+ = .09; Z = 8.42 (see Appendix A).

18. $(863/390) = (Va - 58)/(P+ - L+) = 2.2$.
$(146/94) = (Vb - 10)/L+ = 1.55$.

To do this calculation one has to subtract the unique-manuscript poems from Va and Vb (fifty-eight linked and ten unlinked). See Appendix A for explanation of variables and full synopsis of data.

Chapter 5

1. For *traire* in line 4, *E* gives *raire* (*radere, cancellare*—i.e., erase)!

2. Text for this stanza as edited by Roncaglia. Variants in *A* and *E*: 13 aun dedar *E*; 14 ves la penchura *E*; 15 retraissos *A*, fas *E*; 16 rebuzos *AE*, faun li ric lur veiaire *E*.

3. Literally, "crouchers"; Roncaglia, "poltroni" (1957, 25).

4. Boissonnade, cited in Roncaglia 1957, 4: "On avait vu un empereur acheter l'appui de la cour pontificale par l'octroi d'un tribut et la reconnaissance de la suzeraineté du Saint-Siège."

5. According to Nicholson (1976, 127), the scribe of the unique MS *c* writes the first line of a seventh stanza and leaves blank sufficient space for an eighth and a ninth stanza.

6. *C* and *R* belong to the "western languedoc tradition," according to Zufferey (1987, 103–104): *R* with its Gascon component "probably originally Toulousain," and *C* with its Catalan influence from Narbonne. Other manuscripts in this group (M^4, *GQ*, and a fragment he designates e^5) were made in northern Italy.

7. See Sakari 1956, 81–89, song 4. I return to this song later; all information about the manuscript variants is drawn from the *apparatus criticus*.

8. See Pickens 1978, 88–135, song 2. The editor discusses the "slot strophes" and the imbalance of *coblas doblas* in his introduction to the song (pp. 90–96).

9. Dejeanne prints the versions of *C* and *R* separately (1909, 186–188).

10. See Appendix A, Table A-5. I refer the reader to figures for "poems with linked stanzas" in general, although *coblas doblas* are a subset of this category. At one stage of investigation I separated *coblas doblas* from "more complex" forms of stanzaic linkage to investigate whether *coblas doblas* protected sequence as well as other forms did. The sample size becomes too small at that point, however, to support precise distinctions of a few percentage points one way or the other.

11. The mathematical formula for the number of possible permutations of *coblas doblas*, given a stable first pair of stanzas, and allowing inversion within pairs other than the first pair, is $2\,[(n-2)/2] \times [(n-2)/2]!$.

12. Note that each pair of stanzas has its own set of rhyme words: the first stanza of each pair uses feminine rhymes; the second uses masculine derivatives in retrograde order.

13. Chambers, discussing Marcabru's innovation of derivative rhymes in (293,14) "Contra l'ivern que s'enansa," points out a performance problem created by rhyme schemes in which masculine and feminine endings alternate from stanza to stanza: "A musical phrase which would be suitable for the masculine lines of one stanza would not fit the feminine lines occurring in the next at the same place and vice-versa. In a system of versification less rigidly bound to a strict

syllable count than Provençal, one might say that *enansa* and *trebalh* (in the respective first lines) could easily be sung to the same notes, with a hold for the masculine ending, extending through the final note of the feminine ending, but the correspondence of masculine and feminine endings is so uniformly exact in troubadour verse that one must question the validity of such a solution" (1985, 54). The song of Guilhem de St-Didier just discussed (234,5), however, avoids this problem, as Chambers notes: "the masculine lines are octosyllabic, the feminine heptasyllabic, so that the actual number of syllables is the same in both, and could be sung to the same tune (doubtless with some violation of the stress)" (p. 55).

14. Text, and all information about this poem's manuscript variants is drawn from Toja 1960, 372–385.

15. *Annales du Midi* 22:30, cited in Toja 1960, 201*n*.37.

16. For songs of uncertain or erroneous attribution to Bernart de Ventadorn, see Appel 1915, 277–348.

17. Not that it "should": the point is that the very intricate forms that would have promoted the concept of fixed text were not in widespread use, nor were they particularly usable. Thus, the capability to fix texts by means of form was not exercised, and texts generally were not fixed.

Chapter 6

1. Pattison 1952, 5–6, song 18. I reconstruct the second version from Pattison's *apparatus criticus*.

2. For a diverse selection of studies on *trobar clus* see Pollman 1965; Mölk 1968; and Roncaglia 1969b. Linda M. Paterson (1975, 2–5, 82–85, 88–93, etc.) discusses *trobar clus* as one, but not the most important, of various styles.

3. Ferrante is "inclined to take Guiraut as the sole author, since he names himself so clearly, and since most of the debates we have from the early poets seem to be the work of one poet who often uses the form to make fun of his own postures, putting his cliches into the mouth of another and thereby arguing with himself" (1984, 126*n*.30).

4. See Pattison 1952, 217–218, "Cartulary of Raimbaut d'Orange"; I have given Raimbaut's age at different years on the basis of Pattison's estimation that the poet was born in 1144 (p. 12).

5. See further Pattison 1952, pt. 1, sec. 5, pp. 13–17, "Raimbaut's Economic Position," esp. pp. 16–17.

6. Levy 1961, s.v. *trepeil*, gives "trouble, tapage"; it seems to connote specifically the noise of dancing or stomping: c.f. *trepar*, *trepejar*, *trepir*.

7. For *entendre* see Schutz 1932.

8. R d'Aur 31, 18–19: "ja per los faz / non er lauzatz" (*lauzar* in the legal documents of the period means "to give consent, approval").

9. Riquer (1975, 456) translates *venansal* as *humilde,* summarizes the translations of other scholars, and cites Guilhem de Cervera, who promises "Verses proverbials, / En loch de cells c'ay fayts / Leugers e venesals, / C'ay en cantan retrayts" (Proverbial verses in place of those I composed, light and lowly, that I performed while singing).

10. Riquer (1975, 458) translates *home sesal* as *hombre asalariado,* following Roncaglia, who argues that it means "homo (cantor) stipendarius."

11. Brunel 1926, 97,6; 110,2,3; 298,65; 20,92; 101,3,7. Brunel glosses *natura* in four instances as "famille" (97,6; 110,2,3; 298,65) and once as "peut-être 'droit féodale'" (20,92); *natural* twice means "indigène" (101,3,7) and *omes naturals* means "hommes envers qui on est engagé par serment, par obligation féodale" (144,4).

12. I am indebted to R. H. Bloch 1981 for the framework of ideas leading to my interpretation of *trobar natural;* Bloch 1983 gives a much fuller presentation (the influence of which can be detected throughout this chapter) of medieval notions of legitimacy in language.

13. Compare the formula in the *vidas* and *razos,* "en comtan et en chantan" (Boutière and Schutz 1964, nos. 78,3; 81,1; 321,2, version of *H*).

14. My reading differs from Pattison's (1952) at several points. First, because line 36 explains line 37, I find it more likely that *trop* is in the first person, rather than the third (Pattison, p. 182: "And so that he may not find advantage and may not build up a false tale from it"). Second, while I concur with Pattison that "*Orda* must come from *ordir, ordre,* 'to weave,' or figuratively, 'to construct a tale, to invent a work of fiction,' as in Raimbaut's IV,1" (p. 183), it seems to me that *orda* is a noun: where Pattison punctuates "E qar no·i trop pro, e·n orda," I punctuate "E qar no·i trop pro en orda." Third, *rancas* can just as easily come from *rance* (adj.: *rance*) as from *ranc* (adj.: *boiteux;* Levy 1961) (Levy disagreed with Raynouard, who believed that *ranc* and *rance* were the same word), and the former is more consonant with the verb *sentir,* which generally designates the sense of smell or another sense but rarely the sense of hearing (Pattison, p. 182: "I leave off, for I hear limping words").

15. Bernard of Clairvaux does likewise in his sermons on the *Canticus.* In Brian Stock's paraphrase from the first sermon (1983, 412): "But the Song of Songs surpasses all other sacred melodies. . . . It cannot be heard outside: only the singer and He to whom it is sung, that is, the bridegroom and the bride, can actually hear it, as is fitting for an epithalamium. Above all it cannot be heard or sung by weak and imperfect souls."

16. For *aizi, aiziment,* and *cambra,* see Dragonetti 1964.

17. Minnis (1984, 43 and note 22) recognizes this need: "The apparently erotic encounters recorded by Solomon demanded 'reverent interpretation'—and got it in abundance. . . . The Song of Songs was read as a mystical epithalamium which celebrated the marriage of Christ and Holy Church, a work far superior to pagan poems of merely human love."

Chapter 7

1. Nichols (1976, 32) finds that this pun operates as an essential premise underlying Marcabru's approach to poetry: "Marcabru's *mot* ('words') cannot help but *fan de ver semblansa* because they *are* the *semblansa* (the 'representation' or 'manifestation') and the *ver*. Hence the brilliance of the internal rhyme *vers/ver*, which now becomes more than a rhyme because it *is*—that is, by virtue of existing as a poetic assertion."

2. I give the text of Rudolf Zenker (1901, 795–798). These three lines comprise the *tornada*. This is one of three songs probably by Peire d'Alvernhe that Alberto del Monte does not publish in his edition, presumably because Zenker claimed them for Bernart de Venzac. Despite his interest in establishing a corpus for that poet, Pillet and Carstens (1933) found Zenker's argument convincing for only one song. "Abans que·l blanc poi sion vert" (323,1) is available in Carl Appel's 1882 edition of Peire Rogier; Zenker includes the other two—323,5 "Bela m'es la flors d'aguilen" and 323,6 "Bel m'es lo dous chans per la faia"— among the *dubia* of Peire d'Alvernhe. The more recent edition of Bernart de Venzac is therefore extremely valuable whether or not we accept the poems' attributions to this poet; it contains excellent songs not readily available elsewhere (Simonelli 1974).

3. See Chapter 2 for text and discussion of Bernart Amoros.

4. Marshall (1968, 21) points out that "Com si liman pogues" does not mean "how by filing I could" but rather "as if by filing I could": line 23 is the direct object of *serc*. I have departed from Pattison's text only in adding the parentheses, which clarify the meaning in accordance with Marshall's interpretation of the syntax.

5. Rita Lejeune (1939) argues against this derivation of Raimbaut's nickname, suggesting that it came instead from the comic figure of Ignaure, a medieval ladies' man. Be that as it may, I do not believe that Raimbaut missed the chance to exploit the metaphorical possibilities of the nickname "Linhaure": Raimbaut created his *own* "performing self" and did not merely borrow the persona of a literary character.

6. Arnaut uses the word *rust* only once, carrying its pejorative overtones to the point of obscenity: "entre l'eschine'e·l penchenill / lai on se sangna de rovill" (Arn D 1, 42–43).

7. Payen (1970, 164) discusses the troubadours' use of the opposition of *sai* and *lai;* his perception that these deictics serve the poets as a means of alluding to the relationship between "performing self" and audience might well be applied to Giraut's use of *sai* in lines 43 and 47 here (with an implied *lai* in v. 45, "enviar mo messatge"): "Le jeu subtil sur l'opposition de l'«ici» et du «là-bas» aboutit à un paradoxe: le «là-bas» des troubadours est l'«ici» de leur auditoire, puisqu'il désigne l'univers chevaleresque dans lequel évolue ce public. Jaufre Rudel inverse

ce système et rétablit dans l'éspace courtois une relative cohérence: son «ici» coincide avec celui du public, . . . mais il n'élimine la contradiction qu'en évacuant la *fin'amors* dans un «ailleurs» où elle est d'une certaine manière remise en question."

8. The best edition of this song is Linda M. Paterson's (1975, 60–65). I cite her text for this poem and give her translations, indicating the points at which my reading differs.

9. "Que no·s rompa·l semdiers" retains its literal meaning, I believe, though "broken along the way" differs in meaning from "left half-finished" only in the implied agent of each action: the jongleur might "break the song on the way"; the original author might "leave it half-finished." As a matter of fact, judging from copies in the *chansonniers,* jongleurs also "left songs half-finished" quite frequently.

10. For this use of *acordar,* c.f. Arn D 8, 9: "Qui·ls motz ab lo son acorda." I found three instances from the period ca. 1170 in which the phrase *en bonacort* was used to praise simultaneously the audience and the song performed before them: when one sings *en bona cort* (in a good court), one should sing *en bon' acort* (in good accord): (1) "Be deu en bonacort dir / bo sonet qui·l fai" (Whoever makes a good little melody, he should recite it in good accord [*or* in a good court]; Gr Bor 49, 1–2); (2) "Ben s'eschai q'en bonacort / chan qui chantar sap" (It is fitting that anyone who knows how to sing should sing in good accord [*or* in a good court]; R d'Aur 21, 1–2); (3) "Belh m'es qui a son bon sen / qu'en bonacort lo presen / q'us bes ab autre s'enansa" (It pleases me that whoever has good sense should present it in good accord [*or* in a good court], for one good advances with the other; P d'Alv 14, 1–2). Cf. also Gr Bor 9, 17–19: "Si·m pogues paiar del mazan / Mas volh que·l cor s'acort al chan / e que la bocha rend apres / dels bels dichs" (And I could be contented [paid] with applause, but I want the heart to harmonize with the song [first], and afterwards let the lips return fair speeches).

11. Paterson 1975: "For he ought to be pleasing by speaking consistently without any dark word, since whoever takes a leap in imitation of Maurin falls down mid-way if he does not cling to the sides, as he makes all the words certain to cause toil, so that the whole audience is set to guessing." The phrase "de mauri en miro" has been controversial; Paterson identifies *Mauri* as "the hero of the Provençal *chanson de geste, Aigar et Maurin,*" whose "flaw was overweening pride" (p. 64). Still, it seems to me more straightforward to read, "*from* mauri *to* miro": if *miron* is, as Paterson says, "from the verb *mirar,* 'to admire, reflect, imitate'," then what form of the verb is it? The present participle would be *miran,* not *miron.* "L'auzir de maison" or "maion," as I understand it, refers both to "audience reception" and to the sound of the word *maion:* "The hearing of 'the house.'"

12. I differ with Paterson in the reading of *estiers:* the translation "otherwise"

does not make sense because there is no implicit *condition* mentioned that would permit grain to "be forthcoming." I take *vengua* to mean "become" and read *estiers* as an adjective. Levy (1961) gives *esters* as meaning "exempt, dépourvu," from *esterzer*; the meaning may be closer to *esterle* (*stérile*).

13. This topos was popular among the troubadours: Cnyrim (1887) gives dozens of instances, numbered 148 et seq. in his collection of proverbs in Provençal lyric. I discuss its relation to *trobar natural* in Chapter 6.

14. Hoepffner translates, "Mais fussent-elles encore plus nombreuses, elles ne sont ni 'entières', ni 'brisées'" (1929, 15).

15. *Mogutz,* "in Umlauf gesetzt" (Kolsen 1910, 401).

16. Levy 1961 has *aiguilen* as *églantine, églantier, gratte-cul.* The near homophony with *aiguilha* (pin) may possibly be operative, but the important thing here is that the idiom calls for a worthless object. Other worthless objects used in such expressions are *raba* (rutabaga) and *carobla* (carob bean).

17. For a discussion of Alegret's *vers sec,* see Mölk 1968, 94–98.

18. The phrase is from Ezra Pound, Canto 81 (1972, 522).

19. Pons G 7, 5–8: "E pus a lieys ai ma chanso promeza, / ben la dei far cuenhd'e guay'e prezan, / quar ben conosc que, si·l ven a talan, / qu'en mans bos locs n'er chantad'ez apreza" (And since I have promised my song to her, I must truly make it pleasant, gay, and valuable, for I know well that, if she desires, it will be sung and learned in many a good place).

Conclusion

1. Sarah Kay (1987) offers such a multiple reading as evidence that some versions of Jaufre Rudel's "Quan lo rius de la fontana" may be demonstrably inauthentic because they reflect thirteenth-century, not twelfth-century, themes. Readers of this book will perhaps take issue with her statement that "its insistence on oral rather than written transmission strikes me as more in keeping with a later date than with the mid-1100's" (p. 47). Though she high-handedly berates "the fashion for *mouvance*" and heaps unwarranted "guilt" on its "exponents" (ibid.), she nevertheless profits from their work to the extent of acknowledging the utility of a plural reading—and to the extent of actually performing a plural reading. She sees the "inauthentic" versions as "interesting documents in the history of reception" composed by "a number of not very talented versifiers" (p. 56) whose chief value is to provide literary commentary on the "original." She is not, however, willing to read alternate versions as she finds them. Although disowning "characteristically procrustean" readings of Jeanroy (p. 48), she would rather emend than entertain an unfamiliar lexical item ("Pickens's rendering of *mirimolina* as 'Millview' is unworthy of retention; the original may have had *mi revolina,* with the meaning '[everything] whirls around within [*dinz*] me' [?]";

p. 53). Are twentieth-century readers adequately equipped to establish "the original," and to do so with enough certainty to scoff at an attested manuscript reading?

Appendix A

1. Certain graphs have been omitted. This information comes from the "linear equation" describing the trend line of the extremely regular correlation V vs. M, "number of transposed versions versus number of manuscript copies." (V vs. M: $r = .92$; significance level $= .0001$; $V = .22[M] + 6.18$.)

2. From the trend line of W vs. M, "number of broadly defined versions versus number of manuscript copies." (W vs. M: $r = .95$; significance level $= .0001$; $W = .36[M] + 1.26$.)

3. From the trend line of V vs. W, "number of narrowly defined versions versus number of broadly defined versions." (V vs. W: $r = .98$; significance level $= .0001$; $V = .61[W] + 4.67$.)

4. From the trend line of V vs. T, "number of narrowly defined versions versus number of poems showing stanzaic transposition." (V vs. T: $r = .97$; significance level $= .0001$; $V = 4.36[T] + 5.16$.)

5. From the trend line of W vs. A, "number of broadly defined versions versus number of poems showing alternate stanzaic arrays." (W vs. A: $r = .94$; significance level $= .0001$; $W = 4.46[A] + 4.03$.)

6. Actually, their songs went outside the normal proportion of abridgments to transpositions, on one side or the other of the line.

7. Versions per poem, VP, an index not selected for full presentation because it was too flat, nevertheless showed a significant correlation with Manuscripts per Poem, MS. (VP vs. MS: $r = .59$; significance level $= .0033$; $VP = .15[MS] + .84$.)

8. See the correlation matrices for a synoptic view of the relative strengths of these relationships (Appendix A, Tables A3–A4).

9. T vs. P: $r = .83$; significance level $= .0001$; $T = .42(P) - .44$.

10. A vs. P: $r = .98$; significance level $= .0001$; $A = .75(P) - 3.41$.

11. V vs. P: $r = .85$; significance level $= .0001$; $V = 1.91(P) + .98$.

12. W vs. P: $r = .89$; significance level $= .0001$; $W = 3.26(P) - 8.58$.

13. Where VPb represents "Versions per Poem in Poems with Linked Stanzas," look at LK+ vs. VPb: $r = .36$; significance level $= .0948$. We might expect an inverse correlation.

Appendix C

1. See Zufferey 1987, 80, for a description of variation among scholars in assignation of sigla for Bernart Amoros's songbook. I follow the usage of Pillet and Carstens 1933.

WORKS CITED

Appel, Carl, ed. 1915. *Bernart von Ventadorn*. Halle.

Avalle, d'Arco Silvio. 1961. *La letteratura medievale in lingua d'oc nella sua tradizione manoscritta*. Studi e ricerche, 16. Turin.

———, ed. 1960. *Peire Vidal. Poesie*. 2 vols. Documenti di filologia, 4. Milan.

Barbieri, Giovanni Maria. 1790. *Dell'origine della poesia rimata*. Modena.

Bertoni, Giulio, ed. 1905. *Il canzoniere provenzale della Riccardiana (Q)*. Gesellschaft für romanische Literatur, 8. Dresden.

———. 1911. *Il canzoniere provenzale di Bernart Amoros, complemento Càmpori*. Collectanea Friburgensia, 20. Fribourg.

———. 1912. *Il canzoniere provenzale della Biblioteca Ambrosiana (G)*. Gesellschaft für romanische Literatur, 28. Dresden.

Bloch, Marc. 1961. *Feudal Society*. Translated by L. A. Manyon. 2 vols. Chicago.

Bloch, R. Howard. 1977. *Medieval French Literature and Law*. Berkeley and Los Angeles.

———. 1981. "Etymologies et généalogies: Théories de la langue, liens de parenté et genre littéraire au XIIIᵉ siècle." *Annales: Economies, sociétés, civilisations* 36:946–962.

———. 1983. *Etymologies and Genealogies: A Literary Anthropology of the French Middle Ages*. Chicago.

Bond, Gerald A. 1978. "The Structure of the 'Gap' of the Count of Poitiers." *Neuphilologische Mitteilungen* 79:162–172.

Bondanella, Peter E. 1973. "The Theory of the Gothic Lyric and the Case of Bernart de Ventadorn." *Neuphilologische Mitteilungen* 74:369–381.

Boutière, Jean, and A. H. Schutz, ed. 1964. *Biographies des troubadours*. 2d ed. Paris.

Bowden, Betsy. 1982. *Performed Literature: Words and Music by Bob Dylan*. Bloomington, Ind.

Brunel, Clovis, ed. 1926. *Les plus anciennes chartes en langue provençale*. Paris.

Bunting, Basil. 1978. *Collected Poems*. Oxford.

Calin, William. 1983. "Singer's Voice and Audience Response: On the Originality of the Courtly Lyric, or How 'Other' Was the Middle Ages and What Should We Do About It?" *L'esprit créateur* 23(1): 75–90.

Camproux, Charles. 1965. *Le joy d'amor des troubadours: Jeu et joie d'amour.* Montpellier.

Carroll, Carleton W. 1970. "A Comparative Structural Analysis of Arnaut Daniel's 'Lo ferm voler' and Peire Vidal's 'Mout m'es bon e bel.'" *Neophilologus* 54 338–346.

Chambers, Frank M. 1971. *Proper Names in the Lyrics of the Troubadours.* University of North Carolina Studies in the Romance Languages and Literatures, 113. Chapel Hill.

———. 1985. *An Introduction to Old Provençal Versification.* Memoirs of the American Philosophical Society, 167. Philadelphia.

Clanchy, M. T. 1979. *From Memory to Written Record: England, 1066–1307.* Cambridge, Mass.

Cnyrim, Eugen. 1887. *Sprichwörter, sprichwörtliche Redensarten und Sentenzen bei den provenzalischen Lyrikern.* Marburg University Dissertations, vol. 1, no. 11. Marburg.

Colunga, R. P., O. P. Alberto, and Laurentio Turrado. 1959. *Biblia sacra iuxta vulgatam Clementinam.* 3d ed. Madrid.

Condren, Edward I. 1972. "The Troubadour and His Labor of Love." *Medieval Studies* 34:174–195.

Cropp, Glynnis. 1974. "L'apr. *retener:* Son sens et son emploi dans la poésie des troubadours." In *Mélanges d'histoire littéraire, de linguistique et de philologie romanes offerts à Charles Rostaing,* 179–200. Liège.

———. 1975. *Le vocabulaire courtois des troubadours de l'époque classique.* Geneva.

Dejeanne, J.-M.-L., ed. 1909. *Poésies complètes du troubadour Marcabru.* Toulouse.

Del Monte, Alberto, ed. 1955. *Peire d'Alvernhe. Liriche.* Collezione di filologia romanza, 1. Turin.

Diez, Frédéric (Friedrich). 1845. *La poésie des troubadours.* Translated by Ferdinand de Roisin. Paris.

Dragonetti, Roger. 1960. *La technique poétique des trouvères dans la chanson courtoise.* Bruges.

———. 1964. "Aizi et aizimen chez les plus anciens troubadours." In *Mélanges de linguistique romane et de philologie médiévale offerts à Maurice Delbouille,* edited by Jean Renson and Madeleine Tyssens, 2:127–153. Liège. (Reprinted in Dragonetti, *La musique et les lettres,* 201–227. Geneva, 1986.)

Dumitrescu, Maria, ed. 1935. *Poésies du troubadour Aimeric de Belenoi.* Société des anciens textes français. Paris.

Eco, Umberto. 1965. *L'oeuvre ouverte.* Translated by Chantal Roux de Bézieux. Paris. (Originally published as *Opera aperta.* Milan, 1962.)

Eliot, Thomas Stearns. [1971]. *The Waste Land: A Facsimile and Transcript of the Original Drafts.* Edited by Valerie Eliot. New York.

Faral, Edmond. [1910] 1970. *Les jongleurs en France au moyen âge.* Burt Franklin Research and Source Works Series, 606. New York.

Ferrante, Joan M. 1984. *"Farai un vers de dreyt nien:* The Craft of the Early Troubadours." In *Vernacular Poetics in the Middle Ages,* edited by Lois Ebin, 93–128. Kalamazoo, Mich.

Fish, Stanley E. 1980. "Literature in the Reader: Affective Stylistics." In *Reader-Response Criticism,* edited by Jane P. Tompkins, 70–100. Baltimore. (Slightly revised version of essay printed in *New Literary History* 2[1970]:123–162 and reprinted as Appendix in Fish, *Self-Consuming Artifacts.* Berkeley and Los Angeles, 1972.)

Frank, István. 1953, 1957. *Répertoire métrique de la poésie des troubadours.* Bibliothèque de l'Ecole des Hautes Etudes. Sciences historiques et philologiques, fasc. 305 and 308. Paris.

———, ed. 1949. *Pons de la Guardia, troubadour catalan du XIIe siècle.* Boletín de la Real Academia de Buenas Letras de Barcelona, 22. Barcelona.

Ghil, Eliza Miruna. 1979. "Topic and Tropeic: Two Types of Syntagmatic Development in the Old Provençal Canzo." *L'esprit créateur* 19(4):54–69.

Goldin, Frederick, ed. and trans. 1973. *Lyrics of the Troubadours and Trouvères: An Anthology and a History.* Garden City, N.Y.

Grandgent, Charles Hall. 1905. *An Outline of the Phonology and Morphology of Old Provençal.* Rev. ed. Boston.

Gröber, Gustav. 1877. *Die Liedersammlungen der Troubadours. Romanische Studien* 2:337–670.

Guiette, Robert. 1960. "D'une poésie formelle en France au moyen âge." *Romanica Gandensia* 8:9–32. (Originally published in *Revue des sciences humaines* 54[1949]:61–68.)

Guiraud, Pierre. 1971. "Les structures étymologiques du trobar." *Poétique* 2:417–426.

———. 1979. "La joie d'amour: Analyse étymologique." In J. B. Guiran, *Hommage à Jean Onimus,* pp. 37–40. Annales de la Faculté des Lettres et Sciences Humaines de Nice, 38. Paris.

Hoepffner, Ernest, ed. 1929. *Les poésies de Bernart Marti.* Paris.

Huot, Sylvia. 1987. *From Song to Book: The Poetics of Writing in Old French Lyric and Lyrical Narrative Poetry.* Ithaca, N.Y.

Jauss, Hans Robert. 1982. *Toward an Aesthetic of Reception.* Translated by Timothy Bahti. Theory and History of Literature, 2. Minneapolis.

Jeanroy, Alfred. 1934. *La poésie lyrique des troubadours.* Toulouse.

Jeffers, Robinson. 1925. *Roan Stallion, Tamar, and Other Poems.* New York.

Jernigan, Charles. 1974. "The Song of Nail and Uncle: Arnaut Daniel's Sestina 'Lo ferm voler q'el cor m'intra.'" *Studies in Philology* 74:127–151.

Johnston, R. C., ed. 1935. *Les poésies lyriques du troubadour Arnaut de Mareuil.* Paris.

Kay, Sarah. 1987. "Continuation as Criticism: The Case of Jaufre Rudel." *Medium Aevum* 56:46–64.

Kenner, Hugh. 1975. *A Homemade World: The American Modernist Writers.* New York.

Kleinhenz, Christopher, ed. 1976. *Medieval Manuscripts and Textual Transmission.* North Carolina Studies in the Romance Languages and Literatures, Symposia, no. 4. Chapel Hill.

Knight, William, ed. 1896. *Prose Works of William Wordsworth.* Vol. 1. London.

Köhler, Erich. 1962. *Trobadorlyrik und höfischer Roman.* Berlin.

———. 1970. "Les troubadours et la jalousie." In *Mélanges de langue et de littérature offerts à Jean Frappier,* 533–559. Geneva.

Kolsen, Adolf, ed. 1910. *Sämtliche Lieder des Trobadors Giraut de Bornelh.* Halle.

Lazar, Moshé. 1964. *Amour courtois et "fin'amors."* Paris.

———, ed. 1966. *Bernard de Ventadour, troubadour du XIIe siècle: Chansons d'amour.* Paris.

Lejeune, Rita. 1939. "Le personnage d'Ignaure dans la poésie des troubadours." *Bulletin de l'Académie Royale de Langue et Littérature Française de Belgique* 18:140–172.

———. 1957. "Le troubadour Rigaut de Barbezieux." In *Mélanges de linguistique et de littérature romanes à la mémoire d'István Frank,* 269–295. Annales Universitatis Saraviensis, 6. Saarbrücken.

———. 1962. "Analyse textuelle et histoire littéraire: Rigaut de Barbezieux." *Le moyen âge* 68:331–377.

———. 1965. "La 'Galérie littéraire' du troubadour Peire d'Alvernhe." In *Actes et mémoires du IIIe congrès international de langue et de littérature d'Oc et d'études franco-provençales,* 35–54. Bordeaux. (Prepared 1961.)

Levy, Emil, ed. 1894–1924. *Provenzalisches Supplement-Wörterbuch.* Leipzig.

———, ed. 1961. *Petit dictionnaire provençal-français.* Heidelberg.

Maas, Paul. 1958. *Textual Criticism.* Translated by Barbara Flower. Oxford.

Marshall, John H. 1968. "On the Text and Interpretation of a Poem of Raimbaut D'Orange (Cars Douz; ed. Pattison, 1)." *Medium Aevum* 37:12–36.

———. 1972. *The Razos de Trobar of Raimon Vidal and Associated Texts.* London.

———. 1975. *The Transmission of Troubadour Poetry: An Inaugural Lecture at Westfield College.* London.

Migne, J. P. 1844–1902. *Patrologia cursus completus (series latina).*

Minnis, A. J. 1984. *Medieval Theory of Authorship: Scholastic Literary Attitudes in the Later Middle Ages.* London.

Mölk, Ulrich. 1968. *Trobar Clus/Trobar Leu: Studien zur Dichtungstheorie der Trobadors.* Munich.

————. 1979. "Troubadour Versification as Literary Craftsmanship." Translated by Micheline Nilsen. *L'esprit créateur* 19(4):3–16.

Moore, Marianne. 1951 (author's copyright)/1961. *Collected Poems*. New York.

Mussafia, Adolf. 1874. "Über die provenzalischen Liederhandschriften des Giovanni Maria Barbieri." *Sitzungsberichte der Kaiserlichen Akademie der Wissenschaften, Philos.-Hist. Klasse* 76(1):201–306. Vienna.

Nelli, René. 1963. *L'érotique des troubadours*. Toulouse.

Newcombe, Terence, ed. 1971. "The Troubadour Berenger de Palazol: A Critical Edition of His Poems." *Nottingham Medieval Studies* 15:54–95.

Nichols, Stephen G., Jr. 1976. "Toward an Aesthetic of the Provençal Lyric II: Marcabru's *Dire vos vuoill ses doptansa* (BdT 293,18)." In *Italian Literature: Roots and Branches. Essays in Honor of Thomas Goddard Bergin*, edited by Giose Rimanelli and Kenneth J. Atchity, 15–37. New Haven.

Nicholson, Derek E. T., ed. 1976. *The Poems of the Troubadour Peire Rogier*. Manchester.

Ong, Walter J. 1982. *Orality and Literacy: The Technologizing of the Word*. London.

Paden, William D., Jr. 1975. "The Troubadour's Lady: Her Marital Status and Social Rank." *Studies in Philology* 72:28–50.

————. 1979. "William, Count of Poitou, and the Medium of Troubadour Poetry." Photocopy.

————. 1984. "The Role of the Joglar in Troubadour Lyric Poetry." In *Chrétien de Troyes and the Troubadours*, edited by Peter S. Noble and Linda M. Paterson, 90–99. Cambridge.

Paden, William D., Jr., Tilde Sankovitch, and Patricia H. Stäblein, eds. 1986. *The Poems of the Troubadour Bertran de Born*. Berkeley and Los Angeles.

Pasero, Nicolò, ed. 1973. *Guglielmo IX: Poesie*. Istituto di Filologia Romanza. Studi, testi e manuali, 1. Modena.

Paterson, Linda M. 1975. *Troubadours and Eloquence*. Oxford.

Pattison, Walter T. 1933. "The Background of Peire d'Alvernhe's *Chantarai d'aquestz trobadors*." *Modern Philology* 31:19–34.

————. 1969. "Some Considerations on the Relationship of the Old Provençal Chansonniers." In *Mélanges offerts à Rita Lejeune*, 229–233. Gembloux.

————, ed. 1952. *The Life and Works of the Troubadour Raimbaut d'Orange*. Minneapolis.

Payen, Jean-Charles. 1970. "L'espace et le temps de la chanson courtoise occitane." In *Présence des troubadours*, edited by Pierre Bec, 143–165. Annales de l'Institut d'Etudes Occitanes, ser. 4, vol. 2, no. 5. Toulouse.

————. 1978. "A propos du 'Vocabulaire courtois des troubadours': Problèmes méthodologiques." *Cahiers de civilisation médiévale* 21:151–155.

Pickens, Rupert T. 1977. "Jaufre Rudel et la poétique de la mouvance." *Cahiers de civilisation médiévale* 20:323–337.

————, ed. 1978. *The Songs of Jaufre Rudel.* Pontifical Institute of Medieval Studies. Studies and Texts, 41. Toronto.

Pickford, Cedric E., ed. 1974. *The Song of Songs: A Twelfth-Century French Version.* Oxford.

Pillet, Alfred, and Henry Carstens. 1933. *Bibliographie des troubadours.* Halle.

Pizzorusso, Bertolucci. 1978. "Il canzoniere di un trovatore: Il 'libro' di Giraut Riquer." *Medioevo romanzo* 5:216–259.

Poe, Elizabeth Wilson. 1984. *From Poetry to Prose in Old Provençal.* Birmingham, Ala.

Pollmann, Leo. 1965. *'Trobar clus,' Bibelexegese und hispano-arabische Literatur.* Forschungen zur romanischen Philologie, 16. Münster.

Pound, Ezra. 1926. *Personae.* New York.

————. 1972. *The Cantos.* New York.

Raynouard, M. 1836–1844. *Lexique roman.* Paris.

Regan, Mariann S. 1974. "*Amador* and *Chantador:* The Lover and the Poet in the *Cansos* of Bernart de Ventadorn." *Philological Quarterly* 53:10–28.

Rich, Adrienne. 1979. "Vesuvius at Home: The Power of Emily Dickinson." In *On Lies, Secrets, and Silence: Selected Prose, 1966–1978,* 157–183. New York.

Ricketts, Peter T., ed. 1964. *Guilhem de Montanhagol: Troubadour provençal du XIIIe siècle.* Pontifical Institute of Medieval Studies. Studies and Texts, 9. Toronto.

————. 1968. "A l'alena del vent doussa de Marcabrun: Edition critique, trad. et comm." *Revue des langues romanes* 78:109–115.

Riquer, Martín de, ed. 1971. *Guillem de Berguedà.* Scriptorium populeti, 5 (vol. 1: Estudio histórico, literario y lingüístico) and 6 (vol. 2: Edición crítica, traducción, notas y glosario). Abadía de Poblet.

————, ed. 1975. *Los trovadores: Historia literaria y textos.* Barcelona.

Roncaglia, Aurelio. 1969a. "Due postille alla 'Galleria letteraria' di Peire d'Alvernhe." *Marche romane* 19:71–78.

————. 1969b. "'Trobar clus'—discussione aperta." *Cultura neolatina* 29:5–55.

————, ed. 1951a. "Il 'gap' di Marcabruno." *Studi medievali* 17:46–70.

————, ed. 1951b. "Marcabruno: 'Lo vers comens quan vei del fau' (BdT 393,33)." *Cultura neolatina* 11:20–48.

————, ed. 1957. "Marcabruno: *Aujatz de chan* (BdT 293,9)." *Cultura neolatina* 17:21–48.

Rougemont, Denis de. [1956] 1974. *Love in the Western World.* Translated by Montgomery Belgion. Rev. ed. New York.

Safire, William. 1981. *On Language.* New York.

Sakari, Aimo. 1949. "Azalais de Porcairagues, le joglar de Raimbaut d'Orange." *Neuphilologische Mitteilungen* 50:23–43, 56–87, 174–198.

————, ed. 1956. *Poésies du troubadour Guillem de Saint-Didier*. Mémoires de la Société Néophilologique de Helsinki, 19. Helsinki.

Schutz, A. H. 1932. "A Preliminary Study of *trobar e entendre*, an Expression in Medieval Aesthetics." *Romanic Review* 32:129–138.

————. 1935. "More on *trobar e entendre*." *Romanic Review* 26:29–31.

————, ed. [1933] 1971. *Poésies de Daude de Pradas*. Toulouse/Paris.

Shepard, William P., ed. 1924. *Les poésies de Jausbert de Puycibot*. Classiques Français du Moyen Age, 46. Paris.

Simonelli, Maria Picchio, ed. 1974. *Lirica moralistica nell'Occitania del XII secolo, Bernart de Venzac*. Istituto di Filologia Romanza. Studi, testi e manuali, 2. Rome.

Stengel, Edmund. 1872. "Die provenzalische Liederhandschrift cod. 42 der Laurenzianischen Bibliothek in Florenz." *Archiv* 50:241–284. (Diplomatic edition of MS *P*.)

————. 1898–1902. "Le chansonnier de Bernart Amoros." *Revue des langues romanes* 41(1898):349–380; 42(1899):5–43; 44(1900):213–244, 328–341, 423–442; 45(1902):44–64, 120–151, 211–275. (Diplomatic edition of MS *a*.)

Stevens, Martin. 1978. "The Performing Self in Twelfth-Century Literature." *Viator* 9:193–212.

Stimming, Albert, ed. 1879. *Bertran de Born, sein Leben und seine Werke*. Halle.

Stock, Brian. 1983. *The Implications of Literacy*. Princeton, N.J.

Stronski, Stanislaw. [1910] 1968. *Le troubadour Folquet de Marseille, édition critique*. Geneva.

Sutherland, Dorothy R. 1961. "The Love Meditation in Courtly Literature (A Study of the Terminology and Its Developments in Old Provençal and Old French)." In *Studies in Medieval French Presented to Alfred Ewert*, 165–193. Oxford.

————. 1965. "L'élément théatral dans la 'canso' chez les troubadours de l'époque classique." In *Actes et mémoires du IIIᵉ congrès international de langue et littérature d'Oc et d'études franco-provençales*, 95–101. Bordeaux. (Prepared 1961.)

Teulié, H., and G. Rossi. 1901–1902. *L'anthologie provençale de maître Ferrari de Ferrare*. In *Annales du Midi* 13:60–73, 199–215, 371–388; 14:197–205, 523–538.

Toja, Gianluigi, ed. 1960. *Arnaut Daniel, canzoni*. Florence.

Topsfield, Leslie T. 1974. "The 'Natural Fool' in Peire d'Alvernhe, Marcabru, and Bernart de Ventadorn." In *Mélanges d'histoire littéraire, de linguistique et de philologie romanes offerts à Charles Rostaing*, 1149–1158. Liège.

————. 1975. *Troubadours and Love*. Cambridge.

————, ed. 1971. *Les poésies du troubadour Raimon de Miraval*. Paris.

Várvaro, Alberto, ed. 1960. *Rigaut de Berbezilh: Liriche*. Biblioteca di filologia romanza, 4. Bari.

Werf, Hendrik van der. 1972. *The Chansons of the Troubadours and Trouvères: A Study of the Melodies and Their Relation to the Poems*. Utrecht.

Wimsatt, William K., and Monroe C. Beardsley. 1954. *The Verbal Icon: Studies in the Meaning of Poetry*. Lexington, Ky.

Zenker, Rudolf. 1901. "Die Lieder Peires von Auvergne, kritisch herausgegeben mit Einleitung, Übersetzung, Kommentar und Glossar." *Romanische Forschungen* 12:654–800.

Zufferey, François. 1987. *Recherches linguistiques sur les chansonniers provençaux*. Geneva.

Zumthor, Paul. 1971. "De la circularité du chant (à propos des trouvères des XIIe et XIIIe siècles)." *Poétique* 2:129–140.

———. 1972. *Essai de poétique médiévale*. Paris.

———. 1982. "Le corps du poème." *Paragone* (Letteratura) 33(392):8–25.

———. 1987. *La lettre et la voix. De la "littérature" médiévale*. Paris.

23, 45–46, 193–94; "Lo nous mes
d'abril" (421,6; Várvaro 6), 54; "Pauc
sap d'amor" (421,7; Várvaro 7), 122–
23, 127; "Si co·l solilhs" (337,1; Várvaro dubia 5), 67; "Tot atressi con la
clartatz" (421,9; Várvaro 8), 108–9
Roncaglia, Aurelio, 96
Rupert of Duize, 158

Salut d'amor, 44
Sancho III of Castile, 145, 150–51
Satire, 10–11
Scribes, 61, 62, 63, 68, 88, 108, 128, 222,
256n.15. See also Clerics; Copyists
Scripture, 157–58, 159, 195; miracle at
Cana wedding, 191; parable of the
Sower, 180
Senhals, 54, 73, 110, 248n.13; Bels
Bericles, 73; Bels Paradis, 157; Bertran,
73; Bons Respieitz, 248n.13; Desirat
(for Sancho III?), 150–51; Glove Lady,
148; Joglar, 73, 109, 121; Linhaure (of
Raimbaut d'Aurenga), 134, 138, 172,
260n.5; Messager, 49; Miels-de-
domna, 54, 55, 123; Mos Cortes, 110,
116; Mos Tortres, 110, 116; Tort
n'avetz, 53
Sequence of stanzas: and Arnaut Daniel,
106–7; and closure, 197; and idea of
fixity, 201, 213, App. A; and Marca-
bru, 91–96; and meaning, 72, 92, 127–
29, 202–3, 206; and razo, 92, 126–27;
and reception, 203–5; and song length,
256n.15; and stemmas, 255n.3; and
stylistic complexity, 74–75, 81
Sermons, 158
Sestina, 122, 200, 203
Shakespeare, William, 192
Significance level, defined, 217
Singer. See Cantador; Jongleur; Performer
Sirventes, 29, 38, 92, 97, 145, 188, 190,
197; bastir, 175
Slot strophes, 257n.8
Social class of troubadours, 66–67, 68
Songbooks. See Autograph songbooks;
Chansonniers
Song of Solomon (Canticus), 155, 157,
159, 160, 219–22
Stability and mutability, 5, 28, 79, 89,
198–99, 210, 211. See also Mouvance

Stanzaic arrays, 62, 82, 83, 88, 92, 97,
102, 122, 126, 127, 179, 213–16,
219–22. See also Abridgment; Versions and variants
Stanzaic sequence. See Sequence of stanzas
Stanzaic transposition. See Transposition
of stanzas
Stanza length: and stability, 81, 83–86,
119, 221, 222, 255n.14, App. A; and
stylistic difficulty, 80, 81
Stanza position: first, 99, 108, 117, 166,
200–201, 256n.15 (see also Index of
Provençal Terms: Comensamen); final,
117, 200 (see also Tornada); penulti-
mate, 151
Stanzas, autonomy of: 116, 118, 127; and
of half-stanzas, 92, 93
Stanzas, linked: defined, 74–75, 86; fa-
vored or rejected, 221, 222; and sta-
bility, 83–90, 99, 102–17, 119, 222,
App. A; and stanza length, 81. See also
Cobla; Rhyme, rotating
Stanzas, paired, 86, 98, 102, 103, 108; in-
verted pairs, 99, 257n.11; in threes, 86,
117. See also Cobla
Stanzas, unlinked, 88, 91, 214–21,
255n.14. See also Cobla
Stanza structure, 255n.7; pentastanzaic,
etc., 255n.9; two-part form, 92
Stemma, 71–72, 255n.3
Strophes. See Stanzas
Strophic order. See Sequence of stanzas;
Stanzaic arrays
Stylistic complexity, 72, 80, 83–90; as
control for mouvance, 73, 74, 153,
154; and rhyme, 74, 81, 89, 255n.9
Stylistic debates, 12, 133–63
Stylistic programs, 52
Syllable count, 258n.13

Teissier, Jacques (of Tarascon), 251n.6
Templars, 140
Tenso, 9, 28, 134
Text: authoritative (original), 62, 67, 68,
84, 96, 116–17, 251n.11, 252n.6;
closed and open, 6, 76–77, 89, 163,
201, 203–5; distribution of, 201;
fixed, 81, 91, 127, 165, 201, 203, 206,
258n.17; "irremediable," 253n.6;
moving, 68, 210, 211; sanctity of, 198;

Text (*continued*)
stability of, 81, 86, 122, 202; stemmatic reconstructions of, 71–72
Textual criticism, 61, 63, 209, 253 n.6
Textual integrity, 124; as medieval ideal, 89, 127, 181–82; as modern ideal, 74, 154, 191–95, 209; vs. *mouvance*, 200–203; in transmission, 28, 86, 166, 250 n.4; views of poets on, 75, 83, 185, 187, 202, 218
Thematic continuity, 51, 97
Thibaut de Champagne, 65
Topic development, 141, 205
Topos. See Motifs
Tornada, 6, 26, 29, 44, 45, 53, 73, 98, 106, 110, 113, 115, 116, 122, 123, 150, 165, 193, 250 n.4, 260 n.2; as anti-*envoi*, 43; as signature of performer, 68
Transmission of authorship, 57, 67
Transmitting culture, 86, 89, 126–27, 201, 213
Transposition of stanzas, 67, 71–90, 97, 99, 117, 119, 254 n.2; and verse forms, 75, 86–88, 106–7, 109, 126
Trobar: interchangeability with *amar*, 17, 19, 22; lexical field of, 17. *See also Index of Provençal Terms*

Tropeic development, 140–41
Trouvères, 1, 3, 4, 18, 65, 248 n.1
Typewriter, 197–98

Uc de St-Circ, 59

Value of poetry, 136, 138
Variants. *See* Versions and variants
Variants, word-level, 68, 116, 119–21, 255 n.3; in linking words, 106–7, 108
Version production, 80–81, 87, 213, 218, 222
Versions and variants, 26, 71–72, 204, 255 nn.3,8, 256 n.15; as stanzaic array, 82, 116
Vida (biography), 2, 32, 46, 67, 147, 197, 199, 259 n.13
Virgin Mary, as *hortus conclusus*, 150, 157
Voice, 3, 49, 53, 67, 76, 101, 193–94, 198

Wordsworth, William, 2
Wright, Frank Lloyd, 176
Writing, poets' use of, 40–48, 57, 67, 72, 73, 83, 85, 255 n.4. *See also* Imagery

Zumthor, Paul, 2–6, 18, 204

INDEX OF PROVENÇAL TERMS

Terms have been selected in contexts relevant to the style, creation, transmission, or reception of troubadour lyric. English glosses are given for most terms, to reflect meanings apparent in the cited contexts.

Designer: Barbara Werden
Compositor: G & S Typesetters, Inc.
Text: 10/13 Sabon
Display: Sabon
Printer: Braun-Brumfield, Inc.
Binder: Braun-Brumfield, Inc.